D0086889

HOW HUMANS RELATE

HOW HUMANS RELATE

A New Interpersonal Theory

John Birtchnell

Foreword by Russell Gardner, Jr.

Human Evolution, Behavior, and Intelligence
Seymour W. Itzkoff, Series Editor

Westport, Connecticut
London

HM
132
B546
1993

To Bill, for all his help

Library of Congress Cataloging-in-Publication Data

Birtchnell, John.
    How humans relate : a new interpersonal theory / John Birtchnell.
        p.   cm.—(Human evolution, behavior, and intelligence, ISSN
    1063-2158)
    Includes bibliographical references and index.
    ISBN 0-275-94405-0 (alk. paper)
    1. Interpersonal relations.   I. Title.   II. Series.
    HM132.B546   1993
    158'.2—dc20   93-20296

British Library Cataloguing in Publication Data is available.

Copyright © 1993 by John Birtchnell

All rights reserved. No portion of this book may be
reproduced, by any process or technique, without the
express written consent of the publisher.

Library of Congress Catalog Card Number: 93-20296
ISBN: 0-275-94405-0
ISSN: 1063-2158

First published in 1993

Praeger Publishers, 88 Post Road West, Westport, CT 06881
An imprint of Greenwood Publishing Group, Inc.

Printed in the United States of America

The paper used in this book complies with the
Permanent Paper Standard issued by the National
Information Standards Organization (Z39.48-1984).

10 9 8 7 6 5 4 3 2 1

Contents

Figures

Foreword

John Birtchnell tells us that relating is so essential a part of our being that we never stop doing it, just as our hearts never stop beating. This comparison makes an extraordinary point that signals the importance of this book as well as enlisting the aid of history in setting the stage for his contribution. Before William Harvey demonstrated the circulatory system in 1628, he encountered a cardiology that depended on Galen's metaphor of blood as a river. From its source in the liver, it flowed out via both veins and arteries to the whole body, which then used it up without renewal. In contrast, Harvey focused attention on the heart as a pump for a never ending circle of blood with veins as return conduits. Many odd observations that hadn't made sense before Harvey, finally did as he focused on the heart and blood as a system. As an old man, Harvey told Robert Boyle that his observations of his teacher Hieronymous Fabricus had even then given him the idea that blood must flow from arteries to veins and then back to the heart. That is, Fabricus discovered venous valves in 1603, but called them something else and had no idea himself about their function[1].

I suggest that John Birtchnell's insights represent the beginning of a systematic Harveian science for relating. The body is extraordinarily involved with relating. We speak, listen, and observe with very physical bodies that involve our whole beings. We relate with an enormous repertoire of signals and detect innumerable clues. We use not only language, but facial expressions, movements, and postural communications. Our amplified or diminished body sizes tell volumes instantly, as does how we occupy, arrange, and decorate the spaces we inhabit. Our theories, at some level at least, must feature these bodies. Our communications with other humans achieve biological ends and are the result of biological structures. Our interactions with other members of our species are extraordinarily important and a system for understanding these relationships requires full development. Humans relate to other people intensely and continuously. There is an immense body apparatus to carry out this adaptive behavior. Time dimensions (memories, planning, anticipating) are important components, as is transfer of information to others, something other animals do also, but not nearly to the extent of humans.

The present state of psychiatry, psychology, and the social sciences is similar to pre-Harveian cardiology. Our formulations and therapies continue to be essentially empiric, with explicit or implicit theories similar to Galen's metaphor, as likely viewed by our colleagues of the future. We have speech, movement, and other features of the single organism, but they are not hooked to a central function in whose organizing purpose they operate. To remedy this Dr. Birtchnell tells us in essence that the interpersonal counterpart to Harvey's circulation is relating. Like the venous valves Fabricus observed, many things have been described as altered or affected in the conditions of abnormal interpersonal behavior, but none have so far exhibited the compelling organizing focus of Harvey's circle which, when finally considered seriously, allowed many disparate disconnected observations to cohere together and make sense, to tell a new physiological story that in turn helped form well-founded pathogenic descriptions of heart, lung, and vascular disease, versions of how the disease came about that tallied more with reality.

Until now, we have had no one comprehensive system for organizing and systematizing people's communicational attributes in a clear simple model, one that incorporates the schemata of others and renders them even more useful in their most fundamental form. To this point, the person's social system hasn't been considered part of her/his biological structure. Reciprocity with other people has been taken for granted, not seen as part of an immense body system for mediating these communications, including prodigious quantities of subtle and not so subtle responses to whatever is verbally and nonverbally produced from many others.

This system is not new to family and marital therapists (some of whom have influenced Dr. Birtchnell's thinking). They have considered social and communicational factors at great length and know their power. Much has been written about their observations and clinical interventions, aimed mostly at family dysfunction; but these writings generally consider the body apparatus as being outside their conceptual domain. For Harveian research and intellectual activity to proceed best, we need to have a thorough-going scholar reconceptualize on the socio-level of analysis how the complex and prolix repertoire of our behaviors and experiences can be reduced to common denominators; reduced, but not trivialized. This analysis should proceed with ready connecting links to the known and discoverable systems of the body, and it should be easily applied to the parallel apparatus of other animals. John Birtchnell's schema provides all of this and he describes it in lucid prose.

My personal sense of the pre-Harveian state of affairs in psychiatry evolved as I assumed responsibility for the behavioral sciences course in a curriculum for medical students two decades ago. The offering we provided in the following years was a scattered, poor excuse for a basic science of psychiatry, though very much in line with U.S. national norms, compared to the Harveian models that the other medical specialties possessed. Anatomy, physiology, and biochemistry are straightforward affairs and explain disease conditions of the specialties concerned, but neuroscience, psychology and sociology, at least with respect to psychiatry, were fragmented and only peripherally useful for later instruction in the specialty, except perhaps for medical interviewing, a formal case of human relating. Harvey saw pathology as a branch of physiology, but we who practice in the clinical specialties with prefix psyche- (or equivalents) have not yet made that step. We are still chiefly preoccupied with what is wrong with relating disturbances, but not relating itself.

Because Harvey made macroscopic observations only (the microscope had not been invented) his evidence was incomplete. Thus, he did not know about capillaries, his missing link, without which the proof of a continuous flow of blood was wanting; but from experiment he knew that "porosities" had to exist. Discovery of capillaries thirty years later, with newly developed technology, depended on Malpighi's prepared mind, prepared partly from Harvey's new concepts. Similarly, Birtchnell has not answered all the questions about relating. But in the way that he has developed his formulations, underpinnings are available to line up his formulations with eventual interfaces yet to come, physiological and behavior/experimental. He signals the need for measurement as he notes that we have *appetites* for each form of relating that he lists; we require quanta of each form and can get overloaded, he cites "closeness fatigue" when people are too much together. These are physiological concepts that presage scientific measures and records (and imply brain mechanisms which themselves quantify, time, and record experience in directing the organism's future behavior).

We can guess about some brain areas that will be increasingly focused upon by the physiologists who carry Dr. Birtchnell's work forward; for example, from brain damage studies and across-species comparisons. From neurology, we know that when the frontal and prefrontal cortex is damaged, relating and planning functions are disrupted and the personality of the afflicted person may disappear or become corrupted[2]. For example, a typical sense of humor, *Witzelsucht*, represents offensive, down-putting, teasing aggression. Apathetic interpersonal distance results from other frontal lesions. Prefrontal cortex not only involves affective quality of relationships, but the timing and ordering of behavior and future-orientated mental activities.

In contrast, huge cortical lesions can occur that may severely damage the adaptive capabilities of the person, but if the frontal cortex and related structures are spared, affiliative relationships can continue while impressive planning and deployment of plans can occur, even against considerable odds. This is illustrated by Aleksandr Luria's description of Lyova Zasetsky, "The Man with a Shattered

World," a soldier followed for twenty six years after severe parietal-occipital damage. Though it was distressing and laborious, Zasetsky spent every day writing of his experiences while in the care of his doctors, therapists, and family, with whom he related well. He contrived a plan and he carried it out in the form of telling his story, an important activity for him and his readers![3]. From across-species comparisons, we know these frontal and prefrontal structures are large in humans compared to other primates; they are a late body acquisition. Other species need to budget large amounts of time for foraging and avoiding predation. Our species takes this much more for granted as we have rendered these functions enormously more efficient by group interaction and anticipation of the future. Birtchnell has labelled our needs on his two defined axes to be *appetitive* in nature. I believe this to be accurate and profound: they are exhibits of the creative embroidery human evolution has accomplished upon the neuronal and genomic masterplans of our mammalian ancestors.

I have elsewhere labelled as "sociophysiology" the physiology of relating. John Birtchnell's term of this book is a clear improvement over what I earlier thought of as "intraspecific communication," so labelled because I felt that an adequate basic science should compare human communication to that of other species and that one should specify differences amongst the species. But relating is a better term as it conveys immediately the power and intensity of our interconnectedness with other people, genetically close or distant. The future studies of sociophysiology will surely feature the interfaces of Birtchnell's relating to various components of the frontal lobe, a central structure like the heart for Harvey, not solely but significantly concerned with the tasks of relating.

For our future research, we need to interface social communicational facets of our behavior with concurrent findings in genetics, genomics, neuroscience, and the experiments of nature seen with neurological, psychiatric, and mental retardation syndromes. We need to ask on multiple levels how do organs, cells and molecules that make up the adapting whole individual carry out these activities for sociophysiologic adaptation? What will the next ten years bring by way of new elaborations, connections to other facets of physiology, psychology, sociology, and verifications/falsifications of hypotheses stemming from the sociophysiology of relating? In the meantime, enjoy your reading of this singular offering.

Russell Gardner, Jr.

NOTES

1. Hamilton, W.F. & Richards, D.W. (1982) The output of the heart. In Fishman, A.P. & Richards, D.W. (Eds.) *Circulation of the Blood: Men and Ideas*

(Chapter 2). American Physiological Society: Bethesda, Md.

2. Benton, A.L. (1991) The prefrontal region: Its early history. In Leven, H.S., Eisenberg, H.M. & Benton, A.L. (Eds.) *Frontal Lobe Function and Disfunction*. Oxford University Press: New York.

3. Luria, A.R. (1972) *The Man with a Shattered World: The History of a Brain Wound*. (Translated by L. Solotaroff) Harvard University Press: Cambridge, Mass.

Preface

I can date the origin of this book to the summer of 1982, when I joined the Medical Research Council Social Psychiatry Unit at the Institute of Psychiatry in London. My intention there was to study proneness to depression in young, married women. In a paper titled "Dependence and Its Relationship to Depression" (Birtchnell, 1984) I considered dependence to be an important precursor to depression and, at about that time, decided to develop a questionnaire to measure it. Had I been aware that Hirschfeld et al. (1977) already had done so, the book might never have been written. In fact, being unaware of what other people have done seems to have become a necessary evil for me! John Wing, the director of the Unit, said, "You cannot measure dependence without also measuring independence." That was the beginning of what one might call my dimensional way of thinking.

I began to think that if married women became depressed because they were dependent, they must have husbands who behaved in a way that made and kept them dependent. I called such behavior directiveness and decided to develop a measure of that too. Astonishingly, unbeknown to me, this also already had been done, by Ray (1976). What John Wing had said about dependence, I felt should also apply to directiveness; but what could the opposite of directiveness be? I decided to call it receptiveness; and this was the start of another dimension.

Shortly after arriving in London, I had the good fortune to become a member of John Bolwby's study group. About eight of us met regularly in each other's homes. The word "dependence" was anathema to John. He said, "It will lead you straight into a bog." This made me veer away from Wing's dependence-independence dimension towards Bowlby's attachment-detachment one; so the first version of the system around which this book was written comprised a horizontal, attachment-detachment dimension and a vertical directiveness-receptiveness one (Birtchnell, 1987). Several members of the group were quite taken by it. Maggie Mills told me how excited she had been when she read about it. Andrea Pound said, "One day it will be in all the textbooks." John himself, and Tirril Harris, I remember, remained unconvinced that two dimensions were enough; and Brian Lake objected that receptiveness was not the opposite of directiveness.

Doros Pallis, an old friend from my days at the MRC Clinical Psychiatry Unit in Sussex, told me that the system reminded him of Lorr and Youniss's Interpersonal Style Inventory; so I wrote to Maurice Lorr. In return, he asked me if it had been derived from Leary's interpersonal circle. I had to confess that I had not heard of it, but when I looked it up I realized it had been a case of rediscovering the wheel. Maurice Lorr put me in touch with Jerry Wiggins, who wrote, "I continue to be amazed at the number of people who have proposed similar systems quite independently of each other." This left me with a mixture of dismay and delight: dismay that there was nothing new about my ideas and delight that suddenly I had become part of a movement. Avidly I caught up with the writings of the interpersonal psychologists and, as Donald Kiesler put it, "When the interpersonal bug bites one, it usually has effects for a lifetime."

John Bowlby continued to be uneasy about the system - largely, I suspected, because he saw it as an encroachment upon his attachment theory. Just as I had jettisoned dependence, I saw that I also had to jettison attachment, and with it detachment. The breakthrough came when I realized that both dependence and attachment were hybrid concepts, that had a closeness-seeking part and an upwardly directed part. The answer was simple: the dimensions had to be closeness-distance and upperness-lowerness. Following this, relations became easier with John. He wrote, "Your revised nomenclature seems to me a valuable step forward. Differentiating your emerging theory from attachment theory is valuable since it is then much easier to discuss how they relate to each other and to compare the strengths and weaknesses of each." I finished the first draft of the book early in 1989. I invited John to read it but he was intent on finishing his own book, on Darwin, which came out in 1990. He died shortly afterwards.

The group to whom the system has had the greatest appeal has been the marital therapists. I am especially appreciative of the support of Mike Crowe, Jane Ridley, and Maureen Davies at the Institute of Psychiatry; and Chris Clulow, Paul Pengelly, and Nina Cohen at the Tavistock Institute of Marital Studies.

In 1987 and 1988 Scott Henderson visited the Social Psychiatry Unit. Scott was a link man. He liked my 1984 dependence and depression paper, and it was he who had told me about the dependence measure of Hirshfeld et al. He was an admirer of Bowlby, but more important, he was interested in evolution. He found the system appealing and said it could occupy me for the next ten years. The upperness-lowerness dimension put him in mind of John Price, another evolutionist. Back in the 1960s, John and I had shared an interest in birth order. Re-establishing contact with him made a big difference. He helped me to set the system into an evolutionary context, and reading his writing on depression and evolution fired me with new enthusiasm. He took a keen interest in the book, asking to read each new chapter as I finished it.

John belongs to another study group, which meets from time to time at the locations of its members. Its leader is Michael Chance, a primatologist, and his theories concerning the agonic and hedonic mode of relating form the group's main focus of attention. Presenting my ideas to the group was a rewarding experience and reconciling Michael's position with my own was reminiscent of the exchanges I had had with John Bowlby. Despite their common interest in ethology, John and Michael never met and never referred to each other in their writings. The explanation, I think, is that John was a horizontal thinker and Michael is a vertical thinker. Having had such involvement with both has helped me to integrate the two dimensions.

Through the Michael Chance group I became acquainted with Paul Gilbert, a young clinical psychologist who, through his three books, already has established himself as an authoritative thinker on the evolution of depression. He has been a constant source of encouragement and support. We have met only once, but through an exchange of correspondence and lengthy telephone calls we have forged a valuable working alliance.

On a memorable July day in 1991, at John Price's home in Sussex, I met Leon Sloman and Russell Gardner, American psychiatrists who were there to set up the International Association for the Study of Comparative Psychopathology, an organization concerned with the evolution of mental mechanisms. I had long conversations with both of them and discovered that we spoke the same language. I am grateful to Russell for bringing my ideas to the attention of Seymour Itzkoff, who read the first draft of the book and met me in London a few months later. As a result of our meeting, during 1992 I completely re-wrote the book. This time it came out better. Theories take a long time to grow.

I believe that the theory has wide application and I hope that the book will be read by people from a range of perspectives and areas of interest. The intention is that no specialised knowledge should be required to understand it. Any specialised terms which are used are printed in italics and clearly defined at their first use. This will make it easier to refer back to them when they are encountered later in the book. Whenever a specialised concept is referred to, the chapter in which it was introduced is indicated.

1

Relating:
Some General Principles

Newton did not actually discover gravity, for gravity has always existed, he simply drew attention to it. The point he made was that the apple falls off the tree because the earth pulls it off. The apple also pulls the earth, but its pull is so small as to make no difference. Relating is like gravity in that it concerns the influence of one body upon another. It also is like gravity in that although it has always been there, it has remained largely unattended. The aim of this book is not only to draw attention to it but also to introduce a new theory concerning it.

THE ILLUSION OF PURPOSE AND MOTIVE

In one sense, it could be considered that the apple and the earth relate to each other, but such relating is simply a manifestation of their physical properties. The interactions that occur between the earliest life forms are not a great deal different from this, though they are concerned with both their chemical and their physical properties. At quite an early stage in the course of evolution, the interactions between organisms assumed what would appear to be a sense of purpose. Evolutionary theorists would have us believe that this is only illusory; they maintain that organisms survive simply because they have the characteristics that enable them to do so, and that it is the fact that they do survive that creates the illusion of purpose. Be this as it may, it is convenient to interpret certain interactions between organisms as purposeful; and the more purposeful they appear to be, the more we are inclined to refer to them as relating. When earthworms lie against each other apparently for the purpose of reproduction, it is difficult not to consider this a form of relating. There must surely be something that attracts each worm to the other and something that induces them to lie still while the reproductive process takes place. Dare we assume that they experience something that is equivalent to satisfaction?

Part of our difficulty in conceptualizing the interactions between lower life forms is that we are inclined to attribute to them the kinds of subjective experiences that we ourselves have when we indulge in similar behavior. When a spider constructs its web and lies in wait for its prey, does it feel excited when the web begins to sway as the captive fly struggles to escape? Perhaps it does, or perhaps its behavior is simply automatic and it experiences nothing more than the insectivorous plant does when the fly gets stuck on one of its sticky leaves. It has to be acknowledged, however, that somewhere along the course of evolution, animals, if not plants, came to develop an awareness of what was happening to them in their interactions with others, and later still, to experience satisfactions and disappointments in response to successes and failures in such interactions. Schjelderup-Ebbe's (1935) description of the response of a-birds (previously subordinate to none) to defeat in conflict strongly suggested that they experience something akin to dejection. Dogs certainly show every indication of being saddened when the owners go away and being excited when they return. Although the beginnings of a sense of awareness and emotional responsiveness are clearly apparent in certain animals, it is assumed that such characteristics have become even further developed in humans.

It is tempting to assume that relating has to do with movement, since it appears to take the form of one organism endeavoring to have some influence upon another. In this case, it should be a characteristic of animals rather than plants. However, in a very real sense, the insectivorous plant relates to the fly, that it attracts and captures; and the flowering plant relates to the insects and birds that it attracts by its color and scent and that it rewards with its nectar. Both the insectivorous plant and the flowering plant gain from their seductions. It might be considered that the climbing plant relates to the tree when it entwines itself around it to get closer to a source of light. Because it seems absurd that plants should think out their relating strategies, it may be easier to accept that the so-called motivation that is considered to lie behind human relating is simply something we have imparted to humans in order to make more sense of what appears to be going on between them.

RELATING AND EVOLUTION

Since there seems no doubt that humans form part of the evolutionary chain, it needs to be acknowledged that not only have our anatomy and physiology evolved from that of earlier animal forms, but that our behavior has as well. One implication is that the apparent purposefulness of human behavior must be as illusory as that of earlier animal forms, and this must always be borne in mind. However, if the convenience of assuming a sense of purpose is to be adopted, it must be accepted that whatever purposes we choose to attribute to human behavior must be seen to be linked to similar, or perhaps simpler, purposes that we have attributed to the behavior of our predecessors. Thus, within the most complex human behavior there must be a set of motives that can be traced back through the evolutionary chain. In other words, at each stage of evolution any new motivational pattern is best understood as a modification of one that was apparent in the preceding species. There is an advantage in viewing human behavior in this way: by tracing it back to its simpler origins, it is possible to establish the basic core of motives of which human motives must be adaptations or elaborations. Such a core should provide a basis for both classifying and explaining the infinitely varied attitudes and behavior patterns that are observable in humans. The motives will be considered in the next chapter. The present chapter explores the actual process of relating.

DEFINING RELATING

Throughout this book, relating will be considered an active process; it will be defined as that which one organism or person does to another or to others. It cannot occur without there being at least one other. The other may not be aware of being related to and therefore does not necessarily have to respond. An animal creeping up on its prey is relating just as a distant admirer or a Peeping Tom is relating. The other also does not have to be present. A young animal pining for its lost parent or someone yearning for a loved one is relating. The other may be an individual, a group, or others in general. The other need not be a member of the same species: a cat may relate to a mouse; a man may relate to a dog. In fact, the other need not be a living creature. A young monkey may relate to a fur-covered frame. A child may relate to a teddy bear, a toy soldier, or a blanket. Humans create all manner of machines and devices to which they relate, motor cars and computers for example.

Relating includes being aware of, adopting attitudes toward and attempting to influence other animals, plants, or objects, but particularly animals and more particularly still, animals of the same species. Relating may assume the form of direct action, for example, nestling up close to or hitting out at; but usually it involves simply conveying signals, which may be visual, auditory, or olfactory. In man, such signals usually are conveyed by way of the spoken or written word, though nonverbal signals such as posture, gesture and tone of voice play a significant, albeit less obvious, part. Because they have more contact, gregarious animals relate much more than solitary ones. However, solitary ones clearly are aware of and sensitive to other animals and react strongly to any that come within their radius. It is not so much that they do not relate as that they relate in a negative way by maintaining distance. During periods of mating and the rearing of young, they reveal their potential for close relating. What needs to be stressed is that relating is a process that never stops, just as the heart never stops beating. This may be most obvious in fish swimming in a school: they are continuously checking and adjusting their position in relation to the other members of the school. What may be less obvious is that humans are constantly noting the presence of, developing attitudes and feelings toward and giving out signals and reacting to signals from all those with whom they come into contact. In fact the adjustments of people walking along a crowded street are not unlike those of fish swimming in a school. The point is that people simply cannot stop relating: they do it all the time, without thinking, to every person, animal, plant, or thing with which they come into contact. It is part of being a living being in continuity with the environment. It is perhaps because we never stop doing it that we are so unaware of it.

EXTERNAL AND INTERNAL RELATING

Besides relating to people with whom we are in direct contact, we relate to all the people who have come to be represented in our internal world. People with whom we are in direct contact make stronger claims upon our attention, and when we are alone or asleep we relate most to those who have been internalized. This is in keeping with the principle that we never stop relating, that is, when there is no-one external to relate to we turn to internalized others.

For man in particular, but to some extent for other animals, it is important to differentiate between what will be termed *"external"* and *"internal"* relating. When the young animal is pining for its mother it is retaining, somewhere within its nervous system, a memory or representation of its mother to which it has some form of internal attachment. This reminds it of what its mother is like and enables it to recognize her when it encounters her again in the external world. The pleasure of its reunion with her is due to a matching up of the internal and external experience. It may well be that some gregarious animals retain such internal representations of a number of members of their group, which enables them to remember them and to maintain a constant, long-term relationship toward them; monkeys certainly do. Humans carry within themselves internal representations of vast numbers of others, some of whom may no longer be living, and have internalized relationships of various kinds with them. When they meet these people in the external world they relate with them externally. The internalized relationships originate from external experiences, but if, during encounters with these internalized others in the external world, the nature of the relationship changes, the internalized relationship may become modified. These internal relationships feature prominently in dreams; sometimes in dreams the internalized people may be experienced as they were many years previously, even though the external relationship may have changed. For example, a man whose wife has left him may dream of her as she was before the breakup. Old internal representations therefore may never completely be lost.

Internal relating has much in common with the Freudian concept of *cathexis*. Cathexis is the amount of psychic energy that is directed toward or attached to the mental representation of a person or thing. *Psychic energy* is not the same as physical energy; it is simply analogous to it. It means something like attention, interest, or investment. Cathexis can only flow within the nervous system; it cannot flow out through space (Brenner, 1957).

WHO MAY RELATE TO WHOM?

So far, the assumption has been that relating is that which one organism/individual does to another, though it has been acknowledged that it is possible to relate to an inert object as well. There are two extensions of this, one inward and one outward. Inwardly, a number of writers (e.g., Foa, 1961; Benjamin, 1974) have proposed that it is possible for humans at least to relate to themselves, that is, over and above relating to internalized representations of others and to hallucinations. Children commonly create imaginary companions and seem able to relate to them. Adults commonly talk to themselves; this is not dissimilar from having imaginary companions. To this extent they are able to create states of being related to themselves, and these may serve the same function as states of relatedness to other people. In such states they are able to console or admonish themselves, provoke themselves into action, and calm themselves down. Outwardly, it is possible for a group of animals or people to function as one and to relate either to another group or to an individual. An entire nation can relate to another nation, even though not all of its individual members align themselves with its policies. In fact, it is to be hoped that a clearer understanding of the processes of relating between individuals will contribute to an improvement in international relationships.

SELF-CENTERED AND OTHER-CENTERED RELATING

Relating to the self is not the same as that which will be called *self-centered* relating. This is an extreme form of relating in which there is such a concern or preoccupation with the self that others are considered simply a means to achieving personal objectives. The self-centered relater has only a limited awareness of the existence of others as people with feelings of their own. They are there simply to be made use of. The relating of most nonhumans is self-centered. An equally extreme form of relating is what will be called *other-centered* relating. This occurs when an individual lives for or through another with a total disregard for her/his own interests or needs. Only humans are capable of relating in this way. Most forms of relating fall somewhere between these two extremes, sometimes veering one way, sometimes another.

VICARIOUS RELATING

By identifying with another and following closely the other's failures and successes, it is possible to experience the satisfactions of relating without doing the relating oneself. This happens to the devoted parent. It is probably the main reason why spectators watch sporting events. It is also the principal motive for reading true or fictional stories about others in newspapers, magazines and books and for watching plays, films, soap operas, and the like.

RELATING AND THE CENTRAL NERVOUS SYSTEM

Because relating is an activity that man shares with all animal forms, its representations must be embedded deeply within the central nervous system. Because it is happening all the time, much of it must be taking place in a spontaneous and automatic way, and therefore at a subcortical level. The cortex and the sub-cortex appear to perform different, though complementary, functions in the process of relating. The subcortex is often impressively sensible and logical; in retrospect, its responses and reactions, though taken very quickly, seem to have fitted in exactly with the individual's needs and priorities. The cortex clearly is not geared up to taking quick actions: it operates more slowly and mulls over relational issues, over longer periods of time, sometime after the immediate responses have occurred. Thus, although it is necessary to make immediate and quick adjustments on a minute-to-minute basis, it is also necessary to think out longer-term strategies and plan more devious maneuvers. The logic of the subcortex is often so profound that it feels as though it is the prime mover and that the cortex trundles along some distance behind, long after the main action has taken place. This point of view seems to be in accord with that expressed by Groddeck in his *Book of the It* (1923). Here he maintained that man is animated by "some wondrous force" that directs both what he himself does and what happens to him. This he called the "Es" or the "It" and he proposed the principle that man is lived by the It.

Gilbert (1992) argued that if organisms have biosocial goals, they must have *internal processing modules* for organizing information about how far such goals have been achieved and what needs to be done to achieve them. Cosmides (1989) observed that if the human mind evolved to accomplish adaptive ends, natural selection would have produced *mental algorithms*, including rules of inference, for solving important and recurrent adaptive problems. Such modules and algorithms clearly belong to the subcortex; since they are common to both animals and man, they must be pre-language. Language has an intrapersonal as well as an interpersonal function and humans use language to think things out and conduct dialogues with themselves, but all this happens at the more ponderous cortical level.

In a discussion of social exchange theory, Frude (1991) observed that the choice between alternative actions depends on estimates of the probabilities of possible outcomes and that people often are unaware of the elements involved in making their decisions. They sum up complex social situations "implicitly" rather than by systematically working through a series of calculations, just as when catching a ball they do not explicitly work out the complex mathematics of the trajectory. This process of appraisal, he maintained, is usually automatic and unconscious.

According to MacLean (1973), during evolution the brain of primates has developed according to three basic patterns; thus, there has developed a hierarchy of three brains in one, which he called the triune brain. The earliest, the *reptilian brain* (including the reticular formation and the striate cortex) he considered to be the seat of survival behavior; the next, the *palaeomammalian brain* (including the limbic system), he considered to be the seat of motives and emotions; and the most recent, the *neomammalian brain* (represented by the neocortex), he considered to be the seat of rational thought. The earliest is incapable of adapting to environmental changes; the next is capable of responding to present or past information; but only the most recent is capable of thinking out which response to make to any particular stimulus. It seems likely that relating is represented in all three brains. Although all three are closely interconnected and functionally interdependent, each is capable of operating independently of the other two (MacLean, 1975). This led Vincent (1990) to speculate that sometimes there may be a conflict between what our neomammalian brain knows and what our palaeomammalian brain feels.

BEING RELATED TO

If relating is defined as that which one organism does to another or to others, then it is necessary to consider the reverse process, namely, that of being related to, whiche, is defined as that which another does or others do to the organism. Sometimes this is referred to as *passive relating*. Being related to is every bit as important as relating; just about everything that has been said about relating applies to being related to. Gregarious animals, including man, are continuously being related to by others, though they are not always aware of this. At any particular instant, or over a period of time, an individual is being the other to any number of others and is likely to be aware of much of this. An important difference between relating and being related to is that the quality or nature of the relating cannot be as clearly known by the recipient as it is by the donor; it can only be inferred by the signals being put out. Such signals are received by the sense organs; for this reason, blind or deaf people can sometimes be at a disadvantage.

We also are related to by people in our internal world. This is particularly so for internalized authority figures, who, we feel, make judgments upon our thoughts and deeds. God is commonly experienced as an internalized person who relates to us in either an authoritarian or a comforting way. Internalized others commonly enable us to experience not being alone, as conveyed by expressions such as "God is love" or "God is with me"; we feel loved and comforted by them in conditions of isolation. Internalized figures, however, are not always friendly. In certain psychotic states people are tormented by accusatory voices from which they feel they have no escape.

RELATING AND THE EMOTIONS

Relating is linked with the emotions in a most definite way; this is in keeping with the location of both within the subcortical regions of the nervous system. Emotional states are not normally things we think ourselves into; we simply find ourselves feeling emotional. They develop spontaneously. This places them within the same order of things as the spontaneous relating reactions and adjustments already linked with the subcortex. Emotions are strongest at moments of change; they convey whether such change is advantageous or disadvantageous. It is a common experience to suddenly find oneself feeling happy or sad without being aware of the origin of the emotion. At a cortical level, it may be possible to trace it to a recent incident that could have been interpreted as a success or failure in the field of relating. Somehow our subcortex has decided on our behalf that this event warrants our experiencing joy or sadness. By the time the emotion has reached consciousness the decision has been made; it is a fait accompli.

OBJECTIVE, PERCEIVED, AND SUBJECTIVE RELATING

Objective relating is that which one organism or person appears to be doing to another, in the eyes of an outside observer. Within this category must be included the purposes and motives attributed by man to the relating behavior of other organisms. Closely allied to objective relating is *perceived relating*, that which one person perceives another to be doing to her/him. Animals also are able to have perceptions about what other animals or humans are doing to them. *Subjective relating* may be applicable only to human relating. It is that which one person believes her/himself to be doing to another. The importance of these three points of view lies in the fact that discrepancies commonly occur between them. A husband may perceive that his wife admires him, though his wife's subjective belief may be that she despises him. Her mother's objective opinion, observing the two of them together, is that she does admire him. The wife may truly despise her husband but has successfully deceived both him and her mother into believing otherwise. Alternatively, she may believe that she despises him, though it may be obvious from her actions that she admires him; and when she is drunk, she may admit that she does. It would, of course, be possible for all three to believe that she admires him, even though she really despises him, and when drunk she may admit that she does. There is therefore a further category of relating called *the truth*, which may or may not ever come to light.

CONCEALMENT OF THE TRUE NATURE OF RELATING

The example just given raises the possibility that a person can conceal, even from her/himself, the true nature of her/his relating. Leary (1957) proposed four levels of interpersonal data: the public, the conscious, the private, and the unexpressed. The first two were equivalent to objective and subjective relating; the private was that which might be inferred from reported dream content, artistic creation, or projective tests (equivalent to admitting it when drunk); the unexpressed was that which has so obviously been avoided as to indicate that it has been repressed. There may indeed be such a level of concealment, which is not detectable by ordinary means.

If relating occurs initially at a subcortical level, it would not be difficult to conceive of mechanisms by which awareness (at a cortical level) of certain less-than-acceptable attitudes may be reduced or totally blocked.

STATES OF RELATEDNESS

Notwithstanding the illusory nature of purpose and motive, for the remainder of this book the assumption will be made that relating is a purposeful and motivated activity. If this is so, what is its purpose and what are the motives? It will be argued that its purpose is the attainment of what will be called *states of relatedness*. These are advantageous positions in relation to another or others, which will be fully described in the next chapter. They are roughly equivalent to Gilbert's (1989, 1992) biosocial goals. They may be (1) simply available, (2) willingly offered, (3) negotiated or bargained for, (4) taken forcibly or (5) imposed. Ironically, in example 5, when a state of relatedness is imposed, it is not advantageous to the organism/individual;   it is only advantageous to the one who has imposed it (i.e., taken it forcibly). More will be said of this later.

In man, at least, there is a close association between states of relatedness and the emotions. The attainment of a state of relatedness is accompanied by the subjective experience of elation, achievement, or satisfaction. Danger of its being lost is accompanied by either anger or anxiety; anger if the chance of retaining or regaining it is believed to be good, anxiety if it is believed to be poor. Actual loss of it is accompanied by sadness, defeat, or despair, which may be tempered by hope if there is a chance of regaining it. This interpretation of the function of emotions corresponds with Nesse's (1990) view that emotions have been shaped by natural selection to regulate interpersonal behavior in the direction of increased fitness.

It has to be assumed that in their basic forms the main states of relatedness are common at least to all animals, but that they assume more elaborate variations through the course of evolution. In lower animals, they are attained largely through instinctual behavior. In man, although there seem to be a small number of innate behaviors aimed at attaining them (e.g., the crying, smiling, and clinging of infants), the predominant routes are through Gilbert's (1992) internal processing modules, which are driven by certain general, innate tendencies. The innate tendencies in many ways resemble hunger and thirst; like hunger and thirst, they may originate in specific locations in the central nervous system. Somehow, the individual is made aware of a need for one of them, and this gives rise to a *restless stirring*, which leads to an appropriate form of relating activity directed toward attaining it. Like hunger and thirst, the need appears to be for a finite amount; when this is attained, the stirring subsides. At this point the relating activity changes from an *appetitive* to a *consummatory* form and the individual simply indulges in the state of relatedness.

It is probably true that humans spend long stretches of time in consummatory forms of relating; that is, they are not actually trying to attain particular states of relatedness, they are simply in them and finding the experience pleasurable. A king, for example, is in a particular state of relatedness (i.e., superior) to his subjects and may stay so for all of his life. If he were to be deposed he would experience the distress of losing that particular state of relatedness.

Animals or people may vary in their need for certain states of relatedness. This applies in general terms and at specific times. In general terms, the solitary animal needs less involvement (which might be considered a state of relatedness) than the gregarious one and the autistic child needs less involvement than the normal child. More specifically, the newly born animal or infant may need more involvement than the more mature one, or at moments of danger the need for involvement may increase. Therefore, some centre within the central nervous system must serve as a regulator of these needs and increase or decrease the appetite for them.

It is possible to have too much of a particular state of relatedness, particularly, though not necessarily, if it is enforced. Such excess is registered as *fatigue*, similar to that of an overworked muscle. Such fatigue provokes restlessness, irritation and an increasing need to escape and move towards a contrasting state of relatedness. If this is prevented, the state of relatedness is experienced as increasingly unpleasant and painful and the urgency to escape intensifies. Finally, if no escape is possible, despair and defeat set in and the animal or person may sink into a state of profound depression.

A LINK WITH FREUD'S THEORY OF INSTINCTS

Freud (1911a) maintained that humans, like animals, seek pleasure and avoid discomfort. Pleasure results from the satisfaction of physiological needs such as hunger, thirst, defecation, urination, and the release of sexual tension. The urges to satisfy these needs he called the *life instincts*. An instinct is made up of four components: a *source*, namely a deficiency (e.g., lack of food); an *aim*, namely a wish to eliminate the deficiency (e.g. to remove the discomfort of hunger); an *object*, namely that which is needed to eliminate the deficiency (e.g. the ingestion of food); and an *impetus*, namely the intensity of the craving that derives from the magnitude of the deficiency (e.g. how hungry the person is). These components can be applied to the seeking and attaining of states of relatedness.

There are two important ways in which needs for states of relatedness differ from physiological needs. Firstly, they can only be met by some kind of interaction with another individual, or with a number of other individuals; and secondly, once attained, they can be lost or taken away. The needs of individuals do not always correspond and, when there is a conflict of needs, one individual may lose out. Relating behavior involves therefore (1) bargaining, negotiating or competing for a particular state and (2) defending or warding off competitors once it has been attained.

GIVING AND TAKING AWAY STATES OF RELATEDNESS

One person has the capacity to give a particular state of relatedness to another or take a state of relatedness away from her/him. A person may choose to be friends with another or may chose to break off that friendship. Equally, a person may have a state of relationship given to her/him or taken away from her/him. In this sense, states of relatedness are like commodities that may be passed around, exchanged, bargained for, or fought over.

ACQUIRING SKILLS AND COMPETENCIES

Presumably the transition from purely instinctual relating to relating based upon actions driven by general tendencies has been a gradual one. It seems unlikely that man is the only animal that needs, during a period of maturation and training, to acquire relating skills and competencies. The processes by which these are acquired will be considered in more detail in later chapters, but some general principles are described here. Although it may be assumed that the new born infant has innate needs for certain states of relatedness, it does not know what it feels like to experience them. An important feature of parenting is exposing the child to adequate amounts of them in order that it may enjoy and want more of them. Although it may be desirable to indulge the child in this way, it is also necessary for it to learn how to seek such states by its own endeavors. It seems likely that its innate needs will motivate it to seek them out, but parents can provide opportunities and encouragement for it to do so and offer praise and reward when it succeeds. Accumulating good experiences of the main states of relatedness reinforces their pleasurableness and provides the child with the confidence that it is capable of attaining them whenever it needs to do so. States of relatedness may be attained via different routes and it is important that the child practice and become competent in a variety of strategies and acquire a diversity of skills that can be applied under different circumstances.

When early experiences fall short of this ideal, deficiencies develop that can impair later relating abilities. Despite the child's innate need for a particular state of relatedness, bad experiences may cause it to be frightened of it so that in later life it may try to avoid it. A series of failures in its attempts to attain a particular state of relatedness may lead the child to conclude that it is incapable of attaining it, so in the future it may avoid trying to do so. Having experiences of painfully losing a particular state of relatedness, which was securely held, may lead it to be apprehensive about seeking it again or to be fearful of losing it once it is attained.

The well-adjusted person is competent in a wide range of relating skills and is confident of her/his ability to attain any of the main states of relatedness. Within any area of competency, s/he is able to draw upon a variety of relating strategies according to circumstance. S/he is able to relate one way with one person and another way with another - or with any particular person, one way on one occasion and another way on another. S/he is therefore flexible, versatile, and adaptable. Because of this, it is difficult to classify the relating behavior of a well-adjusted person, to say that s/he is like this or like that. In contrast, the poorly adjusted person has a restricted range of relating skills, tries to avoid some areas of relating altogether, and is anxious and uncertain in others. S/he has a smaller repertoire of relating strategies. S/he finds relating to certain kinds of people difficult; with everyone, she tends to restrict relating to those areas in which s/he feels most competent. This forces them to be accommodating to her/his limited style of relating. S/he is therefore rigid, restricted, and unadaptable. Because of this it is much easier to classify the relating behavior of a poorly adjusted person. Most personality descriptions refer to areas of incompetence.

STORES AND SOURCES OF STATES OF RELATEDNESS

Throughout the course of a lifetime, successes and failures are experienced in striving for various states of relatedness. These become stored in the memory and provide an overall score, positive or negative, of the individual's success or failure in attaining particular states. Such a score represents that person's store or fund of it, which is continually being added to or subtracted from. Continuing the analogy with hunger, such stores may be likened to accumulations of fat, off which the individual may feed when certain states of relatedness are not readily available. States of relatedness may be derived from many different sources; at any particular time, a person will need to know which sources are available to her/him. S/he may rely heavily upon one source or take small amounts from many sources. Whichever s/he does, the overall sum may be the same. Maintaining a broad spread of sources is a safeguard against some drying up. On the other hand, it may be necessary to have at least a few sources from which a substantial amount may be derived. For example, having a large number of casual acquaintances may not be an adequate substitute for having one or two really important friendships. The issue of stores and sources will become clearer in the next chapter when the main states of relatedness are described.

GOOD AND BAD RELATING

The concept of the well- and the poorly-adjusted person already has been introduced. This extremely important consideration will be referred to throughout the book. The relating of the well-adjusted person will be called *good* or *positive relating*, and that of the poorly adjusted person will be called *bad* or *negative relating*. Failure to distinguish clearly between good and bad relating is a serious deficiency of most existing classificatory systems (see Chapter 10). Good or positive relating is the relating of the person who can attain the main states of relatedness with confidence, who is not afraid of any of them, and who is confident that adequate stores of them are readily available to her/him. Because of this, such a person is usually able to attain a state of relatedness without harming or disturbing someone else. There are good and bad versions of each state of relatedness, and good and bad strategies for attaining them; these will be referred to in appropriate chapters. Fear of particular forms of relating already has been considered. Some other versions of bad relating will now be described.

Secure and Insecure Relating

The secure relater is certain of her/his ability to both attain and maintain a particular state of relatedness. S/he will seek it with confidence and, being assured that s/he will not lose it, will freely indulge in and enjoy it. The insecure relater is uncertain of her/his ability to either attain or to maintain it. S/he will seek it with caution and apprehension and when s/he has it, will constantly fear that s/he may lose it. S/he will therefore repeatedly seek assurance that s/he is safe with it; put out gestures or signals to assert her/his position in it; and dispel others who may be likely to deprive her/him of it, take precautions to defend or protect it, and derive little pleasure from having it. The relater is secure because of past and present successes. If a certain state of relatedness has been easily come by in the past, the person will feel confident of being able to attain it again. Circumstances can easily change however: a few recent failures, or even one significant recent failure, can transform the person from a secure to an insecure relater.

Controlled and Desperate Relating

Applying the food analogy, when a state of relatedness is in plentiful supply, the person will seek it in a controlled and orderly manner; but if times become hard and it is in short supply, s/he will become ruthless and adopt desperate measures. The desperate relater may become unscrupulous and undiscriminating, not minding what form the state of relatedness takes or how it is attained. The unloved child, for example, will attach itself to anyone who shows it any sign of kindness.

Respectful and Disrespectful Relating

The respectful relater is considerate of the relating needs of the person with whom s/he is relating and of the effect that her/his relating behavior may have upon her/him. S/he will be careful not to enter into a particular kind of relationship with her/him (i.e., one that will provide her/him with a particular state of relatedness) if s/he believes that this will cause her/him pain or distress. S/he will therefore attempt to (1) determine whether the relationship is what the other wishes, and (2) to establish it on the basis of mutual agreement and understanding. The disrespectful relater is concerned primarily with satisfying her/his own relational needs irrespective of the effect this may have upon the person with whom s/he is relating. S/he is prepared to impose or enforce a particular form of relating upon the other, if need be, perhaps believing that this really is what the other wants or needs, or that eventually the other will come to accept it. S/he may know and not mind that this form of relating is causing pain or distress to the other and may even derive satisfaction from this. Imposed or enforced relating can occur only when, for one reason or another, the other cannot escape from the relationship.

Respectful relating is not necessarily restricted to humans, and humans do not always relate respectfully. Whenever animals behave in a cooperative manner they create the impression that they are relating respectfully, though they may not be experiencing anything equivalent to human concern. There is often a degree of altruism involved in respectful relating, for example when parents protect or feed their young. In humans the respectful relater seems to require the capacity to identify, or even empathize, with the other; it seems unlikely that the small infant is capable of this. Writers such as Kohut (1977) have speculated that early in life others are experienced simply as extensions of the self. This appears to change at quite an early age, for even small children playing together appear capable of considering each other's feelings (Freud and Burlingham, 1944; Wimmer and Perner, 1983). Despite this, even mature adults (e.g., commandants in concentration camps) can behave with total disrespect for others.

True and Deceitful Relating

Sometimes there are advantages to being seen to relate in a particular way, or to have attained a particular state of relatedness when this is not actually so. Because of this, people often attempt to deceive others (and sometimes even themselves) that they are relating in a particular way or have attained a particular state of relatedness, which is not actually the case. This may occur as a means of concealing a negative form of relating (e.g., masquerading as being strong and responsible, while really being weak and irresponsible) or as a way of avoiding causing the other distress (e.g., falsely claiming to love her/him).

Conventional Ways of Describing Bad Relating

What is referred to here as bad relating is relating that generally would meet with disapproval. Within a legal context, it would be considered criminal; within a moral context, it would be considered wicked; within a psychiatric context it would be considered either a manifestation of behaviour or personality disorder or a symptom of mental illness. Since it is intended that the theory proposed in this book be neutral and value-free, any allegiance to these orientations will be avoided.

CONSIDERATIONS OF TIME AND OTHER

In defining or describing relating, it is important to be clear about the time period being considered and the person or persons being related to. An individual, perhaps even a nonhuman, may have a particular relating characteristic that is consistent over time and across relationships. This normally would be considered a feature of that individual's makeup or personality. An extreme example would be that of an autistic child who remains remote and self-absorbed practically all the time in relation to almost everyone. It was stated earlier that most personality descriptions refer to areas of incompetence; thus, if a person does have a predominant relating characteristic, it is more likely to be a negative form of relating than a positive one. Throughout the book, therefore, when the term "personality" is used it is more likely to mean what psychiatrists call "personality disorder".

Alternatively, a particular characteristic might apply either to a specific time period, however long or however short, or to a specific individual. It is not uncommon for a person, or even an animal, to have a predominant way of relating to one particular other. A man may, for example, always relate to his employer in a respectful and deferential manner; a dog may always chase a particular postman down the street.

Over and above these consistent or predominant forms of relating are episodes of relating that may occur during the course of a relationship or even during the course of a conversation. The predominant concern of this book is with the process of relating, irrespective of time or person. However, it must be acknowledged that a relating style that is a long-term characteristic of a particular person is a quite different phenomenon from a momentary gesture, and sometimes it has to be made quite clear which is being described.

INTERRELATING

Interrelating may be described as a bargaining procedure - under certain circumstances, a battleground - in which each of two individuals makes apparent her/his needs, makes an offer, stands her/his ground, or fights her/his corner in order to achieve the best deal for her/himself in terms of satisfying his/her relating needs (i.e., attaining adequate amounts of her/his preferred states of relatedness). If the relating needs of the individuals are compatible, a deal may easily be struck; if they are not, no deal may be struck at all, a compromise may be reached, one participant may choose to indulge the other, or one may force a particular form of being related to upon the other.

Interrelating can be considered within any one of a number of different time scales. An entire relationship may be treated as one protracted interrelating process; on the other hand, a relatively brief conversation may be broken down into a series of interrelating episodes. One participant may simply forge ahead (disrespectfully) with a particular form of relating and ignore the feelings of the other, or some kind of agreement or negotiation may take place. Terms such as "agreement" and "negotiation" are to some extent inappropriate; even if the process extends over a period of years, it is more likely to occur at a preconscious (subcortical) than a conscious (cortical) level, and it is only in artificial settings, such as during the course of individual or group psychotherapy or marital or family therapy, that it may be brought more fully into consciousness.

The process of bargaining or negotiating appears to involve a sequence of stages, that normally would be passed through quickly and automatically. They will be broken down here somewhat artificially in order that terms may be defined. The first stage will be called the *initiation*. This may be a direct action (i.e., the initiator beginning to relate to the other in a particular way); a proposal (i.e., proposing that s/he actively relate to the other in a particular way); or an invitation (i.e., inviting the other to relate to her/him in a particular way, such that s/he would passively be related to). The second stage in the process will be called the *response*. It takes the form of *reactive relating*; it is not a form of behavior that the other would have adopted if the initiator had not taken the step s/he did. The distinction between active and reactive relating is extremely important, since it defines the origin of a particular form of behavior. The response may be positive (i.e., behaving in such a way as to enable the interrelating process to proceed); negative (i.e., behaving in such a way as to block or prevent it) or non-consenting acquiescence (i.e., the respondent does not wish the interaction to proceed but is not in a position to block or prevent it). In other words, s/he is the recipient of imposed or enforced relating. The interrelating process need not stop here, for the initiator may respond to the response, and the respondent respond to this, and so on; but these responses are simply further steps in the bargaining or battling process toward an ultimate outcome. The cycle may be restarted by one or the other participant making an alternative initiation.

As long as the response is not negative, the outcome of the interrelating process is that each participant is in a state of relatedness, even though one of them may be reluctantly or unwillingly so. It is appropriate at this stage to point out that a state of relatedness may be *shared, given, or received.* If it involves doing something together (e.g., having a meal, going for a walk) it is shared. When it is shared, each is in the same state of relatedness. When it is given or received, each may be in a different state of relatedness (e.g., one participant may be in the state of helping and the other in the state of being helped).

The process of negotiating or bargaining is not the only form of interrelating. Two others are competing and challenging. In competing, a number of participants may compete with each other for a state of relatedness that is in short supply (e.g., children may compete for the attention or approval of a teacher or parent, or players in a game may compete for the status of being the victor). In challenging, one person or a number of people may try to diminish or take over another's state of relatedness (e.g., a rival may try to seduce another's lover, or mutineers may try to dislodge the captain of a ship from his position of authority).

SUMMARY

Relating is an activity that man shares with all animal forms. It is an activity that never stops. The distinction is drawn between external and internal relating and between objective, perceived, and subjective relating. It is directed toward attaining states of relatedness, which are positions of advantage in relation to others. Once such states have been attained, relating assumes a more consummatory function, though it also is directed toward maintaining and defending such states. In the main, relating is a spontaneous and automatic activity that is probably under the control of centers in the subcortical region of the nervous system. The emotions are closely linked with relating and represent responses to successes and failures in attaining states of relatedness. The close link between relating and the emotions supports a subcortical location for its control. During the process of maturation, innate tendencies to the main forms of relating are reinforced by the acquisition of skills and competencies. The well-adjusted person is competent in a broad range of relating skills and is confident of being able to attain all the main states of relatedness. S/he has a diversity of sources of states of relatedness available to her/him and has accumulated adequate stores of them. The less well adjusted person has fears and insecurities associated with certain states and is inclined to relate in a desperate and disrespectful manner. Being related to is also a continuous experience. In the process of interrelating, each individual attempts to achieve the best deal for her/himself in terms of satisfying her/his relating needs.

2

The Two Axes
of Relating

More than anything else, it is emotion which creates the impression that actions are purposeful. When an action leads to an advantageous state of relatedness, the person is rewarded by a pleasant emotion; when it does not, s/he is punished by an unpleasant one. This creates the impression that the rewarded actions are preferable to the punished ones and causes her/him to believe that the rewarded ones are fulfilling some kind of purpose. It is difficult to comprehend that most living organisms do not experience emotion; that the spider does not feel excited when it catches a fly, or that the fly does not feel dismay when it fails to free itself from the spider's web, or terror when it sees the spider advancing upon it. It is easier to accept that the insectivorous plant does not feel excited when a fly gets caught on its leaf, and that the flower does not feel excited when a bee successfully pollinates it. It is absurd to suppose that the earth feels excited when it succeeds in pulling the apple out of the tree. Yet human behavior is a complicated extension of the same physical laws that cause the apple to fall out of the tree; and emotion is simply an additional refinement, with which man has been endowed through the course of evolution, in order to reinforce certain advantageous forms of behavior. What must be remembered about evolution is that the so-called higher organisms, namely those that evolved later, are not necessarily superior to, or more efficient than, lower ones. If they were they would have replaced them. They simply perform the same functions but by more complex means, and organisms from all levels of evolution continue to co-exist.

The idea proposed in this book is as follows: at some fundamental level, that which is advantageous to humans is the same as that which is advantageous to all other living organisms; and the objectives of human relating are fundamentally the same as those of the relating of all other living organisms, right down to the very simplest. The continuity from inert matter through plants to animals and ultimately to humans should never be lost sight of, for it compels us to acknowledge that any purpose we might attribute to human behavior has got to have its roots in the functioning of all that has gone before us. We must always bear in mind that plants and animals are essentially of the same order of things; whatever purpose animals may have, plants also should have. Animals have acquired movement to enable them to attain the same objectives as plants but under different circumstances, even though some animals (e.g., sea anemones) have scarcely any more movement than plants have. We are able to identify more easily with animals because we too have movement.

One advantage of movement is that it enables animals to change their environment; this is of value in their search for food and water. Another is that it enables them to interact with each other; this is relating. A central theme of this book is that relating takes place along two fundamental axes, which will be called the proximity axis and the power axis. Seyfarth and Cheney (1992) considered the same two axes in their assessment of the relating of monkeys. Along the proximity axis, animals are able to adjust the distance between themselves and others. Along the power axis they are able to exert influence upon each other. When plants grow, they *are* able to move toward and away from each other; by so doing, they gain support or obtain greater exposure to light. Through differential growth they are able to open and close their petals and, by so doing, allow or deny insects access to them. They are also able to exert influence upon each other. One plant may be parasitic upon another or may so deprive another of light or water that it kills it. With movement, animals are able to do such things to each other to a far greater extent and to much greater effect.

THE PROXIMITY AXIS

Animals, particularly gregarious ones, constantly move toward and away from each other and remain vigilant of the presence of other animals in their vicinity and how far away they are from them. Animals must have an innate capacity to recognize and respond to the appearance and (sometimes) the smell of conspecifics; this ensures that they stay close to members of their own kind. There is enormous variation between species in the general degree of distance maintained between conspecifics; even within the same species, such distancing varies greatly according to time, season, and circumstance. Thus, closeness has no absolute advantages over distance, and both closeness and distance are advantageous in different ways. Animals frequently mass together to feed, sleep, or reproduce; this carries an obvious protective function. Bodies massed together afford protection against the cold in cold climates and against loss of moisture in hot climates (Allee, 1926). Animals massed together create a super-organism that is powerful and intimidating. It is effective in both attack and defense. A swarm, school, or pack of animals is able to overcome and kill prey or fight off predators that are bigger and stronger than the individual conspecifics. Certain insects, by sheer numbers, are sometimes able to create a bridge across a gap that enables other insects to cross over. Often, in mass activities of this kind, many individual animals are killed or die off, but their deaths enable the majority to survive. Clearly such animals are not conscious that they are making sacrifices for the good of the majority: simply, through natural selection the species that have come to function in this way have gained an advantage over those that have not.

Closeness is manifest not only as a massing together activity: it occurs also between two animals of opposite sexes in order that sexual reproduction may take place; or between parent animals and their young, while the young are immature and vulnerable; and between the young of a particular litter or brood. The degree of closeness that develops for sexual reproduction is extremely variable: it may be transient and sufficient only for the fertilization of eggs or it may extend over a period of years. Locating and moving toward a sexual partner is far from easy, particularly for solitary species. Animals that make a noise have a characteristic and recognizable mating call. Animals that do not (e.g., butterflies), need to rely upon smell which must be detectable over very long distances. At closer quarters, innate responses to visual appearance and courtship display become important. Aggressive animals need to make *appeasement gestures* during courtship by covering up aggressive signals or weapons. Grooming behavior, such as licking or stroking, has a calming effect upon an otherwise aggressive animal. Females make appeasement by presenting their posterior for mounting (Eibl-Eibesfeldt, 1970). In the so-called contact species, touching the body serves a greeting function. Chimpanzees have several greeting gestures including shaking hands, embracing and kissing (Lawick-Goodall, 1965, 1968).

In many species, sexual closeness is an exclusive closeness; once pair-bonding has been established, rival partners are driven away and territorial boundaries are imposed. Pair-bonding is important in species in which eggs are incubated outside of the body over a prolonged period of time, or in which the young are born in a weak and vulnerable state. The male may participate in nest building, protecting the female, and protecting and feeding the young. The attachments that develop between parents and their young (e.g., the imprinting of geese), ensure that the young remain close to the parents or are able to regain contact with them rapidly when danger presents itself. From an early age, parents and their young learn to recognize each other, and parents come to recognize and be responsive to the smell, appearance, and separation calls of their young. The bonds that develop between the young, as well as their play behavior, ensure that they remain harmoniously together as a group so that the parents are more easily able to protect and feed them. In primates and humans, the bonds that develop between sexual partners and between parents and their young have laid the foundations for the creation and maintenance of family structures. These may incorporate members of the extended family. Numbers of family structures may coalesce to form social groups; this creates the possibility for shared parenting and other collaborative enterprises.

Distancing

When food and water are scarce, closeness is a disadvantage, since limited resources become exhausted and the entire herd or colony may become extinct. Under such conditions the solitary animal is more likely to survive. Animals massed together are vulnerable to infection and infestation and to powerful predators that can kill off large numbers in the course of a single attack. The solitary animal is more difficult for predators to locate, is less exposed to infection and infestation, and has fewer rivals. Eibl-Eibesfeldt (1970) described a number of examples of overcrowding or overpopulation, particularly in mammals, leading to massive population reduction long before there was food shortage. This he ascribed to stress, which was confirmed by Christian (1959), who observed stress-related histological changes in the adrenal glands of the dead animals.

Distancing, in the form of exploration, enables animals to seek out environments that are more favorable in terms of climate, fewer hazards, greater protection, more plentiful or more varied food resources, fewer sources of infection, and fewer predators. It also ensures a greater diversity of sexual partners.

Distancing, in the form of flight, may sometimes prove a more effective protection against predators than fighting. Animals that can move very quickly survive by escape rather than by defending themselves. Animals do not need to flee in order to distance themselves from predators. They may stay put but produce offensive odors or exude foul tasting substances; or they may survive by camouflage or by having sharp spines, prickles, thick skin, or hard and impenetrable shells. In these ways they are adopting the same protective devices as (immobile) plants.

An important form of distancing is keeping other animals at bay by establishing and maintaining territorial boundaries and by spacing. Territorial boundaries are defined by odorous deposits of feces, urine, or skin secretions. This activity is as important for gregarious animals as it is for solitary ones. It ensures an adequate space for breathing and feeding and reduces contamination, infestation, and infection.

THE POWER AXIS

One animal is able to influence another because, in one way or another, it has the greater power. Such power may take the form of size, alertness, fitness, physical strength, speed, maneuverability, weaponry, or the support and alliance of conspecifics. In the wild, the most common form of influence is aggression; this may be directed at members of another species or members of the same species. When directed at members of another species, it is to kill and eat them. When directed at members of the same species, it is to establish the right of access, either to food or water or to a sexual partner. It rarely involves killing and frequently involves a minimal amount of fighting. This has clear advantages for the survival of the species. It was Lorenz (1981) who first described, in a range of vertebrate species, a form of confrontation between conspecifics, which he called *ritual agonistic behavior* (RAB). This takes place in two stages, assessment and engagement. In the assessment stage, each adversary assesses its power in relation to that of the other. If one assesses itself to be at a major disadvantage, it may back off; this is called by Sloman & Price (1987) *voluntary yielding*. Otherwise the animals proceed to the engagement stage, which amounts to a trial of strength, or a sequence of such trials, out of which there emerges a clear winner and a clear loser. The loser concedes defeat by signals of submission and thereafter avoids further confrontation with the winner. This has been called by Sloman and Price (1987) *agonistic yielding*.

The overall power of an animal, taking into account all its possible advantageous qualities, has been termed by Parker (1974) its *resource-holding potential* (RHP). The RHP of one animal compared with that of another he called the *relative RHP* (Parker, 1984). It is difficult to imagine how animals are able to make accurate assessment of this. For one thing, a lot of deception goes on, in that animals have ways of making themselves look bigger. How are they able to balance an advantage in one area (e.g., size) against a disadvantage in another (e.g., strength)? It is difficult to avoid attributing to animals the kind of reasoning ability by which humans would reach such a conclusion, though presumably they have no such ability. Even lowly animals such as lizards create the impression that they experience something that could be considered the equivalent of human confidence (Carpenter, 1978), though surely this cannot be. When they are in a state of high "confidence" they put out what can best be described as intimidating signals, in the form, for example, of particular forms of posture and gait, which cause adversaries to back away. A lion's roar has an intimidating effect; it must be that those lions that acquired the capacity to roar eventually fared better than those that did not. Following victory in a ritual agonistic encounter an animal will put out further intimidating signals, but following defeat it will put out *signals of surrender*. Defeated lizards may lose their normal colouring (MacLean, 1985).

Hierarchies

In gregarious animals, ritual agonistic behavior is an important precursor to the establishment of hierarchies. These are social systems within which animals of different resource-holding potentials are able to co-exist without harming each other. Animals stay together in hierarchies because they find the closeness (a state of relatedness) satisfying and to their advantage. The more powerful animals could easily kill and eat the weaker ones. If they did, however, (1) the species would rapidly become extinct and (2) the more powerful animals would be deprived of the closeness they need. Two stages in the course of evolution would therefore need to have come about, in order that hierarchies could exist and be maintained. The first was the acquisition of an inhibition on the killing of conspecifics; the second was the introduction of a set of signals, recognizable by all conspecifics, that conveyed the continuous acceptance and reinforcement of each animal's position relative to that of each other animal.

Chance (1988) observed that the assumption of a submissive posture by the loser in a ritual agonistic encounter is essential in order that the loser be retained within the social system. Such a posture inhibits any further attack by the winner and enables the loser to survive. Such a posture would, of course, be inappropriate in an encounter with a member of another species, since it would not have an inhibiting effect and the submitting animal would simply be killed. Following its defeat, the loser does not flee the group. Therefore, it must somehow be aware that it is safe to remain. Its return to the group is called by Chance *reverted escape*. Chance believes that reverted escape is a recursive movement of unique significance because it creates the precondition for social life. The loser's survival within the group is dependent upon its continuing to put out submissive signals to all animals that have defeated it in ritual agonistic encounters. There may well be other animals within the group that this animal has defeated and these animals will put out submissive signals to *it*. Price (1988) has pointed out that animals that have won in ritual agonistic encounters put out what he has termed *catathetic* (putting down) signals to animals they have defeated. Each animal therefore must somehow remember which animals it has defeated and which it has lost to, and on each subsequent encounter must put out an appropriate up-hierarchy or down-hierarchy signal. Since, over the course of time, animals vary in their fitness or their strength, their resource-holding potential will also vary. From time to time there must be repeated encounters, during which their position within the hierarchy may be revised. Seyfarth and Cheney (1992) maintained that there is some evidence that monkeys are capable of *transitive inference* - that is, having seen that A is dominant to B and B is dominant to C, they can infer that A is dominant to C; but they conceded that it is also possible that they simply memorize the outcome of every interaction between other monkeys.

What is being described here is what Schjelderup-Ebbe (1935) first observed in the domestic fowl and what later came to be called the *pecking order*. It invariably determined which birds had precedence in the order of feeding. The principle applies across all hierarchical groups; animals high in the hierarchy (called alpha animals) enjoy a number of privileges such as access to the best feeding and breeding area, feeding and sleeping in the safest places (e.g., in the center of the group), and choice of mates. Animals low in the hierarchy (called omega animals) look away from the direct gaze of the higher ones, withdraw when they approach, avoid their personal space, and may offer their hindquarters for mounting (De Vore, 1965). They eat less, are more furtive, and move more slowly and with greater caution (Crook, 1970).

Begging Behavior

Begging is an expression of powerlessness. The young of some species are able to gain and maintain the attention of their parents and get fed by making appropriate begging gestures. Begging among human adults is not uncommon (Chapter 8), but in the wild, adult animals do not beg. It is interesting that many tame or domesticated adult animals and some adult animals in captivity have learned to beg (Eibl-Eibesfeldt, 1970).

Chance's Distinction between the Agonic and the Hedonic Mode

Chance (1984) observed that different primate colonies have different social characteristics, which suggests that, in primates at least, certain forms of social organization are genetically determined. In Savannah baboon and Rhesus macaque colonies the organization is markedly hierarchical, but in chimpanzee and gorilla colonies it is cooperative. The former mode of organization he called *agonic*, the latter he called *hedonic*. The distinction between these two modes cuts across the proximity and power axes. The primary concern in the agonic mode is with self-security (a distance concept). The animals are spread out, separate from one another, keeping their distance and constantly attentive. They are in a continuous state of high tension and arousal, what Gilbert (1989) called braced readiness, in order to avoid assault from above and challenge from below. The primary concern in the hedonic mode is interdependence (a closeness concept). The animals maintain a closer proximity with one another and the level of tension and arousal is much lower. The more powerful animals, which are described as charismatic, are protective, reassuring, and encouraging toward the weaker ones. They behave therefore in a more parental fashion. When attention is released from rank awareness and self-protective needs, it can be used to explore and integrate many new domains. It is freed for detailed investigation and manipulation of objects in the physical environment, which, according to Chance, facilitates the development of intelligence.

Power (1988) emphasized that the natural world of chimpanzees was a safe and unthreatening one with a plentiful supply of food; the implication was that this contributed to their cooperative social organization. Recently this world has been changed by (1) human invasion and the consequent shrinkage of their environment and (2) the introduction of human-controlled restricted feeding. Since these changes, the behavior of chimpanzees has become more aggressive and competitive.

Parenting

Another power differential exists between parents and their young. In early animal species (e.g., most lizards) the young are left to fend for themselves and there is no parenting behavior at all (MacLean, 1985). In species in which there is, it has been necessary, during the course of evolution, for there to have been introduced two modifications to the behavior of parents: (1) an inhibition of the killing and eating of the young, and (2) the development of responses to specific signals put out by the young (e.g., the gaping beak of the chick) to ensure that they are protected and fed. It has also been necessary, in a number of species, for the parents to be stimulated to construct a nest before the eggs are laid or the young are born. The interaction between parents and their young is quite different from that between adversaries because (1) there is no ritual agonistic encounter, and (2) the parental activity is directed toward reducing the power differential, that is, they attempt to bring the young up to their level. This represents an extraordinary, and extremely important step in the evolutionary process. Parenting activity offers no advantage to the parents themselves (if anything, it renders them more vulnerable to predators); but it offers considerable advantage to the species. Parents will die, and it is essential that their offspring be made strong in order to succeed them.

The parents of many species protect their young, and in some gregarious species (e.g., termites) certain members have a specialist defensive function. Birds of some breeding colonies and members of some herds assist each other in mutual protection against predators. Jackdaws and Rhesus monkeys attack anyone who holds a conspecific (Eibl-Eibesfeldt, 1970).

THE PROXIMITY AXIS AS APPLIED TO HUMANS

Closeness

The tendency of humans to mass together, particularly at times of conflict, may have developed out of the group behavior of our hunter-gatherer ancestors. It was Lovejoy's (1981) opinion that the females foraged together near a fixed base while the males foraged further afield and brought back provisions for their monogamously selected mates and their offspring. The hunter-gatherer period constituted more than 90 percent of man's existence on earth, and such behavior was a characteristic of man's primate ancestors as well (Chance, 1988). The psychology of humans in crowds differs from that of humans acting alone, in that crowd members feel stronger and more confident and are prepared to suppress personal needs in order that the objectives of the crowd be met. In revolution and in warfare, individuals willingly sacrifice themselves in order that victory may be achieved. At the time of the Tiananman Square uprising, a Chinese proverb was told of a community of ants that formed itself into a large ball to roll down the side of a volcano in order that the innermost members might survive. The analogy may not be as far-fetched as it may have seemed. Although those who sacrifice themselves in battle are acclaimed as heroes, it may be that they too are simply driven by the innate tendency of many animal species to mass together in the face of a common adversary, with the inevitable outcome of many perishing as the mass moves resolutely toward its objective.

In groups, personal identity is reduced in order that a group identity may be built up. A group most readily forms among individuals who share a common characteristic (e.g., skin colour), and its cohesiveness is increased by its members assuming group characteristics (e.g., language). It starts because of similarities between individuals and progresses by increasing the similarity of its members. Its stability is maintained by the combination of uniformity and conformity. This is reinforced by the emergence, appointment, or election of a group leader who identifies with the group and with whom the group members can easily identify. Groups may be of varying sizes and complexities, and within large groups there may be subgroups. There may also be groups of groups. Humans derive pleasure from being members of a group; the formation of groups is a feature of all human cultures. Most human groups are not formed, as most animal groups are, for purposes of attack and defense; rather, they promote cooperation between members who share common interests, values, and objectives.

The coming together of individuals of opposite sexes for the purpose of sexual reproduction has developed much more extensively in humans; this is partly due to the relatively continual sexual receptivity of human females. This higher sexual activity serves to strengthen pair-bond adhesion (Lovejoy, 1981). From the age of puberty, the capacity to become sexually aroused intensifies; but in most cultures, free and open indulgence in sexual intercourse between the young does not occur. This is due partly to the inhibitions of the individuals themselves and partly to restrictions imposed upon them by parents and other adults. A common pattern is for alliances and grouping to develop initially between individuals of the same sex, within which sexual attractions and indulgences sometimes occur. Out of these alliances and groupings "forays" into heterosexuality are made, with same-sex peers being used for encouragement and support. The causes of these inhibitions and restrictions are not clearly understood, but because of them, subtler though highly intense involvements develop between adolescents and young adults that are called romantic love (Branden, 1980). Sexual desire remains an undercurrent in almost all romantic love relationships and frequently breaks through, though romantic attachments sometimes continue over long periods without the emergence of overt sexuality.

The evolution of marriage out of animal mating is the subject of a book edited by Reynolds and Kellett (1990). In most industrial societies, over 90 percent of adults eventually marry (Green, 1984); in most western societies, the initial stages of the marital relationship are characterized by high levels of sexual arousal and affection. After a variable interval this gives way to a more subdued form of relating called conjugal love (Oppong, 1979), which ideally involves mutual help, planning and maintaining the home, cooperation in rearing the children, and in the best relationships, development of a long-term companionship based upon shared values and beliefs. Because of the unselective nature of romantic love and the changing needs of marital partners, incompatibilities frequently surface that lead to serious marital disruption (Lederer and Jackson, 1968) and breakdown (Everett, 1991). Recent evidence suggests that two- thirds of first marriages in the United States will end in divorce (Martin and Bumpass, 1989). Despite this, the marital relationship remains the predominant mode of existence for the human adult.

The involvement that develops between parents and children has both a proximity and a power component, but only the proximity component will be considered at this point. The processes of bonding from parent to child and from child to parent are different, though obviously they are interdependent. Within the first month the child becomes able to discriminate between its mother's voice and that of another woman (DeCasper and Fifer, 1980). The parent responds to the cries and facial expressions of the infant in much the same way as the parent bird responds to the gaping beak of its fledglings. The infant's cry is disturbing to the parent, but when the parent responds by comforting or feeding it, the infant rewards her/him by stopping crying. Sometimes the infant does not stop crying and the parent responds by hitting or throwing it, which may result in its death. There is a critical moment when the parent, particularly the mother, needs to take to the infant. Sometimes (e.g., when the mother has had mixed feelings about having it) this does not happen, and the mother cannot bear even to touch it. Whereas the parent can survive without the infant, the infant cannot survive without the parent. Therefore, it has a high priority to get protected and fed, and much activity is directed to these ends. In order to stay close to its mother it clings with hands and feet to whatever part of her it can. Once the infant becomes mobile, it must learn to experience the parent as a safe place to return to and must take to the parent in much the same way as the parent had to take to it. This is what Bowlby (1969) has called *attachment*; it will be considered more fully in the next chapter. The relationship between parent and child is crucial for at least the first fifteen years and may continue to be important throughout life. Lovejoy (1981) observed that monogamous mating in humans ensured a greater male investment in parenting and the eventual establishment of the *bifocal nuclear family*. In the only other primates that practice monogamy (gibbons and siamangs), male parenting is also a prominent feature.

The play between the young from the same brood or the same litter has less relevance for humans than for most animals because multiple births are rare and parents, particularly in industrial societies, have small numbers of children. Children in industrial societies do, however, spend ten or more years in school, in which they are grouped together with age peers. Therefore the school inevitably assumes an important socializing function. Beyond romantic and conjugal alliances, long-term nonfamilial friendships often develop between same- or opposite-sex adults that have no apparent sexual component. They may be more closely linked with peer relationships than with sexual ones.

Distance

In close involvements, the concern is with establishing links with others: with the establishment of a condition of togetherness with other members of a group or of unitedness with another person. In such togetherness or unitedness, self-interest may be less important than the interests of the group or of the relationship. Individual members of a group may sacrifice themselves for the survival of the group, just as a mother may sacrifice herself for her child or a lover for her/his loved one. The solitary animal is concerned only with its own survival, just as the solitary individual is. Humans sometimes need to put themselves first, to protect themselves, be self-centered, self-approving, and self-reliant. Beyond this, much more than animals, they are concerned with needing to experience themselves as separate from others. Within the condition of distance they establish a personal identity and a firm sense of who they are. A group of humans, much more than a group of animals, is a group of individuals, each with her/his distinctive qualities and characteristics.

The exploratory aspect of distance assumes many forms in humans. As soon as it has established its secure base with its mother (Ainsworth, 1963), and at the first moment that any mode of locomotion becomes possible, the human infant, more than the young of many other mammals, begins to make excursions away from its mother and establish physical contact with objects far and near (Rheingold and Eckerman, 1970). Progressively, throughout life, various separations are rehearsed and embarked upon. These include playing with neighbors' children, going to school, going on school outings, leaving school, leaving home, and traveling abroad. In any culture, as soon as new modes of transportation are constructed, they are used to explore and colonize new territories. Although few humans actually become explorers, the exploring spirit manifests itself in the human preoccupation with travel and tales of travelers - and in our present age, with astronomy and space travel. The need to explore motivates much scientific curiosity.

Distancing, in terms of taking flight from predators, is not a prominent form of human behavior because (apart from infection and infestation) humans are not preyed upon by other species. Apart from certain primates, the human species is the only one that preys upon itself. Humans attack and kill each other in vast numbers, though rarely do they eat those whom they kill. Apart from times of war, humans rarely need to take flight or hide from their attackers, though increasingly in the west in recent years wives have started escaping and taking refuge from their aggressive husbands. Humans do escape from unpleasant situations, however, particularly when they involve other people. Children sometimes play truant or run away from home; adults sometimes "disappear" by moving to another town or a foreign country and changing their identity. People sometimes simply travel without knowing where they are going or lose all awareness of their life circumstances or of who they are. Such escapes are called *fugues* (Stengel, 1941, 1943). More commonly, however people escape by staying put but getting drunk, putting themselves to sleep, or ultimately by committing suicide.

The aspect of distancing that is concerned with setting up and maintaining territorial boundaries, with privacy and with personal space, is more firmly established in humans than in any other species. In all but the most crowded conditions, people maintain a space around themselves and do not like to touch or be touched by other people. Apart from formal exchanges (e.g., with trades and service people), they speak only to those who are known to them or to whom they have been introduced. Humans are the only animals that wear clothes; although clothes provide protection against the extremes of temperature, they also serve the important function of maintaining separateness from other people. The removal of clothes, either voluntarily or forcibly, carries considerable significance. People create further protective layers around themselves with lockable rooms, houses, private grounds, boundary fences, gates, moats, drawbridges and so on. Nations establish and guard their frontiers and maintain armed services and arsenals of weapons in order to defending themselves against invasion.

THE POWER AXIS AS APPLIED TO HUMANS

Reynolds (1966) observed that the foraging life mode of humans (which has accounted for over 90 percent of their existence) shares many characteristics of the hedonic existence of the wild chimpanzees; but there remain only a few scattered pockets of this, and even these are rapidly being taken over (Murdock, 1968). Even so, human modes of relating appear to be in a more direct line of descent from Chance's (1984) hedonic mode than from his agonic one, though in some social organizations the agonic influence remains apparent.

Intelligence

Intelligence and interdependence, which have their beginnings in hedonic primate colonies, are carried much further in human societies. "Intelligence" will be used here to refer to the apparent variation between individuals in their capacity to carry out a broad range of mental operations. Raw intelligence may itself bestow advantages in certain kinds of situations, for example when one person is able to outwit another, but its greater benefit is toward the individual's ability to acquire knowledge and learn skills. In the long run, such knowledge and skills contribute more to power than does intelligence itself; and an unintelligent person who has, with greater difficulty, gained these has potentially more power than an intelligent person who has not - though intelligence will contribute further to the use to which they may be put. Acquired knowledge and learned skills may be converted into educational or professional qualifications that are a form of packaged power.

Interdependence

In most animal groups power, or RHP, provides a means of gaining access to food or to mating partners. In all but the most primitive of human groups, its significance is much broader than this. Industrial societies are vastly more complex than any animal groups. In order for societies to function effectively an enormous diversity of tasks has to be carried out, and this requires a broad range of trades and professions. In the normal course of daily living, each individual within a society is dependent upon the services of many of people, all with different kinds of knowledge and different skills and all performing different tasks. Although some tasks might be more essential than others, it does not make very much practical sense to make comparisons between the people within this complex network in terms of their resource-holding potential, since they are all dependent upon each other. Even within a simple relationship between two people, there is such a diversity of ways in which one person can be better than the other, or can do things for the other, that often it is not a particularly useful exercise to attempt to determine, in any absolute sense, who should be considered better than, or being helped by, whom. In fact, in human transactions, either at a macro or a micro level, is usually an arrangement of "I'll do this for you if you'll do this for me"; either at the same time or over a period of time, each is both helping and being helped by the other. This has connections with *social exchange theory* (Thibaut & Kelly, 1959; Bahr, 1982). An extremely important implication of the concept of interdependence is that what is being considered here is not so much who is more powerful than whom (the issue in most animal interactions) as who is doing what for whom. Clark et al. (1989) used the term *exchange relationship* to describe a relationship in which two people benefit each other in specific ways. This introduces the concept of altruism, which will be discussed more fully shortly.

Money and Possessions

An important development in the evolution of human societies has been the introduction of money. Like professional qualifications, money is a way of *packaging power*. It operates very much like electricity in that once it has been generated, it can be stored or accumulated, moved from place to place, transferred from person, to person and used to carry out different kinds of work. When one person performs a service for another s/he is rewarded with money. This s/he may use to pay another person to perform a service for her/him. The money circulates and different people get different things done for them. In none of these transactions does anyone have any more or any less power than anyone else; this creates a more cooperative society. Unfortunately, it does not always work as smoothly as this. Because money is a form of power, people accumulate it for its own sake and the accumulation of money becomes a source of satisfaction in itself. Whole professions are concerned entirely with manipulating sums of money in order to increase its value.

Money and possessions are interchangeable and each may readily be transformed into the other. Certain forms of possession (e.g., precious stones and precious metals) are practically the same as money and are sought and accumulated in the same way. One definition of having power is having that which others want, whether this be food, territory, raw materials, manufactured goods, objects of beauty, personal attributes, knowledge, ability, or physical fitness; and all of these may be traded for money.

Hierarchies

Hierarchies based upon strength or fighting ability, which form the basis of most animal groups, may be apparent in some primitive cultures, but they are rare in industrial societies. Hierarchies similar to these may be found in some criminal and prison populations, but even here, knowledge and skills are likely to play an important part. Even though interdependence is a major factor in human societies, hierarchies do exist, particularly within professional groups. Movement up and down within such hierarchies does not normally occur by ritual agonistic behavior, it occurs by the promotion or demotion of junior members of the group by the more senior members. Promotion is based upon qualification and performance. As in animal hierarchies, members confirm their place within the hierarchy by expressing respect or deference toward those who are senior to them and authority and expectation toward those who are junior. In most hierarchies the more senior members plan, organize, and take responsibility and the more junior ones carry out tasks allotted to them.

Some psychologists continue to consider dominance a useful and meaningful concept in human relating, though Buss (1988) has extended its meaning to include aggression, nonaggressive competition, and leadership. Kalma (1991) has provided evidence that humans, like animals, evaluate relative dominance (mainly on the basis of non-verbal behavior), very quickly, without the intervention of cognitive processing, which is in keeping with the subcortical location of relating described in Chapter 1.

Power Gradients

Human social systems involve not so much hierarchies as what might be called power gradients. One such gradient is the relationship between employers and employees. The most primitive of these existed between masters and their slaves. The slaves were kept alive by their masters so that they would be fit enough to continue to work for them, but they received no rewards. The slaves could not leave their masters because they were their prisoners. During World War II, British prisoners in Burma were treated in this way by their Japanese captors. In early industrial societies the relationship between employers and employees was little different from this; and in some of the less developed nations of today, similar conditions obtain. With the organization of worker power, the establishment of trade unions, and the introduction of industrial legislation, employers have come to treat employees with greater respect and the interdependence between them has become more firmly acknowledged.

Another power gradient is that which (1) dictates or determines which forms of behavior should be considered by the group to be right or wrong, acceptable or unacceptable, tolerable or intolerable; and (2) imposes restraints or controls upon those that are wrong, unacceptable, and intolerable. The hierarchy may be headed by an external deity, in which case that which is wrong is deemed to be sinful, or by a government, in which case it is deemed to be criminal. In certain cultures the two authorities are difficult to separate, but in others they are quite distinct. In communist countries the external deity has been totally suppressed and the only authority is the government. In western societies there are two separate hierarchical systems, the religious and the legal. Within the religious hierarchy, those who are appointed to make clear the judgments and expectations of God may express their disapproval of certain forms of behavior but are not empowered to impose restraints or to punish. Within the legal hierarchy, those who are appointed to make clear the laws of the state are empowered both to pass judgments and to impose punishments. Within societies, organizations exist (e.g., the armed services, schools, and the family), that have their own self-appointed arbiters of what is right and what is wrong; these arbiters make judgments and impose punishments.

Social Attention Holding Potential

Gilbert (1989, 1992) has proposed that over evolutionary time the resource-holding potential system, which involves gaining and exerting control by aggression, or threat of aggression has been added to and to some extent modified by a system by which status depends upon the ability to attract the attention of others in a favorable way. This he has called *social attention holding potential*, or SAHP. He has made connections between this and Barkow's (1975, 1980) concept of prestige. Gilbert's SAHP is a necessary stage between the simple threat-based hierarchies of animals and the much more complex hierarchies, based upon a range of criteria, to be found in humans.

Parenting

The proximity component of parenting already has been discussed. This section deals with the power component. The principal function of parenting is to provide food and protection until the child is strong enough to fend for itself. In humans, this takes longer than in any other animal species. In primitive societies it may take up to ten years, and in industrial societies it may take twice as long. At birth, the power differential between parent and child is immense, but this diminishes as the child grows older. During the early years, parents are in a position to exert enormous control over their children and to intimidate them by threats of punishment. Cultures vary in the extent to which parents are permitted to inflict physical punishment upon their children, but in many cultures their freedom to do so is considerable. The best parent- child relationships are based upon praise, encouragement, trust, and mutual respect, though even in these, there is always the understanding that the parents have the upper hand. As their children grow older, parents need to steer a delicate path between gradually relaxing the restraints they have imposed upon them while continuing to maintaining sufficient restrictions to prevent them from disrupting their own lives. Even though children remain relatively weaker over many years, their innate disposition to gain power induces them, from an early age, to defy and rebel against their parents. If such behavior is not understood for what it is, it may cause the parents great distress and provoke them into making repressive responses. By adolescence, it is not uncommon for children to become physically stronger than their parents, and in certain respects at least, more knowledgeable and more skillful. If a successful transition into adult life is to be accomplished, the transfer of power must be conceded and their new status acknowledged.

ALTRUISM

From an evolutionary point of view, it might be difficult to imagine what advantage altruism has either for the individual or for the species. Much has been written by evolutionists on the subject of altruism (see Badcock, 1986; and Richards, 1987, pages 234-246). The term *"inclusive fitness"* was introduced by Hamilton (1963) to mean the fitness of the individual and her/his kin. He showed that natural selection would favor genes for behaving altruistically toward close kin because copies of those genes had a high probability of being in the bodies of kin; thus, reproductive benefits of behavioral traits can be reaped by kin rather than just by the individual who actually manifests them (Wenegrat, 1984). As Bailey (1988) put it, "Self-sacrificial altruism to close kin serves to perpetuate *our* genes in *them* through succeeding generations." (page 133).

Much of what parents do to and for their young could be considered altruistic; their behavior was called by Hamilton (1964) *kin altruism*. It may be that other forms of altruism, called by Trivers (1971) *reciprocal altruism*, are derivative of the parenting tendency. It is preferable to restrict the term "altruism" to that which one adult does to another. Trivers (1985) argued that helping others may have evolved because the donor would be likely to benefit in terms of subsequent help received from the recipient. Thus, altruism contributes to the overall efficiency of social groups and benefits the species. There are a few examples of animals that care for disadvantaged conspecifics. Porpoises raise those who are wounded to the surface to enable them to breathe (Siebenaler and Caldwell, 1956). There are the beginnings of altruism in primate hedonic colonies. With these possible exceptions, man appears to be the only animal that demonstrates truly altruistic behavior. In the wild, an animal of another species that is ailing or weak would be killed and eaten, and one of the same species would be trodden underfoot or expelled from the group. It is common for humans to respond with compassion to those who are suffering or in difficulties; in most human societies, the ailing and the weak are protected and cared for.

Dawkins (1976) considered that the sacrifice of the phenotypes is of less importance than the survival of the genes. Kin selection (Maynard Smith, 1964; Alexander, 1974) is a variation of natural selection. It is a process whereby an individual favors kin over nonkin or even close kin over self. Kin selection theory assumes that all behavior is genetically selfish whether it occurs be through reciprocal altruism or inclusive fitness. Reciprocal altruism extends kin selection theory because it includes mutually beneficial relations among nongenetically related individuals (Chagnon and Irons, 1979).

Price (1988) has coined the term *"anathetic"* to refer to an act of improving the status of another. It is the opposite of his term *"catathetic,"* which refers to an act of reducing the status of another. Altruism might be called down-hierarchy anathetic behavior. In human societies, much anathetic behavior is not in a strict sense altruistic: it simply forms part of the general pattern of interdependence that characterizes many human interactions. In the so-called helping professions, which include medicine, nursing, teaching, and the hotel and catering professions, workers receive an income for what they do, though it is probably true to say that many are attracted to the work because they enjoy helping people. The altruistic tendency does, however, appear to be quite strong; in times of disaster, people voluntarily work long and hard, sometimes putting their own lives at risk, in order to save others.

Seeking and Receiving Help, Care, Advice

Because animals do not help one another there would be little point in their putting out help-seeking signals. Many animals make noises when they are hurt, but the effect of this probably is to warn other animals of danger. Dogs and cats make whining noises when they are distressed, though these are most likely variants of their separation calls. Humans, however, quite openly seek, help, care, advice and so on, because being the recipient of these is an acceptable form of human behavior.

Altruistic Gradients

Altruistic gradients are a modification of the already described power gradients; like them, they are unique to human societies. The secure child has, in relation to its parents, an understanding that everything is under control and being taken care of, and this makes it feel good. Adults also have this understanding in relation to certain other adults, whose function it is to concern themselves with their well-being. In many organizations, seniority carries with it responsibility; and one important aspect of responsibility is taking the strain of decision making off the more junior members. They are then free to get on with their own tasks, confident that those above and in charge of them have certain organizational matters in hand. The more senior members are paid to do the worrying for them; but the responsibility of the more immediate senior members is limited, for they in turn have even more senior members who carry responsibility and do the worrying for them; and so it goes on up the administrative tree. There is, of course, considerable variation between organizations in the extent to which responsibility and concern for those who are more junior are linked. Some organisations are entirely exploitative; others, while claiming to be concerned about the well-being of their members, reveal little evidence of it.

The principle of the altruistic gradient, although frequently imperfect in practice, does exist, and under certain circumstances it works very well. The attitude of the truly altruistic senior person is, "If you have a problem you only have to come to me and I will do my best to sort it out." Ideally, the parliamentary system is an altruistic gradient and it should be possible to approach a member of parliament in this way. The Church is another, with God, the ultimate all-caring person, at its pinnacle.

SUMMARY

The continuity between the relating of animals and the relating of humans is emphasized. Their capacity to move enables animals to relate in the way that they do. Through movement they adjust their position in relation to one another (the proximity axis) and exert influence over one another (the power axis). Animals move closer in order to create a kind of super-organism; this has advantages for both attack and defense; for sexual reproduction; for enabling parents to protect and feed their young and for their young to stay safely together. They distance themselves as one means of survival, particularly when resources are scarce; for seeking out and exploring new territories; as a form of escape; for spacing and for setting up and maintaining boundaries. The most common way in which animals influence one another is by aggression. Across-species aggression is directed toward killing and eating, and within-species aggression is directed toward determining and defining relative strengths and, therefore, position within the hierarchy. Cohesion within a hierarchy is maintained by the weaker animals submitting to the stronger ones. Parenting is possible because of an inhibition on the killing of the young and the responses of the parents to the needful signals of the young. An important intermediate stage in the evolutionary process was the emergence, among some primates, of the hedonic colony.

Human relating can be classified within the same broad categories as those of animals. Humans group together less for attack and defense than for the pursuit of common objectives and shared interests. Because of inhibitions upon overt sexuality, relationships between individuals of opposite sexes include not only direct sexual involvements but also the more subtle and complex interactions of romantic and conjugal love. Parents and children become united by a combination of the bonding of the parents and the attaching of the children. Children develop important, close relationships with their peers both at home and at school that may form the basis for many adult, nonsexual involvements. Human distancing includes the protection of self-interest and the establishment of personal identity; exploration, travel, and curiosity; escape from stress; concern with privacy; and the defense of personal property and territory. The power axis in humans has developed broadly because of the many forms that human power may assume. The physical strength and fighting capacity of animals have largely given way to intelligence and the acquisition of knowledge and skills. Human relationships and societies are characterized mainly by interdependence. The hierarchies that do exist are based more upon ability and performance, and there are a number of power gradients. Although some parents impose control by fear of punishment, many exert their influence by a more restrained approach. Altruism, the benevolent application of power, has been developed to a far greater extent in humans than in other animals, as has the complementary activity of help or care seeking.

3

Further Development
of the Two Axes

It has now been established that human relating occurs along two principal axes, one concerned with proximity and one concerned with power. For ease of graphical representation (see Figure 1), the first of these will be referred to as the horizontal axis (since people move toward or away from each other in a horizontal plane) and the second will be referred to as the vertical axis (since the more powerful person can be conceived of as being above the weaker one). It will be proposed that each end of each axis represents a *state of relatedness*. The object of relating is to attain states of relatedness. In turn, a state of relatedness is a condition resulting from relating to, or being related to by, another person (Chapter 1). A state of relatedness can be attained only in relation to another person. Since the other person is also trying to attain states of relatedness, a process of bargaining/negotiating/competing has to take place. This is called *interrelating*.

The states of the two ends of the horizontal axis could be called closeness and distance. It is less reasonable, however, to call the states of the two ends of the vertical axis being the more powerful and being the less powerful or being stronger and being weaker. The names need to reflect the fact that the vertical axis in humans is much more broad-ranging and interactive than it is in animals. For one thing, the more powerful or the stronger person is more likely to be able or willing to be of advantage to the less powerful and the weaker one; usually, whereas one person is more powerful or stronger in one respect, the other is more powerful or stronger in another, so that an exchange of benefits often takes place. Thus, it is not always possible to say, in any general sense, which person is the more or the less powerful.

These things having been said, the continuity from animals to humans cannot be lost sight of, and it has to be acknowledged that the vertical axis in humans must have evolved from a more power-based vertical axis in animals. Part of the satisfaction of being the more powerful person probably derives from

FIGURE 1
The Two Main Axes of Relating

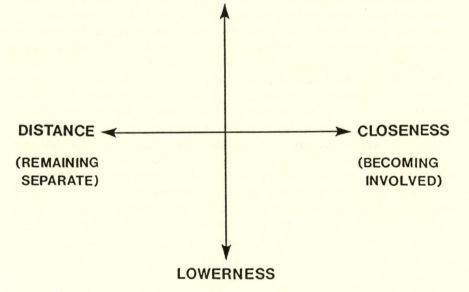

UPPERNESS

(RELATING FROM A POSITION OF RELATIVE STRENGTH)

DISTANCE ←—————————→ CLOSENESS

(REMAINING   (BECOMING
SEPARATE)   INVOLVED)

LOWERNESS

(RELATING FROM A POSITION OF RELATIVE WEAKNESS)

being or feeling superior in some way, otherwise there would be no motivation to seek it; on the other hand, it is not uncommon for the weaker person also to feel good about being weak. What seems to have happened in humans is that the weaker position of the young (who are fed and protected by the parents) of many other animal species has been extended and built upon to apply to adults and that the help- seeking strategies of the young have come to be adopted by adults as well. People perform so many different functions, and there is such a diversity of skills and abilities, that everyone is dependent upon a range of other people for different forms of benefit. Therefore, it is not necessarily a sign of inferiority to be the recipient of that which the more powerful person can provide.

The vertical axis in humans can be viewed in a number of ways. At its simplest, the person moves up it as s/he grows stronger, wiser, more experienced, more skillful, more senior, more responsible. Among other things therefore, it has to be a measure of personal achievement, advancement, improvement, or promotion. There continue to be rewards for coming out on top. In a complex society however, the person at the higher level does much more than simply indulge in the satisfaction of being superior. Such satisfaction, in any case, is usually short-lived. S/he then goes on to play her/his part in activities such as governing, managing, organizing, guiding, teaching, encouraging, passing judgment, rescuing, and nursing. The person at the lower level is the willing beneficiary of such activities. It has to be acknowledged that humans do not always use their power and strength to benefit others; sometimes, as in other animal species, it is used in order to do harm to others. The general names of the two ends of the vertical axis should therefore be neither positive nor negative. They should also be neutral and value-free. Because no suitable words existed, the words *"upperness"* and *"lowerness"* were created. Though such words do not appear in any dictionary, their meaning can readily be understood.

Gilbert's (1989, 1992) social attention holding potential, referred to in Chapter 2, appears to straddle the two axes. In many of the ways Gilbert uses it, it has much in common with upperness; but since it also involves being liked, it has associations with closeness.

AXES RATHER THAN DIMENSIONS

Until now the term "axes" rather than "dimensions" has been used, and this has been done deliberately. A dimension is normally understood to be a range in quality or quantity from one extreme to another such that a high point on one extreme is equivalent to a low point on the other. On the lightness-darkness dimension, it cannot be both light and dark at the same time; on the tallness-shortness dimension, it is not possible to be both tall and short at the same time. In terms of relating, however, opposites can, and frequently do, co-exist. A person may feel both close and distant, or upper and lower, to another at the same time, or s/he may feel close in some respects and distant in others, upper in some respects and lower in others. When there are so many different ways of being close or distant and upper or lower, it is unhelpful to consider these to be dimensions.

The horizontal axis differs from the vertical in one important respect. The way that closeness is the opposite of distance is not the same as the way that upperness is the opposite of lowerness. When one person tries to get close to another s/he is inevitably, at the same time, trying to make the other close to her/him. When one person tries to become upper in relation to another s/he is inevitably, at the same time, trying to make the other lower in relation to her/him. Thus, whereas distance may be the opposite of closeness, lowerness has to be the complement of upperness.

Finally, there is the question of desirability. It is easier to think in terms of dimensions when one extreme is clearly more desirable than the other. Good is desirable, but bad is undesirable; love is desirable, but hate is undesirable; success is desirable, but failure is undesirable. What I hope to make clear through the course of this book is that being close should be neither more nor less desirable than being distant and being upper should be neither more nor less desirable than being lower. The (good) states of relatedness associated with each of the four positions are equally desirable and equally pleasurable. In terms of relating skills or competencies, the good relater needs to be as skillful or as competent in one direction of an axis as s/he is in another. Conversely, the bad relater may be equally bad in both directions on a particular axis. People who are claustrophobic (which might be considered a negative form of distance) tend also to be agoraphobic (which might be considered a negative form of closeness). If an instrument existed for measuring positive forms of relating, a good relater could score high on both ends of a particular axis and a poor relater could score low on both ends; if an instrument existed for measuring negative forms, the reverse of this could be so. This is another reason why it is preferable to think in terms of axes rather than dimensions.

DISTINGUISHING BETWEEN RELATING AND RELATIONSHIPS

In Chapter 1 it was made clear that the book is about relating. It is easier to restrict attention to relating when writing about animals, because although animals relate, they do not form relationships to anything like the extent that humans do. Because the book is concerned with the continuity between animals and humans, it is primarily about relating. Whereas relating is a characteristic of an individual, a relationship is a characteristic of (usually) two individuals. Relating is that which one person does to another and originates within the individual. A relationship is that which goes on between two people and is made up of the combined interrelating (see Chapter 1) of both of them. It may be possible and quite reasonable to describe a relationship as close or distant if both partners are, for the most part, being close or distant. It might conceivably be possible to describe a relationship as upper if both partners are trying to be upper in relation to the other, or as being lower if both are trying to be lower in relation to the other. Although there are relationships such as these, such terminology is unlikely to prove acceptable.

ARE UPPER AND LOWER THE SAME AS RELATING AND BEING RELATED TO?

The vertical axis began (in Chapter 2) as the power axis, and the power axis was referred to as concerning one animal or person being in a position to influence another. The greater part of the description of the power axis concerned the various strengths and capabilities of animals and people that enabled them to exert an influence upon others. Only toward the end of Chapter 2 did we refer to the characteristics of the person who was being influenced.

In an earlier attempt to put together a biaxial theory of relating (Birtchnell, 1987), the vertical axis was described as being concerned with *directiveness* (the upper position) versus *receptiveness* (the lower position). Directiveness was defined as including "attitudes and behavior associated with doing or giving something to another person," and receptiveness was defined as "attitudes and behavior associated with needing, inviting, and being in receipt of affection, approval, support, or direction from others." This distinction proved to be unsatisfactory because it combined two different concepts: being stronger versus being weaker, and being the donor versus being the recipient. Weaker people can do and give things to stronger people, and stronger people can have things done and given to them. Besides this, on the horizontal axis, it is possible to give and receive either closeness or distance.

The introduction of a spatial theory helped to resolve the confusion, since, within a spatial configuration, it is easier to conceive of the horizontal and the vertical axes as being separate. Once the terms "upperness" and "lowerness" had been decided upon, the task remained to determine what they meant. This was made easier with the emergence of the concept of states of relatedness. If these, by definition, are states that should be aimed at or striven for, what should the states of upperness or lowerness be like? Upperness is bound to involve feeling superior to or better than someone in some respect, and lowerness is bound to involve feeling inferior to or worse than someone in some respect; but more frequently in man than in animals, by virtue of being superior or better, the person is in a position to be of benefit to the person who is lower, and the good feelings associated with being upper are not just those of having the edge over someone else. The lower person need not feel bad about being inferior or worse, providing there is an understanding that the upper other is going to use her/his superiority or betterness in order to be of benefit to him/her. The lower person may feel therefore that s/he is in good hands and that her/his interests are being met. Upper people do not invariably choose to use their advantageous position for the benefit of others, and lower people do not invariably experience their disadvantageous position as being of benefit to them, but the extent to which they do is a measure of the difference between animal relating and human relating.

As was explained in Chapter 1, relating is an active process directed toward attaining, maintaining, defending, or indulging in a particular state of relatedness; and being related to is a passive process involving being the recipient of any of these actions. All versions of relating and being related to described in Chapter 1 apply as much to upperness as they do to lowerness (and as much to closeness as they do to distance). Lower people can influence and actively relate to upper people as much as upper people can influence and actively relate to lower ones. Pleading and begging, for example, are ways by which lower people can influence upper ones. Thus, upperness and lowerness cannot be the same as relating and being related to.

A SPATIAL THEORY OF RELATING

Once the names of the axes were selected, it became apparent that they defined the two dimensions of a Euclidian space. This led to the creation of what could be called *a spatial theory* of relating. In a very fundamental way, people can be conceived of as objects separated from each other by space. It is a tantalizing thought that people are spatially separate from each other, that they can never experience being anyone other than themselves, that they communicate with each other across the space that separates them, and that it is never possible to totally bridge the gap. This is related to the existential concept of aloneness - that whatever ties we may have between ourselves and others, we are always essentially alone.

A biaxial conceptualization of one person's position in relation to another is embedded within popular consciousness. People use phrases such as "he feels so close to me" and "she seems so remote" or "I look up to him" and "she looks down on me." When used in this way, the phrases have a more metaphorical than literal meaning. It is always necessary to distinguish between the metaphorical and the literal meaning, though sometimes they overlap. A (metaphorically) distant person frequently does, both literally and metaphorically, keep a safe distance from others and is careful not to become too closely involved with them. When two people experience themselves as being (metaphorically) very close, they frequently give expression to this by staying in close proximity or getting physically close by touching and hugging. A victor in a physical encounter may knock his opponent to the ground or unseat him from his horse and then stand over him, perhaps placing a foot upon his chest, as an indication that he has "come out on top." A person who experiences her/himself as (metaphorically) inferior to another may kneel at the other's feet. This is similar to the submissive posture of some animals.

The literal state can actually induce or enhance the emotion of the metaphorical state it represents. When close people hug, they feel even closer. When a teacher makes a naughty child stand in the corner, the child feels even more abandoned. When a victor stands over his defeated opponent, he experiences the excitement of victory and his opponent experiences the dejection of defeat. This principle is used to good effect in family sculpting, a family therapy technique in which the therapist invites one family member to physically arrange the remaining family members in positions and postures that represent what s/he believes to be the relationships they have with each other. A group of family therapists may also do this with each other so that one therapist can represent to the others the relationships that s/he believes exist within a family s/he is treating. The object of the exercise is to bring out, for the sculpted person, the emotion that being in a particular (literal and metaphorical) position within the family induces. This is particularly effective for exposing the effects of one family member being forced to relate in a particular way by another family member. For this reason it is preferable that family members not be placed in their normal positions. In this way they can, in a make believe way, be compelled to "see what it feels like" to have the position of someone else within the family.

The distinction between the literal and the metaphorical meanings of particular forms of relating is linked, to some extent, with the distinction between internal and external forms of relating, the literal being linked with external and the metaphorical with internal. The tension in the play *Separation* by Tom Kempenski, was created by the circumstances of two people who were separated by being forced to live on opposite sides of the Atlantic but who fell in love during the course of a series of telephone conversations. Thus, literally they were distant, but metaphorically they were close. The reverse situation would occur if a person was forced to spend time in the company of someone s/he did not feel close to.

In terms of spatial relationships, the term "dimension" seems to make more sense. Conceptually, being close *is* the opposite of being distant and being upper *is* the opposite of being lower, thus, the concepts themselves *can* be considered within a dimensional framework. An analogy can be drawn here between the particular and the wave theories of light. Sometimes light behaves as though it is made up of particles and sometimes it behaves as though it is made up of waves. The difficulties arise because of the issue of good, or positive, and bad, or negative, forms of relating (which some might claim should be considered as a third dimension). The policy that will be adopted throughout this book is to consider first the good, or ideal, forms of relating and then to consider various imperfect forms.

EXISTING THEORIES ASSOCIATED WITH THE HORIZONTAL AXIS

Approach-Avoidance Theories

Such theories do not necessarily apply to relating to people, but much of what is written in the approach-avoidance literature has relevance to human relating. People experience involvement with others as both desirable and frightening and many of the conflicts associated with the horizontal dimension are centered around this issue. Stagner (1937) considered that approaching versus withdrawing from a stimulus object was one of the two main dimensions along which variations in human behavior may be plotted. Roth and Cohen (1986) were concerned with approaching and avoiding stressful or threatening circumstances, but their analysis of the coping strategies employed has application to conflicts that arise over human relating. Avoidant strategies serve to reduce stress and anxiety and allow for a gradual recognition of threat. They can result in emotional numbness, unwanted intrusions of threatening material, and disruptive avoidance behaviors when there is a conscious or unconscious attempt to keep threatening cognitions and affects out of awareness. There can be a rapid alternation between approach and avoidance, or certain aspects of threatening material can be avoided while other aspects are approached. Partial, tentative, or minimal use of avoidance can lead to increased hope and courage and a sense of mastery over unpleasant emotions associated with the threatening material.

Hilgard et al. (1979) observed that as people get farther away from a feared object, it seems less frightening, but an attractive object is still appealing from a distance. This, they maintained, is why couples who break up find each other more appealing from a distance, but as they try to resume the relationship their fears drive them apart again. Byrne et al. (1963) suggested that the experiences of individuals throughout life lead to a generalized expectancy of reward or punishment. If the expectancy of reward is greater than that of punishment, other people will be sought as companions, trusted, and highly valued. If the reverse is true, other people will be avoided, mistrusted and devalued. An individual with mixed experiences, who is therefore high on both expectancies, will be in a state of relatively continuous conflict about interpersonal relationships.

Close Relating versus Distant Relating

In an absolute sense, the difference between closeness and distance would be the difference between relating and not relating. However, this book is concerned not so much with the absolute difference as with the relative difference; that is, between what might be called *close relating* and *distant relating*. Such a difference may have been partly understood by philosophers. Bergson (1912), for example, referred to two profoundly different ways of knowing a thing, which he called *intuition* and *analysis*. The first (which would correspond to close relating) involves an "intellectual sympathy" or entering into the object in order to coincide with what is unique in it. The second (which would correspond to distant relating) involves moving around the object, an operation that reduces it to elements that are common to both it and other objects. Buber's (1937) distinction between the *I-Thou* and the *I-It* attitude is very similar. The I-Thou attitude (which would correspond to close relating) involves entering into a relationship. The I-It attitude (which would correspond to distant relating) involves traveling over the surface of something and examining it. "If," he explained, "I face a human being as my Thou, and say the primary word I-Thou to him, he is no longer a thing among things, and does not consist of things" (page 8). It is possible to adopt an I-Thou attitude toward a thing, as a child does toward a teddy bear. It is also possible to adopt an I-It attitude towards a person, as an autistic child does when it moves someone's foot out of its way. Seyfarth and Cheney (1992) observed that monkeys see the world as composed of things that act, not things that think and feel. No monkey has ever been observed to console a grieving companion, for example. It would seem, therefore, that the I-Thou attitude is essentially a human attitude and that humans are capable of greater degrees of closeness than any other animal.

Mackie (1969) linked what he called intimate relating with *primary process* thinking and nonintimate relating with *secondary process* thinking. Primary and secondary process thinking are terms introduced by Freud (1911a) to differentiate between the more spontaneous and less organized thinking of the immature ego and the less spontaneous and more organized thinking of the mature ego. This is an interesting theory because distant relating tends to be associated with precision, logic, and emotional inhibition. A serious objection to it is that primary process thinking is considered to be common in psychotic individuals, whose relating is the most distant. Mackie's theory can be retrieved by postulating that secondary process thinking is a characteristic of moderately distant relating, which will be called *formal* relating, but that when the individual becomes so distant as to retreat into her/himself (becoming psychotic) s/he reverts to primary process thinking.

Suttie (1935) referred to what he called *the taboo on tenderness,* which he considered to be a defensive posture for avoiding excessive involvement with someone else, and which he considered to be the result of experiencing the painful breakup of an early, close relationship. Since he believed that everyone experiences such pain when the early ties to the mother are loosened, he considered this to be a universal attitude, though it is clearly more pronounced in some people than in others. For Suttie, this taboo regulates the degree of closeness with which a person feels comfortable. He considered that the methods of physical science represent a "*flight from tenderness*" but that Christian religion seeks to reconstruct the tender relationships of early childhood.

It needs to be emphasized that whatever the cause may be of the difference between close and distant relating, there are times when one is appropriate and times when the other is - and that neither should be considered superior to the other.

Intimacy versus Solitude

Dowrick (1992) wrote insightfully of the necessity in all close relationships of balancing the need for intimacy with the need for solitude. You want to know that you are capable of devotion without losing your sense of self, she wrote, but you also want to be alone without feeling isolated. It is a question of discovering how to make rewarding, enlivening contact with other people without losing your sense of who you are and what you want.

Other-Interest versus Self-Interest

A number of writers have drawn a distinction between interest focused upon others and interest focused upon the self. Macdiarmid (1989) called this other-cathexis and self-cathexis and reviewed a range of theories that had a bearing upon it. Whereas interest focused upon others is equivalent to closeness, interest focused upon the self is only part of the distancing process. Freud (1914) and Abraham (1924) distinguished between what they called an *anaclitic object choice*, expressed in terms of the libidinal attachment to the mother, and a *narcissistic object choice* expressed as a hypercathexis of one's own ego. Anaclitic object choice leads to the establishment of mature, intimate adult relationships, narcissistic object choice leads to identification and self-definition. Blatt and Shichman (1983) proposed that personality development involves two primary tasks: the *anaclitic*, the capacity to form stable, enduring relationships, and the *introjective*, the achievement of a differentiated and consolidated identity. Beck (1983) considered there to be two major personality dimensions: the *sociotropic,* concerned with a positive interchange with other people, and the *autonomous*, preserving the integrity and autonomy of the personal domain. Jung

(1921) proposed that the psyche could take two general orientations in relating to the world: inward, toward the subjective world of the individual; and outward toward the external environment. He called such orientations attitudes; he named the inward one *introversion* and the outward one *extroversion*. Some people are inclined more toward one than the other. The introvert is quiet, imaginative, and more interested in ideas than in people; the extrovert is sociable, outgoing, and interested in people and things. This distinction subsequently was taken up and operationalized by Eysenck (1970).

EXISTING THEORIES ASSOCIATED WITH THE VERTICAL AXIS

Theories concerned specifically with the vertical axis are few. Adler (1931), who will be further discussed in the next chapter, was essentially a vertical theorist. He considered the ultimate goal of all humans to be superiority or perfection. He believed it is the feeling of being weak, impotent, and inferior that stimulates in the child an intense desire to seek power. Although he maintained that it was normal to feel inferior, he also saw this as something to move away from. Feeling inferior drives the individual toward accomplishment, which provides a momentary feeling of satisfaction; but the awareness of the greater accomplishments of others drives the individual on toward even further accomplishment. For Adler, power and strength were equated with masculinity, and weakness and inferiority were equated with femininity. Therefore, both men and women were expected to strive to become more masculine. This he called the *masculine protest.*

He applied the principle of overcoming inferiority not only to the individual but also to society. He described scientific endeavor as the striving of human beings to know more about the universe and to be able to control it better. He also maintained that in God's nature religious man perceives the way to height.

Adler considered inferiority acceptable as long as it provided the impetus to strive toward superiority; but he described what he considered to be two pathological forms of it, which he called the *inferiority complex*. In the first, while retaining at some level an awareness of an underlying feeling of inferiority, but knowing that nothing can be done to improve the situation, the person tries to deceive her/himself into feeling superior. In the second, realizing that s/he is not strong enough to solve a given problem in a socially useful way, s/he reacts fatalistically to the situation without trying to correct or improve it. Such a discouraged person may use a real or assumed deficiency in order to gain special benefit. This later condition was the closest Adler came to accepting the necessity for lowerness.

Berne (1975), who also will be considered further in the next chapter, was another predominantly vertical theorist. Like Adler, he was concerned with striving to achieve objectives, which is only one aspect of upperness. He defined a winner as someone who accomplishes what s/he sets out to do and a loser as someone who fails to accomplish what s/he sets out to do, whatever this may be. If the person has relatively modest objectives, s/he is more likely to meet them and therefore to succeed. If her/his objectives are more ambitious, s/he is less likely to meet them and therefore more likely to fail. Berne acknowledged that success (like upperness) is a relative concept and considered that people tend to find themselves in, or move themselves into, situations in which their skills and aptitudes are roughly comparable with those of the people with whom they compete. To use his term, they choose an appropriate "league" in which to compete. If they come to excel in a particular activity, they may choose to move into a higher league; if they consistently do badly, they may choose to drop down into a lower league.

Competing in a higher league can itself be a form of superiority, but within that league there is the possibility of gaining further status points from winning against competitors. People seem therefore to have certain *background characteristics* (social class, profession, strength, intelligence) that place them in a particular league and against these background characteristics they match themselves against people of comparable ability. This joins up with Adler's idea that the person needs to be made to feel inferior before s/he is stimulated to strive toward superiority. It suggests that people feel bored if the competition is not intense enough but demoralized if it is too intense. Neither Adler nor Berne were able to explain satisfactorily why some people seek to achieve more and more while others appear content to lead a humble existence.

Limitations of the Approaches of Adler and Berne

Adler and Berne lay great stress upon striving, competing, succeeding, and failing, but these concepts might apply to any one of the four positions within a spatial system. In the theory proposed in this chapter, the objectives - and sources of satisfaction - are the attainment of states of relatedness. The individual may strive or compete in order to attain any one of them, though these are not the only ways of attaining them. They may be attained by mutual agreement or they may even be offered. Adler and Berne are primarily concerned with the attainment of what in the present theory would be called the state of upperness. Berne shows little interest in lowerness, and Adler conceives of lowerness only as a means of coping with the failure to achieve upperness.

EXISTING THEORIES ASSOCIATED WITH BOTH AXES

Hartup (1989) proposed that experience in two major kinds of relationships is necessary to the child's development. The first, which he called *horizontal*, are relationships with individuals who have the same amount of social power. Normally these are child-child relationships. The second, which he called *vertical*, are relationships with individuals who have greater knowledge and social power. Normally these are child-adult relationships, but they also include sibling relationships. He considered that horizontal and vertical relationships emerge at different times and serve different functions. Horizontal relationships are evident only in rudimentary form until about the third year of life. Within them the complexities of cooperation and competition are mastered and intimacy in social relationships is first achieved. Vertical relationships emerge during the first year and provide children with protection and security during the long period that must elapse before they can "make it on their own." Basic skills emerge within them.

Packer and Richardson (1991), in an analysis of the interpersonal movements between children in playgrounds, proposed two classes of movement; intimacy and status. The first affects the degree of "closeness and involvement" between children; the second affects "a child's standing with respect to another." They cited two sources of these classes: de Rivera (1977), whose equivalent terms were "belonging" and "recognition," and Gilligan (1982), whose equivalent terms were "care" and "justice."

Horney (1937) proposed a theory that had certain structural similarities to the present one. She believed that the child who is exposed to imperfect parenting, which she called *the basic evil*, grows up with what she called *basic anxiety*. She considered that the basic evil is invariably lack of genuine warmth and affection, though more frequently than not it is camouflaged. There are in our culture, she maintained, four principal ways by which a person can try to protect her/himself against basic anxiety: securing affection (closeness), withdrawing (distance), gaining power (upperness), and adopting a submissive attitude (lowerness). Each of these had a *motto*. For securing affection it was "If you love me you won't hurt me"; for withdrawing it was "If I withdraw nothing can hurt me"; for gaining power it was "If I have power noone can hurt me"; and for adopting a submissive attitude it was "If I give in I will not be hurt." It is strange that she thought that only people who have been exposed to imperfect parenting would be motivated to relate in these ways. It is also strange that she perceived these ways of relating as defensive rather than simply as aspects of normal behavior. Later (1942) she proposed ten strategies for "minimizing basic anxiety" which she called *neurotic trends* or *neurotic needs*; although these correspond more with normal behavior, they were still conceived of as escaping from a negative experience rather than as being drawn toward a positive one.

They were:

1. Affection and approval
2. A dominant partner to control one's life
3. Living one's life within narrow limits
4. Power
5. Exploitation of others
6. Social recognition
7. Personal admiration
8. Ambition and personal achievement
9. Independence and self-sufficiency
10. Perfection and unassailability

Finally (1945) Horney compressed these into the three categories of what she called *the neurotic's adjustment to other people*. They were:

Moving toward people (combining 1, 2, and 3)
Moving against people (combining 4, 5, 6, 7, and 8)
Moving away from people (combining 9 and 10)

It is perhaps because she saw herself primarily as a therapist that she found it necessary to couch these processes in terms of abnormality. She later referred to them simply as the three *basic personality types* and gave them the alternative names of the compliant type, the aggressive type, and the detached type. There seems to be no good reason for extracting the three personality types from the ten neurotic trends or needs. Her original four ways of "protecting the individual against anxiety" would appear to have been the more useful and came remarkably close to the four positions of the present theory.

Horney's belief that basic anxiety results from imperfect parenting is an extension of Freud's (1926a) view that the infant's separation from the mother at birth is the basis of all subsequent feelings of anxiety; and Horney's preoccupation with protecting the individual against anxiety is a derivation of Freudian theory. Freud (1926a) considered that anxiety is experienced when the psyche is overwhelmed by an excessive influx of stimuli, such as occurs at birth. He also referred to *neurotic anxiety*, which results from the psyche being overwhelmed by instinctual needs (emerging from the id) pressing for attention (see Chapter 1); and he considered that an important function of the ego was the avoidance or reduction of anxiety by holding such instincts in abeyance. Where Freud was concerned primarily with the avoidance or reduction of anxiety arising from pressure from biological, instinctual needs, Horney, like Fromm (1947a and b) and Sullivan (1947), was concerned with the avoidance or reduction of anxiety arising from the individual's experiences of other people. Leary (1957), following in the tradition of Horney, Fromm, and Sullivan, believed that "All the social, emotional, interpersonal activities of an individual can be understood as attempts to avoid anxiety or to establish and maintain self-esteem" (page 59). The theory presented in this book is not based upon an assumption that relating is a defense against anxiety; the assumption is that it is a positive activity aimed at attaining advantageous positions for the individual.

Leary was a member of a group at the University of California at Berkley during the late 1940s. According to LaForge (LaForge et al., 1985), it was never clearly established which member of the group first hit upon the biaxial representation of "interpersonal mechanisms" that first appeared in a doctoral dissertation by Freedman in 1950 and that was first published (in the *Journal of Personality*) by Freedman, Leary, Ossorio, and Coffee in 1951 (see Figure 2). In this publication it was maintained that "all the interpersonal mechanisms considered to be required for systematizing interpersonal behavior" could be represented as sixteen segments of a circle constructed around the two axes of love versus hate (also called affiliation versus hostility) and dominate versus submit. Love and hate, placed in the positions of west and east, and dominate and submit, placed in the positions of north and south, called the nodal points of the circle, made up four of the sixteen segments. The remaining twelve were placed as four sets of three in the spaces between the four nodal points and were intended to represent "discriminable shadings of interpersonal intent," like the colors of the rainbow, between one nodal point and the next. The sixteen segments were labeled from A to P in a counterclockwise direction around the circle, and this form of labeling has been retained through all subsequent modifications of the circle.

The theoretical justification for this arrangement was provided by Leary (1957) in his book *Interpersonal Diagnosis of Personality*. In this he explained that extensive, informal surveys were carried out of many varieties of data from which several hundred terms for describing interpersonal behavior were assembled. These, he maintained, were found to be classifiable under sixteen basic interpersonal headings, which in turn could be accommodated within a biaxial grid. As further support for this arrangement he quoted from Freud's (1950) open letter to Einstein entitled "*Why War?*" In this, Freud proposed that human instincts are only of two kinds: those that seek to preserve and unite and those that seek to destroy and kill. The first he called the erotic instinct; the second he called the aggressive or destructive one; this corresponded with the horizontal axis. Freud also referred to the interaction between the weak and the strong, the victors and the vanquished, the masters and the slaves; and this corresponded with the vertical axis.

The Circumplex

It was also in this open letter that Freud drew attention to a certain G.G. Lichtenberg, who had invented what he called a *compass of motives*. Within this, Lichtenberg explained, human motives "might be arranged like the thirty two winds." This may have been what inspired the Berkley group to construct around their two axes a circular ordering of sixteen interpersonal mechanisms such that each mechanism represented a blending of the mechanisms on either side of it. It was a remarkable coincidence that, in 1954, a mathematician named Guttman made reference to a set of qualitatively different variables that might have an order among themselves that had no beginning and no end. Such a set of variables, he explained, would best be represented in a circular arrangement, and this he called a *circumplex*. Within such an arrangement, any specified variable would have its highest correlation with the variables on either side of it. Its correlations with its more remote neighbors would fall off monotonically to the right and to the left as a function of their sequential separation. In a correlation matrix exhibiting such a circular ordering, the highest correlations would be next to the principal diagonal running from the upper left to the lower right corner; and along any row or column, the correlations would decrease in size as the distance from the principal diagonal increased, until a point of zero correlation was reached; thereafter the correlations would be increasingly negative.

The statistical elegance of the circumplex model is extremely seductive. A number of psychologists, notably Wiggins (1982) and Kiesler (1983), have attempted, both conceptually and statistically, to improve upon the original circle of Freedman et al. (1951). Wiggins (1979) explained that, in principle the "circumplex pie" can be sliced into 16, 32, or even 64 segments, depending upon the capacity of the human mind to distinguish between similar descriptive terms. The distinction drawn above between axes and dimensions is particularly pertinent to the circumplex issue, for it is implicit in Guttman's proposition that segments on opposite sides of the circle be strictly bipolar, that is, that they should be dimensions rather than axes. Wiggins (1979) was concerned that some of the opposing segments of the original circle did not meet this requirement, and consequently he replaced them. He also considered that the task of creating bipolar opposites for sixteen segments was too great, so he reduced them to eight. Kiesler (1983), however, who was more concerned with concepts than with statistics, increased them again to sixteen. It has been argued (Birtchnell, 1990) that the modifications introduced by Wiggins, Kiesler, and others have not improved the original circle, and that an excessive preoccupation with the circumplex model and with bipolarity has obscured rather than clarified Leary's biaxial representation.

FIGURE 2
The First Interpersonal Circle

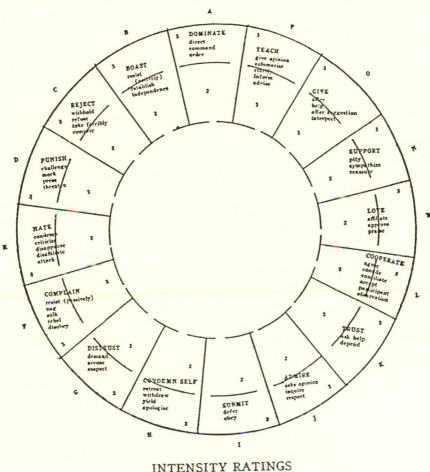

INTENSITY RATINGS

3 = intense or extreme
2 = average or appropriate
1 = mild intensity

Mervin B. Freedman et al., "The Interpersonal Dimension of Personality." Journal of Personality, 20:4, page 151. Copyright Duke University Press, 1951. Reprinted with permission of the publisher.

The Radex

Leary (1957) devoted an entire chapter of his book to the issue of adjustment and maladjustment and was intent on taking this into account in his theoretical system. He considered the contributions of Freud, Jung, Horney, and Fromm; but in the end he was influenced most by Sullivan (1953), who considered there to be a continuum from normal, well-adjusted behavior to psychiatric disturbance. This continuum ranged from what Leary called *consistent moderation* to *intensity*. LaForge and Suczek (1955) constructed an Interpersonal Check List (ICL) for measuring the sixteen characteristics of the interpersonal circle. This comprised 128 adjectival items, with eight items for each characteristic. The eight items were intended to measure four levels of intensity, with one item each for levels 1 and 4 and three items each for levels 2 and 3. Guttman (1954) called the combination of a circular ordering and levels of intensity a *radex*. Lyons et al. (1980), using a multidimensional scaling analysis, confirmed that the ICL did in fact conform to a radex measure. However, from the considerations referred to in Chapter 1, it is clear that the difference between good and bad relating is not a matter of intensity.

Interpersonal Psychology

The circular arrangement of relating characteristics, first published by Freedman et al. in 1951, has given rise to an entire school of psychology called interpersonal psychology. At this stage, it would be inappropriate to describe all the developments and ramifications of this school, but in Chapter 10, after the principles of the present theory have been fully explained, a more comprehensive review of interpersonal psychology will be provided and comparisons with the present theory will be drawn.

Gilbert's Biosocial Goals

Gilbert (1989) proposed the existence of what he called the four *biosocial goals*, which are common to both animals and humans. To some extent they can be represented in the form of a two-dimensional system. In such a system the horizontal dimension would comprise cooperation versus competition; this has an obvious connection with Chance's (1984) hedonic versus agonic distinction. The vertical dimension would comprise care giving versus care eliciting. Cooperation is more likely to occur in a situation of closeness, and competition is more likely to occur in a situation of distance; care giving is clearly an upper function, and care eliciting a lower one. The trouble with these goals is that they are not sufficiently fundamental: they refer only to limited aspects of closeness, distance, upperness, and lowerness. Furthermore, cooperating and competing are not so much goals as means of attaining goals: children may compete or cooperate for example, in order to gain closeness to or distance from a parent. Despite such objections, Gilbert (1992) has retained these goals.

Murray's Needs

As long ago as 1938, Murray published an influential book in which he proposed a set of twenty *manifest needs*. He expressed the view that most of the needs were *social reaction systems*, which lead an individual to form affiliations and cooperate with allied objects or institutions (closeness); reject, resist, renounce, or attack disliked hostile objects (distance); or raise, conserve, or defend her/his status (upperness). There were also needs (e.g., deference, succorance, abasement) that could be linked with lowerness. Murray provided a set of questionnaire items for each need but lacked enthusiasm for questionnaires. Later, Edwards (1959) constructed a questionnaire called the Personal Preference Schedule to measure the needs. Wiggins and Broughton (1985) provided evidence that many of them could be fitted into a two-dimensional system.

Gardner's Psalics

Gardner (1988) is a psychiatrist with a serious commitment to evolutionary theory. He introduced the term *"psalic"* to refer to a primitive communicational state that causes the organism to demonstrate a readiness to assume a distinctive role. (This is a simplification of his longer definition). For each psalic he described a form of animal behavior, a form of normal human behavior, and a form of abnormal human behavior. He considered abnormal behavior to be a breaking free from normal inhibitions under stress. He proposed eight psalics but, like Murray and his needs, did not organize them into any kind of system. However, with little difficulty, they can be fitted into a system. His *sexual* psalic covers aspects of closeness, and his *spacing* and *out-group omega* psalics cover aspects of distance. His *alpha* psalic covers aspects of upperness and his *alpha-reciprocal* and *in-group omega* psalics cover aspects of lowerness. The remaining two psalics, *nurturent* and *nurturance recipience,* are concerned with parental (upper close) behavior and offspring (lower close) behavior.

TO WHAT EXTENT SHOULD INTERMEDIATE POSITIONS BE CONSIDERED?

LaForge (in Laforge et al., 1985) indicated that as far back as 1950, Leary had considered representing interpersonal behavior in terms of the four quadrants derived from the two axes. Later, in his book, Leary (1957) called these the *four blended quadrants* and labeled them *hostile strength* (upper left), *friendly strength* (upper right), *hostile weakness* (lower left), and *friendly weakness* (lower right). He likened them to the four temperaments of Hippocrates, which were called the choleric, sanguine, melancholic, and phlegmatic. There certainly seem to be advantages to examining the interactions between the two main axes in this way. Paddock and Nowicki (1986) extensively reviewed the work that had been carried out on the ICL and carried out further work themselves. They concluded that none of the sixteen scales met the requirements for a true circumplex, but that reducing the system to octants at least produced scales with a reasonable degree of internal consistency. Therefore, a reasonable compromise therefore might be to supplement the characteristics of the four main positions with those of the four main intermediate positions, thus producing eight main classes of relating. This octagonal arrangement (see Figure 3) will be fully described in Chapter 9.

PARADOXICAL POSITIONS

A paradoxical position occurs when a person is experiencing the satisfactions of one position while adopting the posture of the opposite position. There are, of course, four such positions. They are represented with an adjective and a noun, the adjective referring to the posture that is adopted and the noun referring to the satisfaction that is being experienced. An example is *distant closeness*, which occurs when a person is experiencing the satisfaction of closeness from a position of distance, as occurs for instance when lovers speak to each other over the telephone. The paradoxical position is a useful strategy because the person is gaining the advantages of the one position while benefitting from the security of the opposite position. The characteristics of the paradoxical positions will be described in the chapters concerned with the position adopted, not with the state of satisfaction achieved.

FIGURE 3
The Interpersonal Octagon

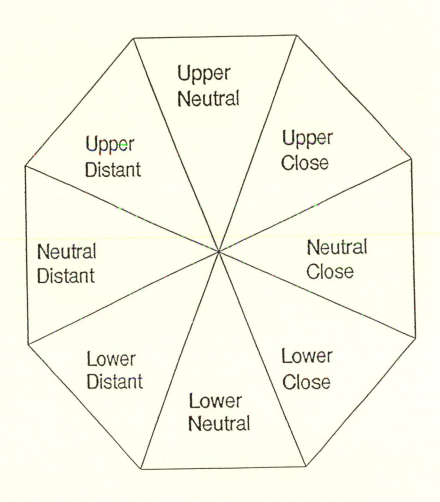

SUMMARY

For ease of graphical presentation, the proximity axis will be called the horizontal one and the power axis will be called the vertical one. Reasons are given why "axis" is a more suitable term than "dimension." It is intended that each end of each axis represent a state of relatedness. The ends of the horizontal axis will be called closeness and distance; those of the vertical axis, upperness and lowerness. An important principle of the theory is that no position be considered preferable to any other. The vertical axis in humans is more interactive than it is in animals. The upper person is more inclined to be of benefit to the lower person, hence the lower position carries greater advantages. Whereas distance is the opposite of closeness, lowerness is the reciprocal of upperness. Together, these terms create what could be called a spatial theory of relating. It is necessary to distinguish between the literal and the metaphorical meaning of each term.

Existing theories associated with the horizontal dimension are of two kinds: those concerning approach versus avoidance, and those concerning interest in self versus interest in others. Existing theories associated with the vertical direction are those of Adler and Berne. They focus predominantly upon striving for success and equate lowerness with inferiority. Of the theories concerned with both dimensions, that of Horney comes closest to the present (spatial) theory. Interpersonal theory, which has a structural resemblance to the present theory, has become excessively concerned with bipolarity and lacks an adequate distinction between good and bad forms of relating.

The final version of the present theory has four main positions, representing the extremes of the two principal axes, and four intermediate positions.

4

Maturational Processes within the Two Axes

The understanding is that humans are born with certain general tendencies in each of the four directions, but that ideally, during the course of maturation, they should (1) become exposed to and gain experience of each of the associated states of relatedness, (2) accumulate adequate stores of each of them, (3) develop relating competencies that enable them to attain each of them, and (4) acquire the confidence that they would be able to seek and attain any of them whenever the need should arise. Under less than ideal circumstances, some of these processes do not take place or take place only imperfectly, and the individual is left with various relating deficiencies. This chapter is concerned mainly with the ideal circumstances.

Psychologists and psychoanalysts rarely show an interest in both the horizontal and the vertical axes. There tend to be horizontal theorists and vertical theorists. This suggests that people's preoccupations are predominantly on one axis or the other, and it reveals the general lack of awareness of most theorists of the importance of there being two axes.

MATURATION WITHIN THE HORIZONTAL AXIS

The characteristics of both closeness and distance have to be acquired and built upon throughout the prolonged period of psychological maturation. This happens as the developing individual passes through alternating phases of closeness and distance, the satisfactory completion of one phase propelling her/him toward the next. It seems to be an important principle in all stages of development that it is necessary to feel secure in (and able to return to) one state of relatedness before being prepared to venture toward the opposite one.

Birth

Some thinkers maintain that the infant's first experience of closeness was the time it spent within the uterus, particularly during the later months of pregnancy. At this time it might have had sufficient proprioceptive sense to register its position, and be aware of the warmth of and hear the sounds from within its mother's body. Klein (1957) has referred to a universal longing for the pre-natal state of unity with the mother. A minority of writers (e.g., Rank, 1923) have considered that being expelled from the warmth and security of the uterus and being forced through the narrow birth canal are experienced by the infant as a trauma of some magnitude that, under certain circumstances, can be recalled and even re-lived. If this is so, it would be the infant's first experience of enforced distance.

The Post-Natal Period

Again, some would maintain (Klaus and Kennell, 1976) that the degree of physical contact established and maintained between infant and mother during the immediate post-natal period plays an important part in creating a condition of closeness that facilitates their later capacity to relate closely; but the larger body of evidence (Myers, 1984) does not support this. It certainly seems likely that the early separation of mother and infant, such as occurs when the birth is premature and the infant needs to be transferred to an incubator, would not improve the ease with which the mother subsequently becomes bonded to her infant.

During the first days or weeks it is important that the mother take to her infant, a process akin to falling in love. Winnicott (1948) referred to the mother as needing to be *there*, to be sensed in all possible ways, and to love in a physical way, providing contact, body temperature, movement, and quiet according to the baby's needs. Winnicott (1952) laid special emphasis on physical contact, which is after all the most direct form of closeness. He wrote of the early anxiety of the infant as a reaction to being insecurely held.

From the earliest days, the infant needs to become closely involved with the mother so that it can be adequately protected and fed. It plays its part in bringing this about by clinging, crying, gazing and tracking with its eyes, smiling, and babbling (Benedek, 1956). It is a point of some interest that for the first few months of life, the infant cannot even crawl. In this sense, it is like a plant and has to attract the mother to it, rather than move toward her. Since feeding plays so crucial a part in the involvement of the parent animal with its young (responding to the gaping beak), it would be odd if it were not also a factor in humans. Freud (1905) considered that for the first year and a half of life the mouth, lips and tongue are the infant's primary organs of sexual satisfaction. To

Klein (1950, 1957) the infant's relationship to the breast or to "its symbolic representative, the bottle" was of overwhelming importance. MacFarlane (1975) has shown that at three days of age the infant can tell the smell of its own mother's milk. The warm milk produced in the mother's body (or in the case of the bottle, prepared by the mother) passes into the infant's body, becoming part of it. A number of writers from Abraham (1924) onward have been preoccupied with the concept of the mother being swallowed by the infant both literally and metaphorically.

A factor that is likely to play a part not only during infancy but also throughout childhood is the mother's (and from a fairly early stage, also the father's) capacity to form close relationships. This may be either a general tendency in her or an attitude that she may have developed toward this particular infant. If, for example, the pregnancy had been unwanted, she may have experienced great difficulty allowing herself to become close to the infant. Although it has yet to be clearly established, it seems likely that human infants vary in the intensity of their need for closeness. The closeness needs of autistic children, for example, are limited, and though this is an extreme example, it may represent one end of a normal continuum.

The First Phase of Closeness

Much has been written by psychoanalysts of the first phase of intense closeness in which the infant experiences itself as being in a state of continuous and undifferentiated, psychological union with the mother. It extends over a period of six months and has been called *primary narcissism* by Freud (1914), *primary love* by Balint (1952), *symbiosis* by Mahler (1961) and *self-fusion* by Kohut (1977). It is not unlike the intrauterine period. Suttie (1935) gave the name *psychic weaning* to the gradual termination of this phase and proposed that it must be accompanied by some degree of psychic pain. If so, it would be similar to the trauma of birth. It was Suttie's view that so intense is this pain that it deters the individual from ever becoming that involved with anyone again. This he considers to be the explanation for the human tendencies to avoid close involvements and to be reluctant to show emotion.

The First Phase of Distance

Freud (1914) considered that the infant passed out of the phase of primary narcissism into one of *secondary narcissism*, during which it withdrew its libido from the mother and reinvested it into itself. Mahler (1963) proposed that the symbiotic phase gave way to what she called the phase of *separation-*

individuation, which extends until about the age of three. This combines the process of becoming more physically separate from the mother with the development and maintenance of a "sense of identity." Kohut (1977) described the same sequence slightly differently. He maintained that following the period of self-fusion the infant incorporates the mother within its own self-system, creating what he called a *self-object.* This means that over a protracted period its own and its mother's identity are intertwined. Gradually, it separates off fragments of its mother's identity and takes them into itself, a process known as *transmuting internalization.* Masterson (1972) stated that a mother may, because of her own symbiotic needs, discourage the separation-individuation process by withdrawing her love as the child tries to separate. These theories incorporate several of the characteristics of distancing outlined in Chapter 2: the creation of space between infant and mother, the turning in on the self, and the development of a separate identity. They emphasize the vital role of the parent in letting the child go.

Eibl-Eibesfeldt (1989) observed that at the age of five to six months the infant begins to show its first indication of fear of strangers. We must, he maintained, accept the fact that a child is phylogenetically programmed to act as though strangers are potentially dangerous. Smith and Martinsen (1977) confirmed that a child selectively chooses its mother's presence. Waters et al. (1975) showed that at between five and ten months the pulse rate increases dramatically upon the approach of a stranger, even if the stranger speaks with a friendly voice. Fraiberg (1975) observed the same reaction in children who were blind from birth. Feinman (1980) showed that white children displayed more fear toward black strangers than white ones.

Gender Differences in Separation

Rubin (1985) made the point that gender identification complicates the separation-individuation process. This is because closeness and identification are interconnected. The girl, because she is the same gender as the mother, needs to separate less completely than the boy. As a result, the process of defining and experiencing herself as an autonomous, bounded individual is more difficult. The boy, because he has to both separate and change his identity, has to become more completely and therefore more painfully separated. As a result (in line with Suttie's view) males are less inclined to form close relationships and are more reluctant to show emotion. On the other hand, they have more clearly defined identities. Rubin used the term *"ego-boundary"* to mean both a boundary around the self and a restraining of involvement and emotional expression. She described women as having "more permeable" ego boundaries so that they can get closer to others and others can get closer to them.

A number of writers have concerned themselves with the processes and consequences of this gender difference in separation-individuation. Greenson (1968) used the term *"dis-identification"* to describe the boy's reduced identity with his mother and "*counter-identification*" to describe his increased identity with his father. Hudson and Jacot (1991) introduced the term the *"male wound"* to emphasize the traumatic effect of this enforced realignment and pointed out that it gave rise to both strengths and weaknesses in men as compared with women. Lynn (1969) proposed thirty eight hypotheses that followed from it.

Attachment Theory

Bowlby's (1969) attachment theory runs counter to those just described in that it proposes that for the first six months the child remains relatively unattached and only develops a firm *attachment* to the mother from six months onward. His theory stems as much from ethology as it does from psychoanalysis and lays great stress on the processes of clinging (Harlow and Zimmermann, 1959) and following (Lorenz, 1957). It is perhaps no coincidence that attachment behavior becomes manifest at a time when the infant is able at least to crawl, for it seems that an important feature of attachment is the establishment of the mother as a *secure base* from which to explore and to which to return. Attachment becomes established as a result of repeated interactions between mother and infant involving the mother being attentive and responsive to the infant's expressions of need. By this process the infant warms to the mother and becomes trusting of her. Bowlby (1980) proposed that when the infant's (or young child's) approaches to the mother are not appropriately responded to, frequently and over a prolonged period, the psychophysiological system controlling attachment behavior may eventually become deactivated. This could be achieved by the defensive exclusion of sensory inflow of any or every kind that might activate attachment.

Main et al. (1986) devised what they called the "Strange Situation Test" for determining the extent to which attachment between young children and their mothers has taken place. The children are left with a stranger, left on their own, then reintroduced to their mothers. On the basis of their reunion behavior children are grouped into three categories. The majority (some seventy percent) approach their mothers with pleasure and make good physical contact; a second group (called *anxious, resistant* or *ambivalent*) alternate between clinging and being angrily resistant; and a third group (called *avoidant*) turn away from their mothers and turn either to someone else or to an object. Grossmann et al. (1986) observed that avoidant children, even when distressed, are less likely to communicate their distress directly to their mothers or to seek contact with them. Patterns observed at one year of age have been shown to be consistent at least until age six and to correlate with the observed behavior of the mothers at home. Ainsworth et al., (1978) and Egeland and Farber (1984) observed that the mothers of securely attached infants were warm, sensitive, and consistently responsive to their signals; those of the ambivalent infants were insensitive, inconsistent, and inept in dealing with them; and those of the avoidant infants were rejecting, unemotional, and rigid and compulsive in their care-giving behavior. An avoidant form of behavior has also been observed in toddlers who have been abused, which might be construed as a form of enforced closeness (George and Main, 1979).

The Internalized Close Parent

Although Bowlby has tried to focus attention on observed behavior, the essence of attachment, as it is of all forms of close involvement, is what psychoanalysts have called the *internalization of the object*. This is a difficult concept: it means that somewhere within the psyche is a representation of the person being related to and that somehow the individual relates to this representation (internal relating) in the same way as s/he relates to the actual person in the real world (external relating). The individual is also *related to* by this representation. The advantage of this for the infant is that it can carry an image of the mother around within itself as though it is still with her, which enables it to leave her without feeling it has lost her. This establishment of a good and loving internalized parent is known as *object constancy*. A slightly different concept, referred to by Erikson as *basic trust*, is that when the mother goes away the infant is confident that she will return. Therefore it can allow her to go away without creating a fuss. Winnicott (1958) laid great stress upon the internalization of a good internal object in the acquisition of what he called the *capacity to be alone*. From these ideas the important principle emerges that one route to distance is a good experience of closeness that can be incorporated into the individual. It has to be remembered, however, that the autistic child has an infinite capacity for being alone that has not come from the good experience of closeness.

Transitional Objects

Winnicott (1953) considered that the infant could use objects as substitutes for the mother in her absence. These he called *transitional objects*. They include the thumb, a blanket, a teddy bear, or some other soft toy that can be clutched or sucked. It is questionable whether these need to be associated with the mother. It may simply be that the need for closeness is so intense that closeness to things is better than no closeness at all. Young children talk to their toys and even create imaginary companions to which they can talk. Relating to objects is not restricted to humans. Harlow and Zimmermann (1959) showed that orphaned baby monkeys developed a strong and persistent attachment to cloth-covered wire frames, which they preferred to wire frames that were not covered with cloth.

Progressive Extension of Distancing

Rheingold and Eckerman (1970) have stressed the biological importance of separation for both animals and man and have emphasized that detachment should not be considered a negation of attachment. The separation and the individuation components of Mahler's (1963) phase of separation-individuation (which extends up to age three) will be considered separately. The separation component is only the first of a series of stages in which the developing child makes progressively more adventurous excursions away from the parents and the parental home. To some extent such excursions are driven by the child's innate curiosity and urge to explore its environment, but the encouragement of parents, siblings and friends also plays a part. There are of course serious dangers outside the home territory. The child may get lost, abducted by strangers, knocked over by traffic, and so on. It is realistic therefore for parents to impose restraints upon such explorations and to make arrangements to ensure the child's safety. With each excursion, the child builds up an *interior map* of where it has been, which enables it to find its way again. Explored territory assumes a familiarity that reassures the child that it is a safe area to venture into again. Such familiarity is also a kind of closeness, so that distant places, as they are "conquered," get converted into close places. Being accompanied to new places by parents, siblings or friends is a way of taking closeness with it and makes such exploration easier. Frightening experiences send the child running back to base and, temporarily at least, inhibit its exploratory tendencies. As close areas become familiar they become absorbed into its home territory, which then provides a broader base from which the child may explore further afield. The parent plays a crucial role in providing a friendly presence and waving good-bye as the child sets off and in being there to welcome it on its return. Releasing the child under these circumstances can be a frightening experience for the parent. In providing the experience of distance for the child s/he is denying her/himself closeness. An insecurely close parent may therefore be unable to let the child go, and this can seriously impair its capacity to experience pleasurable distance. So-called *school phobia* is commonly a result of the parent's inability to let the child go; all too easily the parent's anxiety gets picked up by the child. A child will try extending its range of distancing only when it feels safe to do so and when it feels confident that the parent will be there on its return. A parent can seriously interfere with the child's distancing activities by pushing it too hastily away, encouraging it to go further than it feels safe to go, or not receiving it warmly on its return.

Individuation and the Development of a Personal Identity

The individuation component of Mahler's (1963) separation-individuation phase, like the separation component, must be considered only the first of a number of stages in which the developing child acquires its own sense of being an individual who is distinct from other individuals. In fact, it can reasonably be said that individuation is a process that continues throughout life. The possibility that there may be other individuals in the world is not likely to occur to the infant initially, because its entire existence centers around itself. Its first rude awakening may be the realization that there are other siblings or peers who may compete with it for attention, affection, approval, and so forth. Thus, one way of acquiring a consciousness of oneself as a separate person is becoming aware of the differences between oneself and other people and between the way one is treated compared with the way other people are treated.

More important than this, however, is being given credit by others for having a mind of one's own, with one's own wishes, likes, and preferences. Parents are able to bring this out in their children by offering them the opportunity to decide what they would like to play, where they would like to go, what they would like to eat, to wear and so on. As with exploration, such wishes cannot always be granted, but when they can be they should. Parents often thwart their children's efforts to become individuals by having their own ideas about what they ought to like and having dreams and expectations for them. In this way they are treating their children as extensions of themselves. Drawing an analogy with separation, they may be afraid of their children being different from them and for this reason they try to stop the individuation process from taking place.

Laing (1965) wrote insightfully of the importance of creating a secure sense of who one is. He coined the term "*ontological security*" to describe this. Fraiberg (1969) proposed that on the basis of *good-enough mothering* (a concept developed by Winnicott), successful separation-individuation results in a firm sense of identity and the capacity for developing intimate, nonsymbiotic object relationships. This is an example of the principle that security at one end of an axis is necessary for the successful movement to a position at the other end. Without a firm sense of self, moving close to another person carries the risk of what Laing called *engulfment*, namely, the complete loss of being by absorbtion into the other person.

The child who is allowed to be different (is given distance) may not necessarily be capable of allowing other children to be different (of giving distance). If it is allowed always to have or do exactly what it likes, it may never need to consider the wishes of other children. It may therefore need to have experiences of not having its wishes granted in order to be able to appreciate what this may feel like for other children. This may dispose it to allow them sometimes to have their own way. Thus, the capacity to give distance (in the form of identity) has to be acquired as much as the capacity to be distant (to have an identity).

Receiving and Giving Closeness

Closeness is a state of relatedness that may be received or given. The developing child is open to closeness and readily accepts it when it is offered. Providing the parents have the capacity to give closeness, the child feels loved. Being loved is being the center of attention, being treated as someone special, and being valued and appreciated for oneself and for one's qualities. Fenichel (1945) observed that the child gains *self-esteem* when it is loved, and Storr (1983) maintained that the child acquires a built-in self-esteem from an early positive relationship with its mother. Coopersmith (1967) observed that one of the most important antecedents of a child's high self-esteem is total or near total acceptance of it by its parents. He found that a child who feels accepted in this way finds it easier to identify with and model itself upon its parents. Love tends to feed upon itself. When the child feels loved it is happy, and when it is happy the parents are inclined to love it all the more. The child loves its parents because they love it, and so a process of circular reinforcement develops. Love accumulates with the sharing of experiences and with the exchanging of kindnesses.

The establishment of a firm sense of self makes possible the development of a close relationship between child and parent which is more that between one individual and another. This involves what psychoanalysts call the *transfer of cathexis*. Cathexis is the directing of interest toward and development of an emotional involvement with an object (an object in psychoanalytic parlance being the person, or sometimes the thing, toward whom attention is directed, both externally and internally). Since an object can both love and be loved, part of the experience of closeness is carrying around within oneself loving objects and objects that one loves.

It might seem that a child who has been freely loved will feel disposed to love other people. To a very large extent this may be true. Certainly the reverse seems likely to be true, that is that a child who has been deprived of love will find it hard to give love freely to others. Issues such as this have yet to be resolved. What of the *spoiled* or *overindulged* child? It may acquire a sense of *entitlement* and feel no obligation to be loving to others. As with the experience of distance, it may be necessary to feel unloved in order to appreciate what wanting love may feel like and to feel more disposed to offering it to others. Zilboorg (1938) warned that if the omnipotent child learns the joy of being loved without adequate guidance in reality testing, it may develop an expectation that life is nothing but being loved and admired.

The Acquisition of a Sense of Privacy and of Personal Space

Privacy and personal space may not be important for the small child, but from middle childhood to adolescence they become increasingly so. Sharing a room, a bed, a bath may at first feel chummy and enjoyable, but over time it may erode the child's sense of being a separate person. Wishing not to be seen undressed, locking the bathroom door, refusing to share toys and clothes are expressions of the child's emerging need for personal space. Fear of penetration, either physical or psychological, is a manifestation of the need to keep others out; and the devastation of sexual abuse is largely due to the brutal disregard of this. Parents may feel disappointed that their children stop sharing their personal thoughts with them, but keeping secrets and telling lies become an effective means for the child to maintain a private inner world.

Adolescence

Adolescence involves the dual processes of separating from parents and developing close involvements with peers outside the home. Blos (1967) referred to it as the second individuation process (i.e., following from Mahler's first) and considered that without a successful disengagement from infantile internalized objects, the finding of new extrafamilial love objects in the outside world is precluded, hindered, or remains restricted to simple replication or substitution. However, Ryan and Lynch (1989) emphasized that teenagers who are attached to their parents (in Bowlby's sense) experience them as emotionally accepting and supportive of independence and autonomy. Cumming (1961) observed that the family of orientation must, like other socializing institutions, be resigned to expelling its members when their socializing reaches an adequate level. Bowen (1978) considered that the adolescent, or young adult, needs to become disconnected more from the family as a unit than from individual family members; he used the phrase *differentiation of the self* from the family of origin to describe the experience of breaking away. Differentiation is a useful term; like Mahler's earlier concept of separation-individuation, it combines the processes of becoming separate (both physically and emotionally) and becoming a different kind of individual with different values, aspirations, and so on. Bowen drew a distinction between what he called *fusion* and *objectivity*. Fusion is to the family what Mahler's symbiosis is to the mother-infant relationship. Family members are perceived as being fused together in what Bowen called an *undifferentiated ego mass*, and objectivity is being able to stand outside of the family and feel not part of it. He considered attaining the state of objectivity to be an essential stage in the process of leaving home. It needs to be emphasized that parents play an important part in enabling this to happen. They need to be neither too ejecting nor too clinging; they need to make it clear that there will always be a place for the young adult should s/he wish to return. In ideal arrangement the separated adult should always be free to come and go within the parental home, feeling neither pushed away nor sucked in.

Early Adult Life

Mahler (1963) made reference to Freud's conviction that a lifelong, albeit diminishing, emotional dependence on the mother is a universal truth of human existence. "Involvement" would be a better word than "dependence" and such involvement would be with all family members rather than simply the mother. The relationships that adults have with their families can be mutually satisfying and advantageous, but often, because the separating process has been incomplete, this is not the case. A number of writers (incorrectly) have used the term "symbiosis" to refer to a parent-to- adult relationship in which the parent has not felt able to release the adult child. Tabachnick (1961) described the mother of a 25-year-old man who had always indulged and pampered him. She kept him living with her by emphasizing her need for him and playing upon his guilt feelings. Taylor (1975) described a 22-year old single girl who lived with her mother and who experienced overwhelming feelings of anxiety, guilt, and fears of going mad whenever she contemplated separating from her mother. Other adults who have not succeeded in achieving Bowen's condition of differentiation or objectivity attempt to cope with this lack of resolution by living a long way away, neither communicating with nor returning to the parental home.

The Forming of Adult Close Relationships

Following separation from the family of origin, the young adult enters into a new phase of seeking close relationships with other adults. Raskin (1985) and others have stressed that s/he is incapable of doing this without first attaining a firm sense of who s/he is. Erikson (1965) proposed that the achievement of an identity is both precursor to and partial prerequisite for the establishment of an

intimate mode of interpersonal relationships. This is a further example of needing
to become secure at one end of an axis before being able to move to the other
end. Closeness for a person with a poorly established identity and weak ego
boundaries constitutes a threat to her/his autonomy. It is equivalent to Bowen's
(1978) fusion. Closeness between two ontologically secure adults represents a
state of interdependence and mutual empathy. Laing et al. (1966) wrote that
under such circumstances "each has a source of strength from within and is
capable of taking responsibility for her/his own person while, at the same time,
being responsive to the other." (page 50).

MATURATION WITHIN THE VERTICAL AXIS

The characteristics of both upperness and lowerness also have to be
acquired and built upon throughout the prolonged period of psychological
maturation. As with closeness and distance, this happens as a result of the
developing individual passing through alternative phases of lowerness and
upperness. The satisfactory completion of one propels her/him toward the next.

The Weakness and Needfulness of the Infant

During the early days, weeks, or even months of life the infant has one
primary objective: to be protected and fed. This is a state of pure lowerness, and
the infant employs all the ploys with which it has been endowed by evolution to
achieve this. Striving toward upperness could not be further from its mind. This
early phase of total indulgence (providing, of course, that its needs are met)
creates in the infant an immense sense of satisfaction. It is one of the paradoxes
of the vertical axis that during the course of many upper to lower relationships,
the upper person becomes more lower and the lower person becomes more
upper. (Though it may seem grammatically incorrect to add the word "more" to
what already is a comparative word, the words "lower" and "upper" are being
used here to describe relative states, of which there may be greater or lesser
degrees.) In its lowerness, the infant (and subsequently the child) is being helped
by its parents toward upperness, because it is growing bigger and getting
stronger.

A number of writers have developed the idea of the paradoxical position of
the helpless infant. Ferenczi (1916) wrote of the first, limitless sense of
omnipotence in which its every need is met; and Kohut (1971) described this
phase as the phase of the *narcissistic, grandiose, exhibitionistic self*. What is
needed in this phase, he argued, is for the parents to enjoy the infant's emerging
delight in self and to indulge it in its grandiosity and exhibitionism. He wrote

that to get what you want makes you feel good, and that the parent who is prompt to cater to the infant's needs keeps it feeling good and confirms its sense of goodness and well-being. He called this promptness and accuracy of response *mirroring*. In promptly and accurately responding, the parent is mirroring the baby's own fantasy image of itself. What the infant seeks and responds to, he maintained, is "the gleam in the mother's eye" that affirms it as good and loveable. The infant expects to be able to perfectly control objects, which are still experienced as part of the self. When they refuse to be controlled it responds with what Kohut has called *narcissistic rage*. Freud (1914) carried the paradox further by suggesting that the infant evokes in its parents a response of adoration, which prompted him to introduce the phrase "His Majesty the Baby." This carries associations with the Christian concept that the infant Jesus was adored as a king.

The Bliss of Childhood

The phase of total indulgence is of limited duration, and its gradual termination (on the vertical axis) must be as painful to the infant as is Suttie's (1935) *psychic weaning* on the horizontal axis. Beyond this, however, loving parents continue to indulge their children to varying degrees throughout childhood and adolescence. They do so because it gives them pleasure and because it is rewarding to witness the pleasure in their children that such indulgence generates. One reason why parents are prepared to indulge their children so is that they identify with them; thus, to some extent, it is like indulging themselves.

It has already been observed that self-esteem (on the horizontal axis) results from feeling freely loved and accepted. Coopersmith (1967) further observed that the parents of children with high self-esteem were genuinely interested in them, were concerned for their welfare, attentive to their needs, loyal sources of affection and support, and willing to exert themselves on their behalf. In one sense, particularly in industrial societies, the entire period of childhood and adolescence is one long experience of lowerness. Children live in the parental home where they are protected, kept warm, provided with a room and a bed, clothed, fed, entertained, taken on outings and holidays, and cared for when they are ill. They are sheltered from responsibility. If they are frightened, upset, or hurt they are able run or turn to their parents, who will console and comfort them. They have no need to worry because they know that everything is under control and being taken care of. Obviously not all childhoods are like this, but those that are are *blissful*. To some extent, in society at large, adults organize their institutions so as to emulate the secure structure of the family home, but adult life is rarely as carefree as childhood itself.

Parental Control

Although children are indulged by their parents, they are not usually allowed the freedom to do as they please. There are places they cannot go and things they cannot do. Both at home and at school, the child receives from adults what Price (1988) has called down-hierarchy catathetic signals, which keep it in its place and keep it aware that it is a child. Parsons and Bales (1955) and Minuchin (1974) have, in different ways, emphasized the structural demarcation within families, between the domain of the parents and the domain of the children, and the importance for the parents of establishing and maintaining such a demarcation. A further observation of Coopersmith (1967) was that children with high self-esteem have parents who set clearly defined and enforced limits but who permit within this structure a considerable degree of freedom. Children who have been treated in this way are more likely to view their parents with affection and respect and to require less harsh treatment from them.

This introduces the important issue of the *security of lowerness*. One reason for childhood being blissful is that the child feels secure in its lowerness. It has every reason to believe that its parents know what they are doing and that it can rely upon them to protect and look after it. Just as when the child feels securely close it has the confidence to make excursions into distance, when it feels securely lower it has the confidence to make excursions into upperness.

Coopersmith (1967) observed that most parents of children with high self-esteem had high self-esteem themselves. One implication of this may be that they were secure in their upperness. They therefore acted reasonably and calmly toward their children; and because their children respected and trusted them as reasonable beings, they were happy to allow themselves to be controlled by them. Parents who are less secure in their upperness may resort more to the promise of reward and the threat of punishment implied in Fenichel's model (see subsequent discussion), and be more erratic and less consistent. They may be half-hearted in the instructions they give and may appeal to their children to cooperate with them. In their erraticness they will be more likely to behave unreasonably and unfairly. Their children, not knowing where they stand with them, will be less likely to respect them and more likely to defy and rebel against them. As a result, the parents will resort even more to rewarding, punishing, and appealing, and a vicious cycle will become established.

Parental Approval

Fenichel (1945) argued that the promise of necessary narcissistic supplies of affection under the condition of obedience and the threat of withdrawal of these supplies if the conditions are not fulfilled are the weapons of authority. What Fenichel is describing here may be the beginnings of the complex issue of judgments imposed upon those who are lower by those who are upper. What Fenichel is suggesting is that the parent, or other authority figure, conveys to the child the idea that, "if you do certain things I will like you, and if you do certain other things I will dislike you." The child rapidly assimilates the idea that certain actions are approved of and certain others are disapproved of. Being approved of therefore becomes one of the child's primary objectives. Though initially this will apply specifically to parents, gradually it will come to apply to anyone who is perceived of as being relatively upper (e.g., an older sibling or playmate), and approval and disapproval will easily become linked with being rewarded and punished.

This is not far removed from issues of right and wrong. If the child is brought up in a religious family, the idea can readily be extended to "if you do certain things God will like or reward you, and if you do certain other things God will not like or punish you." It seems likely that initially the child's criteria for determining what should be considered right or wrong would derive from whether or not an action would meet with parental approval. From quite an early age, the child also seems able to determine whether or not certain acts should be considered *fair*; and it is far from clear whether this also derives from parental attitudes or whether, in fact, the child has an innate sense of fairness. Certainly, from quite an early age a child is capable of protesting to a parent (or other upper figure) that the parent is treating it unfairly. From its lower position it is assuming the upper role of passing judgment upon someone who in every other respect is upper to it.

The Internalized Upper Parent

The internalized upper parent of the vertical axis is the equivalent of the internalized close parent of the horizontal axis. They may both be the same parent (but performing different functions) or each may be a different parent. The close parent is more likely to be maternal and the upper parent, paternal. The internalized upper parent may be an amalgam of a number of authority figures, though predominantly it is likely to be the father. Like the internalized close parent, it is carried around within the child, and later the adult. It exerts a constant pressure of upperness and therefore imposes a constant state of lowerness upon the individual. Its characteristics are those of the parent and other authority figures in the real world and may range from benign and tolerant to severe and punitive. What some would call the conscience is part of it, but it has the more general function of determining how the individual responds to pressures (particularly judgmental pressures) from people who are experienced as upper. Its influence may be modified by variations in the upper attitudes of others. It remains a powerful force throughout life, determining how the individual feels about her/himself, particularly in relation to authority figures and to society as a whole (see Chapter 8).

It is related to the psychoanalytic concept of the *superego* (Freud, 1923), which, it is said, is formed when the child is caught between feelings of aggression toward the parent and fear of the parent's retaliation. This is presumed to occur at any one of the three stages of psychosexual development. At the oral stage, it is considered to grow out of the conflict between coercive rage and submissive fear (Rado, 1951); at the anal stage, the infant's libidinal and aggressive urges are considered to be converted into remorse, guilt, and fear of punishment (Bibring, 1953); and at the phallic or oedipal stage, it is considered to result from the fear of punishment for incestuous wishes toward the parent of the opposite sex (Freud, 1921). The superego ranges from the benign to the severe, and its influence ranges from reassuring and facilitating to inhibiting and punitive.

Adlerian Theory

Adler (Ansbacher and Ansbacher, 1958) believed that at the beginning of every psychological life there is a more or less deep inferiority feeling, which is a consequence of the child's lowly position within the family. Because it is exposed to the environment of adults it is inclined to regard itself as small and weak and to appraise itself as inadequate and inferior. He therefore considered that there is one basic, dynamic force behind all human activity, which he described as a striving from a felt minus situation to a plus situation, from below to above, from inferiority to superiority. The impetus to move upward never ceases; it begins in early childhood and continues to the end of life. Adlerian theory is acceptable as far as it goes: it ties in well with the (across-species and within-species) striving of all animals toward supremacy over rivals and with the equivalent striving of humans toward upperness. Its limitation is that it has nothing to say about the human tendency toward lowerness - the need to be governed, protected, guided, instructed, helped, and cared for.

In various ways, the child inevitably moves upward during the course of childhood and adolescence. It grows older, taller, stronger, and more experienced; it acquires the skills of crawling, walking, running, climbing and so on; it learns to talk, read, and write; and at school and college it passes through successively numbered classes and grades. With the acquisition of each new skill, it is motivated to attempt more difficult skills. Progressive moving upward on the vertical axis parallels progressively moving toward further and further distance on the horizontal axis. It accumulates knowledge and gains new competencies.

As on the horizontal axis, the child consolidates its upperness base before using this as a launching pad toward further achievement, knowing that if it should fail, it has its existing achievements to fall back on. As on the horizontal axis, it needs the reassurance and encouragement of parents and teachers to maintain its motivation. Adler viewed laziness as ambition joined with discouragement, ambition so high that the child can see no hope of realizing it. In consequence, it loses belief in itself and the will to go on trying. Adler considered that people select certain routes by which to attain success (upperness) that dictate a certain life plan or life style and that become their primary source of satisfaction.

Berne's Theory

Berne (1975) acknowledged a degree of continuity with Adler. He was concerned with the concept of winners and losers; like Adler, when he thought this way he was inclined to believe that up is good and down is bad. He proposed that within the first six years of life the child lays down what he called *a script*, which - like Adler's life-style - sets a pattern for the way it lives its life. He believed that the individual remains true to her/his script throughout life, unless s/he makes a determined effort to change it (through the process of script analysis). The script is created by what Berne called *parental programming* and is continually reinforced by the individual repeatedly playing out the role that is determined for her/him by the script and by daily contact with the parents. Parental programming is the result of *injunctions* and *directives* that convey to the child what it may expect of life. The two main kinds of scripts are what he called *winner scripts* and *loser scripts*; they have the effect of pushing the person toward upperness or lowerness. A winner is determined to learn from her/his mistakes and do better next time, but a loser adopts an attitude of resignation, believing that failure was inevitable. Because there are so many different routes to upperness, there should be no need for any child to acquire a loser script. The good parent (or teacher) will steer and reinforce the child in those directions in which it appears capable of making progress.

The Relativity of the Vertical Axis

It was noted in the last chapter that the attainment of upperness or lowerness in relation to another person has the effect of pushing that other person in the opposite direction. In any particular area of activity, therefore, the child gains upperness at the expense of the lowerness of others who are less successful, and others gain their successes at the expense of pushing the child toward lowerness. The motivation to strive toward success is complex. Being in a class of relatively unsuccessful others may lull a child into a sense of complacency, since the class already is providing it with an adequate experience of upperness; whereas being in a class of relatively successful others may provoke it into more determined activity in order that it may improve its position. However, it will not try to move upward unless it believes it is capable of making progress. A certain amount of lowerness will stimulate it into activity, but too much will cause it to feel hopeless and defeated. Having a conspicuous degree of lowerness in one direction may stimulate it to strive toward upperness in another: a child who is short for its age may study hard; one who is failing in classwork may bully weaker children.

Berne's Ego States

Berne (1975) considered that maturation within the vertical axis involved the progressive development of what he called the three *ego states*. These he defined as coherent systems of thought and feeling, manifested by corresponding patterns of behavior. Once they have developed they remain and gain expression throughout life. The ego states represent the less competitive side to Berne. The first to develop is the *Child ego state*. This comprises acting, talking, and responding as a child between two and five years of age. It assumes three forms: the *Natural*, the *Adapted* and the *Rebellious*. The Natural Child is acting according to personal inclination; the Adapted Child is acting in a way that conforms with parental wishes; and the Rebellious Child is rebelling against parental wishes. The second state to develop is the *Parent ego state*. This comprises feeling, thinking, acting, talking, and responding in the way that the parents did when the individual was a child. It is apparent at quite a young age when the child behaves in a parenting way toward younger siblings, pets, and toys. It assumes two forms: the *Nurturing Parent* and the *Controlling Parent*. The third and final state is the *Adult ego state*. This develops as the child tries to make sense of the world. In it the child appraises its environment objectively and calculates its possibilities and probabilities on the basis of past experience. Each ego state is capable of relating autonomously. For example, during the course of interrelating the Parent state of one person may relate to the Child state of another. Any ego state may be either under- or overdeveloped so that the individual may relate excessively or insufficiently within any one of them.

Loosely, the ego states correspond with stages from lowerness to upperness: the Child state represents lowerness, and the Parent and Adult states represents aspects of upperness. Berne's theory offers an alternative way of conceptualizing development on the vertical axis, without making direct transpositions from one theory to the other. One similarity between the two theories is that both the Child state and lowerness are considered to be essential components of the adult mentality.

Adolescence and Upperness

At adolescence, the renewed surge toward distance on the horizontal axis is paralleled by a renewed surge toward upperness on the vertical one, but the surge is not uniform. Although many adolescents become increasingly aggressive, competitive, and assertive, others become indolent and apathetic. Their tendency to challenge and defy parents, teachers, and other authority figures may be a way of breaking free from their position of lowerness. Ironically, they set up alternative figures to admire and idolize, but these are more likely to be outrageous and revolutionary - and therefore easier for them to identify with. Parents and other adults commonly misunderstand the nature of adolescent revolt and respond to it with repressive measures.

Easing the Child toward Adulthood

In order to ease the child upward through adolescence toward adulthood, parents, teachers, and other influential adults adopt a policy of gradually relaxing controls over it and permitting it more freedom and responsibility. This provides progressively greater exposure to upperness. As with movement on the horizontal axis toward distance, the child should not be presented with more upperness than it can handle and opportunities to return to the security of lowerness should be available to it. As with the clinging parent on the horizontal axis, the insecurely upper parent or teacher can frustrate the child's efforts to attain upperness by remaining protective and nurturant beyond an age when it is appropriate. Doing things for or making decisions for the child deprive it of the opportunity to do or decide things for itself. Parents and teachers who cannot tolerate those in their charge drawing level with or overtaking them fail to acknowledge, or make little of, their achievements and continue to relate to them as though they were still children. Remarks such as "You will always be my little girl," though well meant, may have the effect of forcing the emerging adult back toward childhood. Some ritualistic act may be needed by which the parent or teacher accepts the young person as an equal and welcomes her/him into the world of adults. This is part of the function of the celebration of the twenty-first birthday. Beyond this there needs to be a continued attitudinal change of both parent and child.

Continuing Lowerness into Adult Life

It needs to be stressed that moving into adulthood does not mean relinquishing lowerness. The well-adjusted adult is happy to seek the help, care, guidance, and advice of others, even if they are children. Just as the condition of secure lowerness provides the child with the confidence to make excursions into upperness, so does the condition of secure upperness provide the adult with the confidence to move toward lowerness. Insecurely upper people tend to avoid assuming the lower role and always try to coerce others into adopting a lower attitude toward them. It can be one of the advantages of the adult parent/child relationship that the adult may, at any age, return to the parental home and regress to the condition of being the child again, but such regression needs to be by mutual agreement and understanding and the child must feel free to resume her/his adult status when s/he chooses, without resistance from the parent.

SUMMARY

On both axes, the individual passes through phases that alternate from one end of the axis to the other. This links with the principle that the secure establishment of a maturation stage at one end of an axis facilitates movement toward and development of the other.

On the horizontal axis, security within the uterus might be considered the first experience of closeness and birth, the first experience of distance. During the immediate post-natal period the immobility of the infant requires it to attract the mother by clinging, smiling, and so on. The mother in turn needs to take to and *be there* for the infant. Closeness is mediated through holding, feeding, and swallowing. In the first phase of closeness, mother and infant are enveloped in a psychological oneness. This gives way to the phase of separation, in which it is thought that males separate more completely than females. At about six months of age, attachment takes place; this involves the internalization of the parent and the development of the capacity to be alone. Progressive exploration of the environment requires a combination of parental supervision and encouragement. Individuation involves the establishment of identity and the creation of ontological security. With this comes the ability to form a close relationship between child and parent, which is more like that between one individual and another. During the later half of childhood the need for privacy and personal space becomes more compelling. With adolescence comes a further surge toward separation and the differentiation of self from the family of origin. The final emergence into adulthood requires a further process of letting go by the parents so that the young adult may establish close relationships with other adults.

On the vertical axis, the infant begins life weak and helpless, which is a condition of extreme lowerness. In the phase of narcissistic omnipotence, all its needs are met by parents who enjoy caring for it. To varying extents the indulgence of lowerness continues throughout childhood, and the bliss of childhood comes from being sheltered and provided for by caring parents. Parents also have the function of imposing limits and controls. By expressing approval and disapproval of the child's behavior they introduce to it a sense of right and wrong; this is further reinforced by the internalized upper parent and the development of the superego. Two important vertical theorists were Adler and Berne, Adler being concerned with striving to overcome feelings of inferiority and Berne with winners and losers. Berne also introduced the concept of the Child, Parent, and Adult ego states. In some respects, moving up the vertical axis is an inevitable consequence of moving toward adulthood. At adolescence, there is an additional surge towards upperness. Parents and teachers perform the vital function of relaxing restraints and permitting the child to draw level with and even overtake them.

5

Closeness

The need for closeness varies enormously between species. In humans, one of the most gregarious species, it is considerable. At its simplest, it is like magnetism (or gravity): animals are drawn toward conspecifics, and for this to be possible they must have innate neural processes that enable them to recognize and respond to them. Insofar as there appears to be some kind of closeness seeking tendency in even the simplest organisms, the underlying mechanism must be extremely basic: something like being in the presence of, or in contact with, conspecifics evokes pleasurable responses. For humans, this has become expanded and elaborated to include a range of feelings and satisfactions concerning involvement and interaction with others (which is the state of relatedness of closeness). The motivation behind the drive to seek closeness appears to be of two (overlapping) kinds: (1) a (positive) striving towards a closer involvement with others because of its various advantages and benefits, and (2) a (negative) avoidance or fear of distance, or an inability to tolerate it.

THE POSITIVE STRIVING TOWARD CLOSER INVOLVEMENT

Some advantages of closeness have been described in Chapter 2. What Chance (1988) said about the hedonic mode in monkey colonies has much relevance to the more positive forms of closeness. Closeness enables animals and people to work or strive cooperatively, within families, communities, and societies. Seyfarth and Cheney (1992) concluded that monkeys are not capable of comprehending what other monkeys are thinking and feeling, so they cannot empathize with each other or console each other. This suggests that man is capable of attaining much greater degrees of closeness than any other animal. Language is a mediator and facilitator of closeness. Through language, humans are able to convey their thoughts and feelings to each other in great detail; this enables them to get much closer than any other animal to knowing what is going on inside each other's heads. The very act of talking (chattering, nattering), irrespective of what is said, binds people together. Writing (typing, printing) enables people to record their thoughts, feelings, observations, theories, and fantasies for others to read, at different times and in different places. By this means, people have been able to draw upon, extend, and develop the ideas of others. This has led to enormous theoretical, scientific, and aesthetic advances within civilized societies.

Almost all humans are capable of communicating to a far greater extent than even the most highly evolved primates; but within humans, the capacity to become closely involved with others or with a specific other varies considerably. It is because of this capacity that they have become so needful of and dependent upon closeness. In industrial societies there is a tendency for people to want to be with and in contact with others excessively; to spend time in crowded places; to listen to the radio, watch television, read books and newspapers. People also have become vulnerable to being emotionally disturbed when deprived of closeness either to others in general or to a specific other. They are capable as well of *closeness fatigue*, an equally disturbing condition that arises from overexposure to closeness - particularly when it is enforced, which induces an increasingly compelling desire to escape into distance.

THE AVOIDANCE OR FEAR OF DISTANCE

Sullivan (1953) described loneliness as the exceedingly unpleasant and driving experience connected with an inadequate discharge of the need for human intimacy (i.e., closeness). Von Witzleben (1958) used the term *"primary loneliness"* to describe the loneliness of the self, which he considered to be inborn in everyone and which is the feeling of being alone and helpless in the world. Weigert (1960) maintained that primary - or, as she called it, *existential* - loneliness is seldom fully experienced, since the interdependencies of daily life protect the individual from recogniZing it. Kierkegaard (1944) believed that people do everything possible to keep lonely thoughts away. Fromm-Reichmann (1959) considered loneliness to be such a painful experience that people will do practically anything to avoid it. The philosopher Heidegger (1927) was concerned with the nature of being. Unlike Descartes (who said, "I think, therefore I am") he considered that what he called my *being-in-the-world* involves my *being-with-others* who are also in the world. My full self-consciousness and self-affirmation, he maintained, derive from my consciousness of others. Thus, a major consequence of the experience of closeness is a confirmation of one's existence.

Schachter (1959) observed that autobiographical reports of people such as religious hermits, prisoners of war, and castaways make it clear that the effects of isolation can be "devastating." After relatively short periods the person experiences what amounts almost to physical torture.

A fear related to the fear of being alone is the strangely anthropocentric fear that man may be all alone in the universe: that there is no point or purpose to life; that it does not matter what we do because there is no one to notice or care. Those who are able to convince themselves that there is a god derive comfort from the thought that they are not alone in the universe, that their god is there for them and cares about them. This gives meaning to their existence. Those who are not, suspect that humans have created their gods as a defense against this kind of fear. They ask why other animals do not have gods and what might provide animals with a purpose for their existence. This fear can be understood as a projection onto the universe of the child's fear of separation from its parent, and of its need to be told what to do, and responded to, by its parent.

THE RESPONSE OF OTHERS

Beyond needing to be aware of the presence of others, people need to feel that they are getting some response from them. Ellis (1985) included the fear of having no impact among what she called the six primitive fears. "It has to do" she wrote, "with being heard, being seen, being felt." In other words, being taken notice of. The question is sometimes asked: If a tree falls in the middle of a desert, and no one hears it fall, does it make a noise? One might similarly ask: If a man screams in the middle of a desert, and no one hears him scream, or hears him but takes no notice, does *he* make a noise? Worse still, does he exist? Imagine a nightmarish situation in which you are among a group of people who are behaving as if you do not exist. They speak through you or across you, and when you speak it is as if you have not spoken. The child or adult who feels s/he is being ignored will do anything to draw attention to her/himself and will not even mind if the response is one of anger or disapproval, because the pain of being ignored can be intolerable.

Beyond being noticed or responded to, what people appear to appreciate most about closeness is being wanted, liked, or valued. May (1953) observed that people get much of their sense of their own reality out of what others say to them and think about them. The state of relatedness that we call closeness is, in its most intense and satisfying form, one of being related to, rather than one of relating. That is, it is a passive state. For most infants or young children, closeness simply comes their way, because parents in particular like to be close to them. As they grow older, it may continue to come their way because they grow into likeable children whom others want to be with. If they are lucky they will grow into likeable adults and will always have plenty of people enjoying their company and wanting to be with them. The satisfaction of the condition of closeness is not entirely derived from passively receiving closeness from others. People also find it pleasurable to be aware that others want them to be close to them, and in actively responding to and satisfying the closeness needs of others they are deriving a particular form of gratification.

OFFERING CLOSENESS AND INVITING CLOSENESS

Closeness may be attained either (actively) by making an approach to another or (passively) by waiting for another to make an approach to oneself. The approacher makes a gesture of interest to which the other may or may not choose to respond, and the waiter tries to convey that a response might be forthcoming if an approach were to be made. The disadvantage of approaching another is that it carries the risk of being turned down. The disadvantage of waiting to be approached is that there is less control over who makes the approaches, though it is sometimes possible to target invitations. A common sequence is for each to start with fairly minimal signs of interest and to progress to more definite signs if these are met with sympathetic responses. Nonverbal communications such as smiling, opening the lips, raising the eyebrows (Eibl-Eibesfeldt, 1970), opening the eyes widely and making eye contact (Argyle, 1972) provide additional reinforcement of positive intentions to become close. The fact that people proceed so cautiously indicates how apprehensive they are about being rejected; however, this kind of sequence is common in the mating rituals of many animal species.

DONATIVE AND RECEPTIVE CLOSENESS

When considering closeness, the distinction between relating and being related to is important. Relating is *donative closeness* (i.e., giving closeness) and being related to is *receptive closeness* (i.e., being given closeness). The distinction is often difficult to sustain, and a particular action can sometimes be both at the same time. The most satisfactory close relationships are likely to be those in which each partner sometimes gives and sometimes receives and in which neither is conscious of who is doing the giving and who the receiving. Doing or giving something pleasant to, is perhaps the most clear-cut form of donative closeness; having something pleasant done or given to oneself, the most clear-cut form of receptive closeness. Stroking might be considered a form of doing something pleasant to, yet the act of stroking itself can give pleasure. The main flow of closeness, however, would be from the stroker to the person who is being stroked; this would determine who should be considered the donor and who the receiver.

Being listened to attentively is another form of receptive closeness. The (donative) listener gives her/his attention and the (receptive) person being listened to finds this helpful. The listener however, may well find that having personal feelings revealed to her/him is a pleasurable experience. Thus, the person who gives closeness attains the state of relatedness called closeness (i.e., actually gains closeness) simply from giving closeness. This is a remarkable but important fact. According to Waldroop and Hurst (1982), a number of authors have argued that psychotherapists frequently use their relationships with their clients as a means of safely satisfying their own need for closeness. They called this "one-way intimacy" (which it clearly is not, for both client and therapist derive closeness from the encounter). There is, however, a power (vertical) differential between the therapist and the client, for the implication is that the therapist's need for closeness is less than the client's. The client comes to the therapist for the closeness that is on offer and may even have to pay for it. The therapist is ostensibly the donor, though nevertheless, s/he is deriving closeness from the encounter.

CLOSENESS, SHARING, AND FAMILIARITY

Not all aspects of closeness are concerned with giving and receiving. When one gives and the other receives, one is being an I to the other's Thou (see Chapter 3). Much closeness involves the participants behaving as though they were a We, such as when they share living space, possessions, activities, feelings, ideas, values, objectives, hopes, crises, and so on. People who are close want to share, and the experience of sharing reinforces their closeness. The accumulation of shared experiences creates a common memory that contributes further to the state of We-ness. A related aspect of closeness is familiarity. Familiarity is comforting and reassuring (though it may sometimes give rise to closeness fatigue). It is an important component of closeness to nonpersons (see Chapter 6). People become fond of, and therefore close to, familiar objects and familiar surroundings (though they sometimes become fed up with them and want to change them).

CLOSENESS AND PHYSICAL CONTACT

Physical contact is the most direct form of closeness. Apart from exceptional circumstances (e.g., during physical examinations by a doctor) people who are not close do not make physical contact. Lovers usually enjoy physical contact and it, in turn, intensifies their experience of closeness. It has been argued by Hollender et al. (1969, 1970) that women in particular agree to sexual intercourse in order to experience being held and that this accounts for some forms of promiscuity. People hug on reunion after periods of separation and at times of crisis and celebration. Being touched, stroked, or massaged by another person is a soothing experience (Downing, 1973; Montagu, 1986). Professional masseurs give this particular form of closeness even though they do not have a close relationship with their clients.

SEXUAL CLOSENESS

Sexual closeness is a form of closeness that has been passed, by evolution, directly from animals to humans, though in the process it has undergone certain changes. Whereas in most animals it is possible only at certain times of the year, in humans it is possible at any time. Sexual closeness is one of the earliest forms of closeness out of which many of the other forms of closeness may have developed. The relationship between sexual closeness and what might be called more *amicable* forms of closeness is complex. Sexual closeness can occur between strangers who have no other form of close involvement at all. This feature is in keeping with its direct line of evolution from animals. In cultures in which it is permitted, the casual sexual behavior between adolescents can be understood as a precursor to the more committed, amicable involvements of early adulthood. The need for sexual closeness may be different from that for amicable closeness and each may have to be satisfied separately. A person can have a predominantly sexually close relationship with one person and a predominantly nonsexually close (amicable) relationship with another. Sometimes a sexual relationship between two people seems to run parallel to a more amicable relationship and the partners appear to shift from one to the other, almost as though they have two separate existences. In such an arrangement, the quality of one relationship may be quite different from the quality of the other. Ideally, a sexually close relationship and a more amicable relationship become totally integrated and each feeds from and reinforces the other.

An essential component of sexual closeness is *sexual arousal* or *sexual excitement*. This is a highly specific emotional state, though it can link up with other emotional states such as elation and anxiety. It can be evoked by a variety of circumstances, some of which may be the consequence of experiences in childhood. Sometimes an expression of interest or willingness to participate by one partner will arouse excitement in the other, but sometimes teasing can be more exciting. Because of the many inhibitions and restrictions imposed upon sex in various societies, the defiance of such inhibitions and restrictions (or the danger of being found out) becomes exciting. Even getting drunk often facilitates sexual arousal.

Because the sexual act involves penetration of the woman by the man, much enactment of the penetration theme occurs between men and women in industrial societies. Typically the woman provokes the man, in much the same way as the bullfighter provokes the bull. By their gestures and styles of dress, women convey hints that they might permit the man to enter them, either from above (neckline) or below (hemline); but the convention is that unless certain other conditions are met, the man should not consider himself entitled to respond to such hints. By dressing attractively in this way women play a dangerous game, laying themselves open to the risk of assault or rape. There appears to be a direct evolutionary link between this kind of enactment and the posturing of female monkeys to indicate their willingness to be mounted (Lancaster, 1975, page 32).

Exposing, and being exposed to, parts or all of the body can be sexually exciting. Men appear to be more affected than women by such exposure, but the issue is complicated. Such exposure by women may belong to the same category of behavior as hinting that penetration may be permitted. It is the communicational aspect of exposure that is important. In a naturist community, nudity is not sexually exciting; but if a woman in a long dress exposes her ankle it can be exciting. Men pay to watch women exposing themselves and become sexually excited by it. Women pay to watch men exposing themselves, but it is less clear that they find this sexually exciting. When men expose themselves to women in public places, women feel frightened and offended, but apparently not excited. Men spy upon women when they are undressing and find this exciting, but women tend not to spy upon men when they are undressing.

EXISTING THEORIES OF CLOSENESS

Intimacy versus isolation was described by Erikson (1963) as the sixth of his eight "ages of man." It was, he considered, a feature of early adult life. He defined intimacy as the capacity to commit oneself to concrete affiliations and partnerships and to develop the ethical strength to abide by such commitments, even though they may call for significant sacrifices and compromises. He used the word *"distantiation"* to refer to the counterpart of intimacy, defining it as the readiness to isolate and, if necessary, destroy those forces and people whose essence seems dangerous to one's own and whose "territory" seems to encroach on the extent of one's intimate relations. Thus, he described intimacy in much more positive terms than isolation. Orlofsky et al. (1973), who were influenced by Erikson, defined four classes of individual: (1) *intimates*, who have attained true intimacy; (2) *preintimates*, who have some close relationships but who experience conflict over commitment and are ambivalent about the risk involved in intimate sexuality; (3) *stereotyped individuals*, whose relationships lack significant depth and who treat others more or less as objects; and, (4) *isolates*, who have a few acquaintances but who tend to withdraw and isolate themselves from others. This classification carries an unfortunate implication that closeness is good and distance is bad.

Attachment theory, as elaborated by Bowlby in his book *Attachment* (1969), like the classifications of Erikson and Orlofsky et al., places greater value on closeness than on distance, particularly on closeness from a position of lowerness. He (1977) defined attachment as "attaining or retaining proximity to some other differentiated and preferred individual who is usually conceived of as *stronger and/or wiser*" (page 203, emphasis added). His main concern was with the success or failure of the young animal or infant to establish and maintain such attachment and the part played by the parent in bringing this about. The assumed opposite of attachment is detachment; this carries the unfortunate implication of failure of attachment and tends to underplay the more positive aspects of the detaching process. Bowlby's subsequent two books *Separation, Anxiety and Anger* (1973a) and *Loss, Sadness and Depression* (1980), albeit authoritative and scholarly, continue to place too great a stress upon the disadvantages of inadequate or lost attachments. A number of others (e.g., Ainsworth, 1989; Collins and Read, 1990; Hazan and Shaver, 1987, 1990; Mikulincer and Erev, 1991) have attempted to apply attachment theory to the relating of adults, but they too have paid insufficient attention to the equally important process of distancing.

Heard and Lake (1986) modified attachment theory in order to more easily apply it to the relating of adults. Although they included the terms "closeness" and "distance," they placed greater emphasis on closeness. Their main concern was with what they called *interactions;* these could be either *companionable* (based upon shared interests or skills) or *supportive* (involving one partner behaving in a parental way toward the other). Closeness or distance could be either *comfortable* or *uncomfortable*. A satisfactory interaction was associated with the condition of *assuagement;* an unsatisfactory one with the condition of *disassuagement*. Such a condition is a shared state of relatedness.

REVEALING AND BEING REVEALED TO

Revealing and being revealed to are components of closeness that are not necessarily donative or receptive, though revealing is active and being revealed to is passive. It seems likely that the processes of revealing and being revealed to of more amicable forms of closeness have developed out of the exposing and being exposed to of sexual closeness. Exposing and making revelations induces the other to expose and make revelations in return. When people feel close, they are disposed to make revelations and to have revelations made to them. Just as exposing and being exposed to intensifies sexual excitement, revealing and being revealed to intensify the condition of closeness. It seems likely that exposing and revealing are linked with the acts of submission and appeasement that characterize the courtship behavior of many animal species (Eibl-Eibesfeldt, 1970). The message being conveyed is that, "I am rendering myself weak so that I cannot harm you."

SEEKING AND IMPARTING INFORMATION

Wanting to understand and know about the other, or know what it feels like to be the other, is the opposite of wanting to make revelations to the other. It is an active form of closeness seeking, a psychological penetration, that might be a symbolic enactment of - or even a development out of - sexual penetration. When people first meet (e.g., at a party) they ask each other questions as a way of getting to know each other, thus becoming closer. When the other asks questions it is more difficult to withhold information. Curiosity needs to be a carefully judged form of behavior. Excessive curiosity is not experienced as kindly or respectful, and interrogation is totally unkindly and disrespectful, fitting into the category of enforced closeness.

Duck (1992) observed that self-disclosure confirms a desire to develop a relationship. Imparting information to another renders a person vulnerable to abuse should the other choose to misuse it. Agreeing to impart information is a form of entrustment of the other. When a close relationship breaks up, it can be a source of distress that the other retains information imparted during a period of entrustment. Imparting information that reveals certain deficiencies or weaknesses is called *confiding*. People confide because they wish to unburden themselves of certain aspects of themselves they feel bad about. When this is something they also feel guilty about, it is called *confessing*. In the Roman Catholic Church, the ritual of the *confessional*, which is conducted under conditions of absolute trust, serves an important unburdening function, though it also carries the additional function of *forgiveness*, which is an upper-to-lower procedure. Self-disclosure is a complex issue that has been extensively covered in a book edited by Derlega and Berg (1987).

The processes of confiding and confessing carry the risk that when certain undesirable aspects of the person are revealed, the other will want to break off the relationship. When people become close they often vow that they will keep no secrets from each other. There is an understanding that the degree of closeness is so great that either could confess anything and the other would forgive them. This is not necessarily so: confessions of infidelity are particularly hard to tolerate.

CLOSENESS AND IDENTITY

It was explained in Chapter 4 that it is necessary to have a firm sense of who one is before one can safely enter into a close relationship with another; otherwise one's identity simply becomes absorbed into that of the other. Laing (1965) explained: "A firm sense of one's own autonomous identity is required in order that one may be related as one human being to another. Otherwise, any and every relationship threatens the individual with loss of identity" (page 44). This is equivalent to Bowen's (1978) state of fusion. When two people have secure identities they are able to *lose themselves in each other,* creating a state of total we-ness, but being confident that should they need to, they can extricate themselves from this and regain their autonomous separatenesses. The (ontologically insecure) person who has an insubstantial identity is faced with two choices: (1) to avoid close involvement altogether, or (2) to use Laing's terminology, to become *ontologically dependent* upon another, namely, "dependent upon the other for one's very being." In this way s/he becomes totally identified with the other person, adopting all her/his beliefs, opinions, values and so on.

One aspect of becoming or being close is having an interest in and a curiosity about the other, which involves experiencing what it feels like to be the other which in turn, leads to developing varying degrees of *identification* with the other. Identification also involves sharing the pleasures of the other's successes and the disappointments of the other's failures. Given that people tend to get close to those who are like themselves, closeness inevitably results in the respective identities, or selves, coming into close proximity, overlapping and merging. This experience of the *two becoming one* can be one of the most exciting features of close involvement; it is particularly so when men and women become close, because it creates an intermingling of the two genders.

People who are close sometimes feel as though they know what each other is thinking and often find themselves about to say or suggest the same thing. It is called *thinking as one.* This they find pleasurable. In the presence of a third person, they may give each other a knowing look to indicate that each knows what the other feels about what the third person is saying. Associated with this is the belief that they can communicate by a kind of *telepathy;* they may feel they can do this across long distances, such that one might know when the other is in difficulties. A further extension of this is the conviction that one can communicate with the other even after s/he has died.

EXTENSIONS OF THE IDENTIFICATION PROCESS

Understanding

Understanding someone is a stage beyond getting to know about her/him. It is necessary to distinguish between understanding what s/he is saying and understanding what s/he is experiencing or striving for. Being understood is a potent component of being the recipient of closeness. Describing another as being understanding, or as someone who understands, is acknowledging that the other has taken the trouble to listen in an interested and concerned way and has grasped some essential truth about the person. Being "got right" is one way of describing being understood. The understander needs to make some gesture or remark to convey that s/he has understood. The person who feels understood inevitably feels close to the person who understands. This is linked to the idea that the infant readily becomes attached to the parent who correctly perceives its needs and responds appropriately to them (Bretherton et al., 1989).

Sympathizing

Sympathizing with is similar to understanding but carries a more emotional emphasis. The sympathizer not only understands but feels for, shares the same emotion as, aligns her/himself with, or sides with the other.

Empathy

Empathy is, at least temporarily, almost assuming the same identity as the other. The empathic person watching another fight may clench her/his fists and make punching movements.

Empathic Attunement

Empathic attunement was introduced by Rowe and MacIsaac (1989) to describe the psychoanalytic technique of becoming immersed within the patient's experience as a means of understanding what it is like to be her/him. The technique is derived from the writing of Kohut (1984), who defined empathy as "the capacity to think and feel oneself into the inner life of another person" (page 82). The technique enables the patient to experience the therapist as a needed extension of her/himself. Kohut emphasized the powerful therapeutic effect of the therapist conveying to the patient that s/he has been correctly understood. He described the process of empathic immersion as an *experience-near* form of gathering information and contrasted it with the *experience-distant* approach of scientific enquiry. He considered the empathic stance to be essential to the therapeutic process. This has connections with the close relating versus distant relating discussed in Chapter 3.

CLOSENESS AND EMOTION

It was explained in Chapter 1 that emotion is closely related to gaining or losing states of relatedness. Because of this, emotion is associated with all four of the main forms of relating. There is, however, a special association between closeness and emotion. Self-disclosure includes allowing feelings to show. Close people and people who are close find it easy to be openly emotional; in turn, the open show of emotion predisposes people to closeness. Crying is easier between people who are close, and crying together often brings people closer. Smiling and laughing are especially linked with closeness. Smiling is a signal that indicates a preparedness to become close. People commonly say they fell in love because they could make each other laugh, and lovers often are able to end a quarrel if one can manage to make the other one laugh.

THE SELECTION OF SOMEONE TO BECOME CLOSE TO

When the need for closeness is intense, selection is either nonexistent or minimal. The newly born infant readily accepts whoever happens to be its parent. The person who believes her/himself to be unattractive, or the repeatedly or recently rejected person, is inclined to accept the closeness of whoever may offer it. The emerging adolescent falls in love easily and uncritically with members of her/his immediate peer group. The person in a conflictual marriage falls easy prey to the extramarital affair. When the need for closeness is less intense, a greater degree of selectivity is possible, though such selection commonly occurs at a subcortical level.

There is a complex interrelationship between being similar to, liking, and wanting to be close to. People are more inclined to like people whom they believe to be like themselves (Byrne, 1971), providing, as Duck (1992) observed, they like themselves. They may like people who are not like themselves, if they consider that such people have admirable qualities that they themselves do not have. They are also more inclined to get close to people they like, though there are many people they like whom they may not wish to get close to, either because they have enough close relationships already or because they consider these people would not want to become close to them. Generally, then, they are more likely to want to get close to people who are like themselves; but there is a further complicating factor here. People who are ontologically secure (see Chapter 4), who have well established identities of which they are certain, are relatively comfortable in the presence of people who are not like themselves and may even find them interesting and attractive. People who are ontologically insecure will find the differentness of others disturbing and therefore may prefer to become close to people who are like themselves.

In the establishment of close relationships, vertical considerations come into play. People are inclined only attempt to get close to those whom they consider to be likely to want to get close to them; to use Berne's (1975) phrase, whom they consider to be in their "league." Desirability may be affected by age, sex, race, physical attractiveness, social class or social position, and a range of indices of upperness. This is linked to the principle that people tend to get close to those who are like themselves. Thus, in assessing their chances of forming a close relationship, individuals engage in a procedure similar to that of the ritual agonistic encounter (see Chapter 2). If they consider the other to have qualities superior to their own they may back off, in the expectation that the other will reject them; if they consider the other to have qualities inferior to their own they may also back off, considering the other not to be worth getting close to. In turn, being someone who is, or has been, successful in establishing close relationships, or a particular close relationship, is one form of upperness.

CLOSENESS TO A SPECIFIC OTHER

Closeness to a specific other can occur between people of similar status, from upper to lower or from lower to upper. The present chapter is concerned mainly with closeness between people of similar status. The other two forms of closeness will be dealt with in Chapter 9. Closeness between people of similar status can range from being central and of high significance to being peripheral and of low significance and from having a strong sexual component to having no sexual component at all. Central and highly significant forms of closeness tend to develop under conditions of high emotion. Living together through a crisis, when there are shared high levels of anxiety, is one route to such closeness. It may be that under conditions of this kind people are compelled to shed their usual, formal facades and get on with whatever is necessary to resolve the crisis. It may also be that when people are anxious they need someone to hold on to and grab whoever happens to be nearest. The development of closeness under such conditions was the theme of a classic film, featuring Humphrey Bogart and Katharine Hepburn, *The African Queen*.

A person only needs, or can only cope with, a small number of central and highly significant forms of closeness at any one time and having got them, does not seek more (i.e., her/his closeness stores are full). One important requirement, therefore, if two people are to come together in a form of closeness of this intensity, is that both be needful of a close relationship at the same moment in time. The infant, the adolescent, someone who is in a failing relationship, or someone who is emerging from a broken relationship would be in such a needful state. Such people probably put out signals indicating their availability, just as people who are not needful, probably put out signals indicating their nonavailability. Because the need for such closeness is great, people rarely stay in this state for long: they rapidly become involved with an equally needful person who happens to come their way.

An emotion that commonly propels people into an intensely close relationship is sexual arousal, though this is not always openly acknowledged. Extreme needfulness combined with sexual arousal are the likely ingredients of that most precipitate and intense form of coming together called *falling in love*. Many have drawn parallels between falling in love and the early involvement between the infant and its mother, though unlike the infantile experience it is between participants of equal status. Some have likened it to Mahler's (1961) condition of *symbiosis*, while others (e.g., Hazan and Shaver, 1987) have likened it more to Bowlby's (1969) attachment. The part played by sexual arousal in the mother/infant relationship is a contentious issue. Mothers are capable of being sexually aroused by their infants, though not to the same extent as fathers. Though some (e.g., Brenner, 1957) would argue that what psychoanalysts call infantile sexuality is essentially the same as adult sexuality, it would be misleading to suggest that infants become sexually aroused by their mothers.

Falling in love is like making a parachute jump: it is not possible to half jump. One has to let oneself fall and trust that "the parachute will open." Falling means allowing oneself to become emotionally dependent upon the other person (Birtchnell, 1991a), to the extent of needing frequent and prolonged contact, and being capable of getting badly hurt should the closeness be broken off. One will not fall unless one is prepared to allow it to happen. One needs to *open oneself to love*, to let the other into one's heart, under one's skin. People who have allowed it to happen but who have been badly hurt when the relationship failed have difficulty allowing it to happen again.

Being in love bears a certain resemblance to being addicted to a drug; emotional dependence is similar to drug dependence. Periods of separation are accompanied by painful restlessness and obsessive thinking about the other. The greater the separation, the greater the obsession becomes. The pain of separation is relieved as soon as contact is re-established. The infant left alone suddenly begins to shout and scream and is consoled only by the return of a familiar figure who picks it up and holds it. The pain of separation of people who are in love may be similar to this. Gradually the infant and lovers become able to tolerate increasing periods of separation. The infant is said to achieve a state of *object constancy*; it incorporates inside itself an image of its parent to which it can relate when the parent is not there. Perhaps something similar occurs with the lovers.

In the case of the infant, there may be a kind of blending of the need for closeness and the need for food. When it is well fed, it survives on its food stores; but as they become depleted, hunger pangs return and it begins to crave more. This link between loneliness and hunger persists to some extent into adult life. Bruch (1957) observed that people often attempt to compensate for loneliness by overeating. Blatt (1974) observed that people with anaclitic depression (see subsequent discussion) crave food. Lovers (and other friends) commonly eat together (and sometimes even feed each other) as a means of consolidating their closeness. To a larger extent, the satisfaction they gain from re-establishing contact is sexual, but they also gain the experience of being wanted and appreciated by each other.

The closeness need is probably the most intense of the four main needs, which explains the extreme euphoria associated with being in love. Romantic love is characterized by the sharing of experiences, the exchange of kindnesses, childlike playfulness, the idealization of the other's qualities, the abandonment of privacy, self-exposure, self-disclosure, physical contact, and sexual indulgence; but living at this level of intensity is intolerable for long and closeness fatigue rapidly sets in. A critical point is reached when (1) the relationship breaks up and the partners go their separate ways, or (2) a position of compromise is reached in which there is a "polarizing out" of identities in order that each may retreat back toward autonomy, and the partners negotiate a more subdued, long-term relationship.

COMMITTED, LONG-TERM CLOSENESS

Orlinsky (1979) defined romantic love as "an explicitly time-limited engagement that carries its partners through a relatively unstructured period between formal commitments of one sort or another." Although some long-term commitments may become established without an initial phase of romantic love, most western marriages (or their equivalent) develop out of such a phase. The more subdued love that is maintained over long periods of time between marital partners is sometimes called conjugal love (Oppong, 1979). It seems likely that somewhere deep within conjugal love there remain elements of the original romantic love, just as somewhere within the butterfly there remain elements of the original caterpillar (Birtchnell, 1986). An important feature of conjugal love is that the intense craving for the other during periods of separation, which characterizes romantic love, is absent. Partners may miss each other but they do not pine, unless the separation is prolonged. Somehow, each develops a confidence that somewhere the other exists for her/him. That this is so is brought out by the immediate and acute distress that is evoked when there is any threat to the relationship, such as learning that some harm has come to the other, that the other has been having an affair or has died.

The longer the relationship survives the more extensive the common memories of the partners become. Living through and surviving crises feeds into and reinforces the shared closeness. The stresses that develop between marital partners are due mainly to the fact that two people with separate relational needs have such overlapping existences. In a sense, they are like escaped prisoners who are handcuffed together: one cannot act without it affecting the other. In order for the relationship to survive, each must be able to obtain, and allow the other to obtain, adequate amounts of each of the four states of relatedness. Strains arise when one partner imposes upon the other a state of relatedness that the other does not want in order to attain a state of relatedness s/he wants. Each should become attuned to the other's needs and be prepared sometimes to make concessions to the other.

Ironically, issues of distance play an important part in the stability of long-term commitments. Closeness fatigue becomes a problem when people lead overlapping existences, and marital partners need to allow each other time to be on their own. Gibran (1968) put it: "Let there be spaces in your togetherness." Having employment outside the home is one way of reducing involvement, and problems sometimes arise when one partner becomes unemployed or retired. When people fall in love they are happy to allow their identities to fuse, but when they enter into a long-term commitment the retention of their separate identities (each accepting the differentness of the other) becomes an essential requirement for their survival. One aspect of identity is expressing preferences, and there are many instances (where to live, what kind of accommodation, where to spend holidays) in which preferences may differ. Reaching agreements and making compromises impose strains upon the relationship. Marriages can and sometimes do survive by one partner consistently making concessions to the other.

FRIENDSHIPS

Marriages and friendships are not necessarily the same thing, though in the best marriages the partners are also friends. Friendships are forms of long-term closeness that are commonly asexual and develop between partners of the same sex. Friendships differ from marital relationships in that friends do not have to share the same existence and therefore do not encounter the sorts of strains that marital partners do. Some friendships are more secure than, and perhaps even closer than, marital relationships and sometimes survive longer. They may survive because they are less intense and do not carry the same commitments and responsibilities as marriages. They may lie dormant over long periods and become reawakened when the need arises. Extramarital sexual liaisons, which may or may not also be friendships, similarly survive because they are not subject to the strains and responsibilities of married life.

CLOSENESS AND PSYCHOTHERAPY

Rogers (1957) maintained that the therapist-patient relationship was the crucial factor in psychotherapy and that theories about psychopathology were of minor importance. He believed that the successful psychotherapist required only three qualities: genuineness, unconditional positive regard, and empathy, all of which are facets of closeness. Mitchell et al. (1977) found, from a research review, a significant link between genuineness, warmth, and empathy in the therapist and positive therapeutic outcome. Lambert et al. (1986) considered certain *common factors*, such as warmth, attention, and understanding, to be central to all varieties of psychotherapy. Ferreira (1964) considered the therapeutic value of what is talked about in psychotherapy to be secondary to the experience of the fulfilment of the client's intimacy needs. Luborsky et al. (1988) showed the therapist's quality of closeness to the patient to be the best predictor of a favorable outcome. It can be concluded that the provision of closeness is an essential component of psychotherapy, though in many forms, ranging from behavior therapy to psychoanalysis, a lowerness component is also important (see Chapter 9).

Psychotherapy, however, is an unusual kind of closeness. One of the risks of entering into a close relationship is that the person is uncertain of her/his acceptability. In psychotherapy the client's acceptability is guaranteed, particularly if s/he is required to pay a fee (exchanging upperness for closeness); but s/he may worry that the therapist has accepted her/him only because it is her/his job to do so. In a normal close relationship there is always the risk that the relationship will break down and cause pain. In the psychotherapeutic relationship, the client knows from the outset that there will be a termination date, which is usually carefully negotiated. Despite these restraints, the client may get very close to the therapist, who may become incorporated as a good internal object.

An important distinction between therapists and clients is that clients make personal revelations to therapists but therapists do not make personal revelations to clients. This is why Waldroop and Hurst (1982) described the closeness as being "one- way." They proposed that this renders clients more vulnerable than therapists. Most clients prefer it to be this way because they feel they are being indulged by being allowed to make revelations to which the therapists attentively listen. Mostly they would not want to hear the therapists' revelations. Making personal revelations does not necessarily render people vulnerable. When they do so in the course of writing their autobiographies, they do not render themselves vulnerable. Clients usually *are* more vulnerable than their therapists, but the reasons for this are complex: they have to do with their greater needfulness, their emotional dependence and their tendency to regress (all of which are vertical considerations).

On reason why, as a matter of policy, therapists do not make personal revelations to clients is that the less clients know about them the more they are able to establish a *transference relationship* with them. Many therapists consider the understanding and interpretation of the transference to be an essential component of therapy (Stone, 1984). Transference involves relating to the therapist as though s/he were some key figure in the patient's past or present life. Through this process the patient's relating to an internal object and her/his perception of the way the internal object relates to her/him become manifest in the way s/he interacts with the therapist.

Freud (1937) referred to transference as a libidinal attachment of patient to therapist and considered it essential for therapeutic work; but he also (1915a) proposed what he called the *rule of abstinence*, which stated that the patient's craving for love should not be satisfied by the therapist because her/his unsatisfied longing provided the impetus for therapy. Nunberg (1948) cautioned that *transference gratification* can occur in the absence of any therapeutic progress. Blatt and Behrends (1987) considered effective therapy to involve a constant oscillation between gratification and deprivation. It may be that different conditions require different degrees of gratification. Dublin (1985) described an extreme approach for the treatment of terrorized or brutalized patients, which he called loving the hell out of them. Of one patient he wrote, "When she kissed me on the cheek and I could feel her slight trembling, I held her as tenderly as I ever have my own daughter, and she exploded into a quivering hurt that lasted through two weeks of crying." (page 79).

KINSHIP

Bailey (1988) made the important point that our predecessors in phylogeny who failed to develop effective kinship strategies for distinguishing between *familiars* and *strangers*, and for classifying familiars in terms of degrees of closeness, became extinct. It seems likely therefore that what has been described here as closeness has evolved out of such kinship strategies. Animals treat kin differently from nonkin and, at some level, are aware that it is safer to approach kin than to approach non-kin. The phrase "blood is thicker than water" indicates that the same applies to humans. The kind of helping that members of a kinship provide for each other Bailey called *natural helping*. He postulated that under stress individuals turn to kin to avail themselves of such natural helping. The evolution of closeness in humans must have been the result of the transfer of kinship strategies to selected nonkin. Boyd-Franklin (1984) called such strategies nonbilogical kinship ties; a number of writers have referred to the *"as if family"* phenomenon.

Bailey (1988) observed that although clients may seek kinship from therapy, most psychotherapists (particularly behavior therapists and psychoanalysts) try to avoid offering it, and this creates what he called a *kinship asymmetry*. The therapists who come closest to creating what he called a *sense of familiness* are the humanistic therapists. If kinship were the essential ingredient of therapy, clients would seek it from their family members and there would be no professional therapists.

CLOSENESS TO ONE VERSUS CLOSENESS TO MANY

From consideration of the accumulation of stores of states of relatedness (see Chapter 1), it might be concluded that many small doses of closeness (as might accumulate from casual acquaintances) could add up to the equivalent of one large dose (as might result from one intense, central relationship). Weiss (1969) suggested that close relationships might be rated either by number or intensity and proposed what he called the *fund of sociability* hypothesis, which stated that people require a certain amount of interaction with others and experience stress when the total amount is too little or too great. The infant relies entirely upon one, intense, central relationship; some adults are able to sustain themselves on just casual acquaintances and no intense central ones. In the normal course of events, people relate in different ways to different people (e.g., closely to family members, more distantly to tradespeople). Ideally, therefore, people should have the capacity to relate at different levels of closeness.

People vary considerably in the general level of closeness they feel comfortable with. There are those who thrive on closeness, who try to get close to almost everyone they meet; those who avoid it at all costs, and the majority who fit somewhere in between. There is a particular category of person who has a lot of fairly close friends but no really close ones. Such a person resembles in many respects what Jung (1921) and later Eysenck (1947) called the *extrovert*, described variously as outgoing, sociable, having many friends, likes parties, craves excitement, quickly forms attachments, needs to have people to talk to, and prefers to keep moving and doing things. Jung and Eysenck have never been very explicit about how close extroverts are capable of getting to others. Perhaps some are capable of getting very close, whereas others simply flit from person to person, apparently afraid of committing themselves to any one. Such people have much in common with those who in the sexual sphere would be called promiscuous.

Murray (1938), one of the earliest to define a set of relating needs, included one that he called *affiliation*. This was later taken up by Schachter (1959), who also called it *gregariousness*. It includes all manifestations of friendliness and goodwill and the desire to do things in the company of others. Bowlby (1969) was careful to distinguish between this and his concept of *attachment*, which, he explained, could be directed only to one or a few particular figures.

In the *Diagnostic and Statistical Manual of Mental Disorders of the American Psychiatric Association* (1980), commonly abbreviated as DSM III, Axis II is concerned with the classification of disorders of personality. Within this, one of the Basic Personality Disorders is called the *histrionic personality: the gregarious pattern.* This has much in common with what is here referred to as extroversion, affiliation, or gregariousness. The histrionic personality is dissatisfied with single attachments; lacks fidelity and loyalty; and is perceived by others as being shallow, lacking genuineness, and superficially charming and appealing. S/he has a need for constant stimulation and attention and exhibits a seductive, dramatic, and capricious pattern of relationships.

CLOSENESS TO A GROUP

The *togetherness* of a group resembles the we-ness of two people in a relationship. A group functions most effectively if it has a well-defined group identity. Though its members may have identities of their own, they also are required or expected to assume the identity of the group. Groups vary enormously in the extent to which members are enabled to retain their own identities while remaining identified with the group. As a general rule, the larger the group the less well defined is its identity and the freer are its members to retain their own identities. In a group with a well-defined identity, individuality is disruptive and is not encouraged. An ontologically insecure person may either avoid a group for fear of losing what small degree of identity s/he has or join one in order to provide her/himself with an identity. Thus, the group identity may be the only identity s/he has.

The smaller the group and the stronger the group identity, the greater may be the feeling of closeness derived from it. Each member is expected to relate primarily to the group. Close ties between group members are discouraged since this weakens the cohesiveness of the group. For some people, joining a group may be a substitute for and a way of avoiding a close relationship with another individual. This is similar to the idea of extroversion discussed earlier. In Orwell's novel "*1984*" an entire society functioned as a group and close relationships between individuals were prohibited. A person who is strongly identified with a group is prepared to sacrifice her/his needs for the good of the group. Patriotism is a form of strong group identity.

A group with a well-defined identity is capable of functioning as though it were a single person. In order to do this it needs (1) a central nucleus of individuals who determine group policy and communicate this to the rest of the group, and (2) group representatives who are empowered to act and speak on behalf of the group. Once these conditions are met, all that has been and will be said about the relating of individuals applies to the relating of groups.

Although conformity is a characteristic of groups, a group may be formed of people who do not conform (i.e., to a larger group). There may be a group of criminals, rebels, or outsiders. The group members are united by their nonconformity. They derive closeness from not wanting to conform, but they may avoid conforming in certain characteristic ways, and this gives them their group identity.

It is possible to relate to a group without actually being a member of it. The political or military leader, the preacher, the entertainer, the stand-up comic, the stripper all relate to the group as though they were relating to a single other person; and every individual member of the group relates back to them. An extension of this is the person who speaks over the radio, through television, or by some recording device, or who writes a book or an article in a magazine or newspaper. The listener, viewer, or reader responds to these communications though the person has no immediate awareness of this.

PACKAGED CLOSENESS

Making recordings; writing books, articles, poems, letters; having photographs taken of oneself; composing music; painting pictures; or creating other aesthetic objects are all ways of packaging closeness that any other person may receive. These are ways of packaging closeness in the way that having money is a way of packaging upperness.

RECEIVING CLOSENESS IN THE ABSENCE OF A DONER

The person who speaks on radio or television or who produces a form of packaged closeness is being a donor of closeness (and perhaps deriving some of the experience of being close) in the absence of an immediate recipient. When another person receives the closeness from such packaging, s/he is doing so in the absence of an immediate donor. The idea of receiving closeness in the absence of a donor is indeed a strange one, but there are a number of ways in which this can happen. A person can derive closeness from a much-loved place or object (e.g., a familiar landscape or street; her/his own home, room, or garden; an armchair, motor car, or scarf). S/he can receive closeness from the memories, possessions, or presents of a much-loved other person. A baby's comforter may provide closeness in this way, as do a child's toys, especially dolls and teddy bears. A stage beyond this is the creation of imaginary companions. Finally, s/he may continue to receive closeness from a person who has gone away or died, partly by retaining cathexis to the internalized object and partly by relating to continuing reminders such as photographs, possessions, or the grave.

All of these closenesses gain by having fantasies projected onto or into them; sometimes these projections enable the person to believe that the object of closeness can and does communicate back; that the toys, the imaginary companion, or the dead person actually speak to her/him. Auditory and visual hallucinations of the dead person are common accompaniments of grief.

CLOSENESS TO GOD (OR GODS)

To the nonbeliever, gods are imagined into existence as a protection against primary loneliness. Therefore, they belong strictly to the category of receiving closeness in the absence of a donor. They have characteristics in common with imaginary companions and phantom lovers (see subsequent discussion). An important feature of gods is that they are conceived of as upper and, because of this, are related to from a position of lowerness. Only the closeness aspect of gods will be considered here. The Christian God can be an immense source of closeness, as is conveyed by the phrase "God is Love." Allowing yourself to become involved with God is similar to falling in love; phrases such as "opening yourself to God" and "letting God into your heart" imply a preparedness to allow yourself to become needful of Him in a way that you might become needful of a lover, which is strange if He does not function as a donor. In certain religious orders, nuns undergo the ritual of becoming married to God, though not in any sexual sense. Jung (1964) referred to God as an *archetype of the collective unconscious*, that is an inherited tendency that is part of man's nature. An alternative view is that He is an amalgam of all good internalized objects, which is in keeping with the observation that different people have different conceptions of Him (i.e., some kindly and some severe). In one sense, men of the Church serve as intermediaries between God and the rest of the population, and this reinforces the illusion that love flows from God to us. People speak to God in prayer, but only a few believe that He speaks to them.

CLOSENESS IN RELATION TO THE VERTICAL AXIS

This topic will largely be covered in the sections on upper closeness and lower closeness in Chapter 9, but some issues are more appropriately considered here.

The capacity to form close relationships, like any other capacity, contributes to a person's sense of worth and therefore to her/his upperness. Some people have a natural and easy manner that enables them to make friends easily. This makes them popular. Being popular feeds upon itself because people like to be friends with people who are popular. People of this kind are successful in occupations that require the capacity to get along with people. In radio and television they are in demand because listeners and viewers are able to relate easily to them and therefore can derive closeness from them. Being endowed with qualities that are associated with conventional physical attractiveness contributes to the capacity to form close relationships and therefore to that particular kind of upperness. Success in any sphere adds to a person's attractiveness and to her/his ability to form close relationships. Physically unattractive people may therefore be more strongly motivated to seek success in other directions.

An important consideration in any closeness transaction is the question of who needs the closeness most. This involves the vertical axis, for one distinction between upperness and lowerness is the distinction between having that which the other needs and needing that which the other has. The person who needs the closeness least has the upper hand and is in a position to dictate terms. The person may need the closeness least because of her/his greater attractiveness. Alternatively, it may be because s/he has a more self-reliant (distant) personality. Thus not needing people (being the John Wayne type) can make a person attractive, but at the same time frustrating, to someone who has quite reasonable closeness needs.

The person who has the closeness that the other wants may be willing to trade it for money, in which case s/he offers closeness and receives upperness. The stripper, the masseur, and the prostitute do this, but so also (besides other things) do the counselor and the psychotherapist.

Permitting Closeness

The term "permitting" implies that an element of power is involved. Permitting closeness implies that the permitter is the more powerful and can decide whether or not the close act may take place or continue. Yet, strangely enough, what the permitter permits is usually a form of receptive closeness: for example "I will let you give me a present, walk me home, see me, touch me, kiss me, enter me." Having permitted it, the permitter actually experiences the closeness. Sometimes the power differential between the permitter and the permitted may be so great that the permitter experiences minimal satisfaction from the experience, as when a mistress permits her maid to dress her, or when a girl lets a boy kiss her because she feels sorry for him.

CLOSE DISTANCE

Close distance is one of the four paradoxical positions. It involves experiencing distance while adopting the posture of closeness. It is not as important, or as easily attainable a condition as distant closeness (see Chapter 6). A person tries to attain it when in a position of closeness that s/he does not want, as in an unwanted relationship, in an unappealing social gathering, entertaining friends who have overstayed their welcome, or unwillingly being made love to. In an unwanted relationship it may involve actually maintaining distance by working late, staying out late, or spending long periods away from home. Alternatively it may involve getting drunk, entering into dissociative states, pathological wanderings or fugue states, making suicide attempts, or committing suicide or murder. In more transient unwanted closenesses it may involve fainting, going to sleep, or imagining being somewhere else or with someone else. Vomiting is a symbolic separation from an unwanted situation and commonly follows being sexually assaulted.

CLOSENESS AND RESPECTFULNESS

In Chapter 1, respectfulness was included as a form of good or positive relating. As such, it ought to be applicable to the relating of any one of the four main positions. Yet it seems to be more aligned to closeness than to any of the other positions, being linked with sympathy and empathy. Being respectful involves being considerate of what the other's relating needs might be and of the possible effect that one's relating behavior might have upon the other, which seems to be a characteristic of closeness. It is possible, however, to be respectfully distant (i.e., respecting the other's need for privacy) and disrespectfully close (i.e., forcing one's company upon the other when it is not welcome).

CONFLICTUAL CLOSENESS

It is appropriate to place conflictual closeness between close distance and negative forms of closeness since it has links with both. Being closely involved with someone does not necessarily involve having feelings of good will toward that person. One characteristic of closeness is not being able to stop thinking about someone, even if the thoughts may be thoughts of hatred. Can the victim of torture, rape, or physical or sexual abuse be said to be close to the perpetrator of these acts? In one sense, the answer must be yes. There are examples of women who choose to stay close to men who abuse them and of children who choose to stay close to parents who abuse them. People who are bitter rivals are in some way caught up in each other. The emotions of love and hate are, in some strange way, interchangeable: one can readily turn into the other, and just as readily turn back again (Anna Freud, 1949). Quarrels between lovers are common and vicious fights sometimes break out between married couples. Such quarrels and fights are sometimes interpreted as substitutes for intimacy and sometimes they lead on to acts of intimacy. Feldman (1979) has described how, in some marital relationships, conflict and intimacy alternate as a distance-regulating process. Friends and lovers sometimes agree to have physical fights as an expression of their closeness. Competitive games (tennis, chess, etc.) are often played between people who are close. Professional fighters not infrequently like each other.

CLOSE PERSONALITIES

In the *Diagnostic and Statistical Manual of Mental Disorders of the American Psychiatric Association* (1980), there is no personality type that is purely associated with closeness. Aspects of the *dependent personality: the submissive pattern* are summarized in the DSM IIIR (revised), Axis II (American Psychiatric Association, 1987) as follows: feels uncomfortable or helpless when alone, or goes to great lengths to avoid being alone; feels devastated or helpless when close relationships end; and is frequently preoccupied with fears of being abandoned. They correspond with what in an earlier analysis was called affectional dependence (Birtchnell, 1984). The remaining features of this personality type will be described in Chapter 8.

NEGATIVE FORMS OF CLOSENESS

Many negative forms of closeness occur from an upper close or a lower close position. These will be explored (in Chapter 9) when the intermediate positions are considered.

Giving or Receiving Disrespectfully Imposed Closeness, Invasiveness or Intrusiveness

Disrespectfully imposed closeness occurs when a person comes or remains close to someone who does not wish it. Disrespectfully imposed invasiveness or intrusiveness occurs when a person invades or penetrates the other's personal space, or physical or psychic interior, against the other's wishes. Mostly these behaviors occur from a position of upper closeness (power or strength), but there are circumstances under which force does not have to be exerted. For fear of causing embarrassment or offense, the other may not make her/his objections clear. The person may be aware of the other's discomfort, but her/his need for closeness may be such that, as long as the other does not openly object, s/he is prepared to persist. Examples of this include asking personal questions, overstaying one's welcome and coercing an unenthusiastic marital partner to have sex.

Nunberg (1961) referred to the condition of pathological curiosity and described a patient who had an excessive need to ask questions. It was his belief that conditions such as this have their origins in the sexual curiosity of childhood. It seems likely that excessive inquisitiveness, particularly about a specific other person, is a particularly predatory, noninvolving, and therefore safe kind of closeness. It may be linked with voyeurism.

Mindreading. This term is sometimes used by family therapists (Lange and van der Hart, 1983) to refer to the tendency, on the part of certain family members, of assuming they know what a certain other member is thinking or feeling and of speaking on her/his behalf. When carried to excess it can be extremely disturbing to the recipient, who feels s/he is being penetrated.

Insecure Closeness

It is not always easy, but it is important to try, to distinguish between two forms of insecure closeness: (1) that resulting from the disinterest or unreliability of the other, and (2) that resulting from to the person's lack of confidence in her/his attractiveness or acceptability to others, or to a specific other. The latter may be a consequence of early, or earlier, experiences of the former. The insecurely close person becomes anxious when the other shows interest in other people or when other people show interest in the other. S/he finds it hard to allow the other to have friends or interests of her/his own and may try to sabotage these. The strategies that the insecurely close person may adopt to ensure or maintain the other's closeness will vary according to the power differential between the two. These will be considered in the appropriate sections of Chapter 9.

Jealousy (Friday, 1986; Mullen and White, 1989) is a common accompaniment or extension of insecure closeness and tends to be focused upon one specific third party (Buunk and Bringle, 1987). It may be contributed to by the behavior of any one of the three people. The insecurely close person becomes obsessed by the other's relationship with the third party and endlessly quizzes her/him about her/his comings and goings. Sometimes the third party is entirely imagined; in rare instances, a complex delusional system (*morbid jealousy*) is constructed around the suspected relationship (Shepherd, 1961; Cobb, 1979). The emotion accompanying jealousy depends upon the power differential. Hansen (1991), observed that for men, because they have more power, the emotion is more likely to be anger but for women, it is more likely to be depression.

The Misperception of Closeness

The misperception of closeness is, in a sense, the reverse of jealousy. The person, usually a woman, incorrectly perceives that she is loved by someone. It may be someone who has previously loved her, someone who has simply shown an interest in her, someone unknown to her or someone to whom she has never spoken. The term *"phantom lover"* applies to loving and feeling loved by someone who does not exist. The term *"erotomania"* applies to a delusional belief of being loved passionately by another, commonly of high status. Seeman (1978) distinguished between two forms of delusional love: one comprising intense, brief, recurrent episodes to different men; and one comprising a sustained, fixed belief concerning one man, extending over a number of years. Extensions of the delusion are that the man visits and has intercourse with the woman during the night and that she is made pregnant by him.

Negative Forms of Closeness that Are Consequent upon Deficiencies of Distance

When a person is deficient in the capacity to attain various forms of distance s/he may move excessively in the direction of closeness.

Excessive Identification with Another. A person who has a poorly formed identity may so identify with another as to live entirely for or through her/him. This is equivalent to Laing's (1965) condition of ontological dependence. S/he may adopt the other's gestures, mannerisms, style of speech, opinions, and values and abandon all personal satisfactions, deriving satisfaction only from the pleasures and achievements of the other. In the rare, psychotic condition of *folie à deux* (Rioux, 1963) s/he may even believe the other's delusions.

Escaping into the Identity of Another. Some actors maintain that they spend their lives assuming the parts of different other people because they do not like being themselves. In this sense they are escaping from themselves, and since the self is part of the condition of distance, they are escaping from distance; but if the part they are playing is that of a fictitious person they can hardly be said to be getting close to that person. There is, however, a further twist to this form of behavior: in the assumed role they have the confidence to get closer to other people than normally they could, and many stage performers adopt this strategy. It could be argued that this is not true closeness because the real self is hiding somewhere in the background and is not doing the relating.

Separation Anxiety. This term, used first by Freud (1926a) and later by Bowlby (1960), refers to the anxiety experienced by the infant when it is separated from its mother. The condition assumes pathological proportions, later in childhood and during adult life, when the individual becomes frightened of separating from a trusted other person.

Fear of Being Alone. A person who lacks the capacity to spend time alone (due either to a poorly formed identity or to inadequate internalized objects) always needs to stay close to others. Such a person behaves similarly to the infant before the establishment of object constancy. S/he dreads the departure of important close others and anxiously awaits their return. S/he may keep on the radio or television as a substitute for close others and may make repeated telephone calls to close others. S/he may be overcome by attacks of panic that are relieved only by making contact with someone, either by phone or running to a neighbor.

The Infantile Syndrome. Blatt and Shichman (1983) used the term "infantile syndrome" to refer to an impairment in the process of internalization and the development of *object representation.* As a result of this the individual manifests a constant demand for the visible and physical presence of the object (in the psychoanalytic sense). They proposed that the infantile individual becomes involved in a series of transient and superficial relationships, which are highly sexualized. S/he is afraid to entrust her/himself to another in a long-term committed relationship. The inability to tolerate delay and postponement leads to emotional lability. S/he feels ecstatic when her/his closeness needs are met but angry and frustrated when they are not. S/he has certain features in common with the extrovert.

Agoraphobia. The agoraphobic (Gournay, 1989) person feels secure inside her/his own home but becomes anxious upon venturing outside. S/he seems to have developed a close relationship to the building itself. S/he may be able to go out if accompanied by a trusted friend or even by a child. Thus, s/he has to take a visible and physically present object (trusted friend or child) with her/him as a substitute for an internalized object.

Reactions to the Absence or Loss of Closeness

Loneliness. Primary loneliness (Von Witzleben, 1958), the feeling of being alone and helpless in the world, was considered at the beginning of this chapter. Secondary loneliness is the feeling of being abandoned or deserted. The lonely person has experienced closeness but no longer has it; would like it but feels unable to attain it. Loneliness is common among the elderly and the infirm who are not sufficiently mobile to go out and seek closeness. Zilboorg (1938) has argued that some lonely people harbor a degree of grandiosity and expect the world to come to them. The converse of Zilboorg's theory is that many lonely people feel they are unattractive and have nothing to offer. Zilboorg is right to the extent that they tend to wait to be related to rather than try to relate to others. They are self-absorbed, do not go out much, and are nonresponsive and ineffective in their interactions with strangers (Jones et al., 1985). They tend to relate in such a way that other people do not feel inclined to relate to them (Spitzberg and Canary, 1985).

Being Separated from a Secure Base. There are a number of situations in which anxiety or despair set in because the person has become separated from a secure base. Being lost is a common experience in childhood when the child becomes detached from its mother. Adults also sometimes get lost when they cannot find their way back to familiar surroundings. Being *homesick* is experienced by children when they are sent away to school or when they go on holiday. It is also experienced by young adults when they begin working away from home or serving in the armed forces. It is an interesting fact that sports teams do not play as well when playing away from home, when they no longer have the support of the home crowd.

Grief and Mourning. Grief, which may assume many forms (Parkes, 1965), is a direct response to the loss through separation or death of a loved other person. The pain of grief results from the discrepancy between the person's continuing relationship to the internalized representation of the other and the noncontinuity of the relationship in the external world. Surges of grief arise each time the person encounters associations with the lost other, which normally would have evoked pleasure. Freud (1917) considered mourning to be the protracted period of decathexis of the internal object that results in a matching up of the psychic interior with external reality. There is a sense in which mourning is the reverse of the process of establishing the close relationship. Each memory has to be separately decathected, and the final stage of letting go is the reverse of the initial stage of deciding to become involved.

Anaclitic or Deprivation Depression. Blatt (1974) used the term "anaclitic depression" to refer to depression that results from failure of the anaclitic task (see Chapter 3) of forming stable, enduring relationships. Beck (1983) used the term "deprivation (or reactive) depression" to refer to that form of depression to which his sociotropic type, concerned with positive interchanges with others (see Chapter 3), is prone. The symptoms of the two forms of depression are similar: Blatt's include helplessness, weakness, depletion, and feeling unloved; Beck's include self-criticism related to the notion of social unacceptability and a tendency to react in a positive or negative direction in response to the positive or negative behavior of others. In Chapter 1 it was proposed that depression results from the loss of any state of relatedness. Both Blatt's and Beck's depressions conform with this principle and represent the form of depression that is associated with the loss of closeness. It corresponds with the melancholia, that Freud (1917) contrasted with mourning in his essay *"Mourning and Melancholia."* It could usefully be referred to as *horizontal depression.*

SUMMARY

The motivation to seek closeness is compounded of the need for greater involvement with others and the fear and avoidance of loneliness. The experience of interacting with others provides confirmation of one's existence. People need to be taken notice of, responded to, wanted, valued, and liked by others and to be aware that others want these things from them. People may actively approach others or wait passively to be approached by them. They may give closeness or receive it, but the distinction between donative and receptive closeness is not always easy to make. Beyond giving and receiving, closeness involves sharing, which creates the experience of we-ness. Sexual closeness differs from other forms of closeness because it involves sexual excitement. Its penetrative aspect is played out at a symbolic level in the social behavior of men and women. The main existing theories of closeness derive either from Erikson's consideration of intimacy or Bowlby's of attachment. The willingness to reveal aspects of oneself and the wish to learn about aspects of the other are central characteristics of closeness. When people become close they lose themselves in each other and create a condition of we-ness. If they do not have secure identities, this becomes fusion. Identification can become extended to the processes of understanding, sympathizing with, and empathising.

There is a complex interrelationship between being similar to, liking, and wanting to be close to. People are inclined to become close only to those who they consider would want to become close to them. Considerations of status play a part in selecting whom to become close to. Central and highly significant forms of closeness tend to develop under conditions of high emotion, but mutual

Closeness   113

needfulness and sexual arousal also play a part. People will not fall in love unless they are able to open themselves to love. The intense relating of romantic love is a transient state that either terminates or gives way to a long-term commitment in which the partners become more separate. If this is to survive, each must be able to obtain - and allow the other to obtain - adequate amounts of the four states of relatedness. Nonmarital friendships are under less strain because the partners are less involved. Psychotherapy is a special kind of closeness in which only the patients make self-disclosures. In some respects many casual closenesses add up to the same amount of closeness as a few intense ones, but closeness to many may be a way of avoiding intense closeness to one. Closeness to a group involves assuming the group identity. Closeness may be packaged and received in the absence of the original donor. Closeness may be attained from objects, imaginary others, or people who have died. Closeness to God is a special kind of closeness from a nonperson. The capacity to form close relationships is a form of power, as are needing the closeness least and being in a position to permit closeness.

Negative closeness assumes the following forms: giving or receiving imposed, invasive, or intrusive closeness; insecure closeness and jealousy; misperceptions of closeness; close behavior resulting from deficiencies of distance such as excessive identification, fear of separation, and fear of being alone; and reactions to the absence of or loss of closeness.

6

Distance

For a number of writers, distance is simply the absence of closeness, in the way that darkness is the absence of light. If closeness were to include all forms of involvement with others, then distance would constitute total uninvolvement. Although it is true that one of the objectives of distance is the avoidance or reduction of involvement with others, this does not make it a negative process. Although some distant people appear to be disinterested in and only vaguely aware of the presence of others, distance is very much a response or a reaction to others, and even the most disinterested or unaware people can be provoked into defensive action if they are encroached upon by others. Besides however being a protection of the self against the threat of others, it is also a building up of the self and an investment of interest in the self.

It is a principle of spatial theory (see Chapter 3) that there be advantages to each of the four main positions and that each should be viewed positively. It is argued that distance is a condition that is just as necessary and just as important as closeness; in Chapter 2 the principal advantages and positive characteristics of distance were briefly described. These are further elaborated in the present chapter. In Chapter 5, the motivation for closeness was considered to be of two types: the positive striving toward close involvement and the avoidance or fear of distance. The motivation for distance could be viewed as the mirror image of this, namely, the positive striving toward distance and the avoidance or fear of closeness. This is one of the distinctions that will be adopted in the present chapter.

Because the need for closeness is so strong, in all but the most extreme forms of distance the motivation toward closeness is also present. Sometimes, when the motivations toward closeness and distance are fairly evenly balanced, the term "*distant closeness*" is appropriate. To use an analogy with physics, closeness and distance are like the centripetal and centrifugal forces acting upon a ball that is being swung around on the end of a piece of string. It helps to understand the motives and mechanisms of closeness and distance better when they are described in separate chapters, but in practice they rarely exist in isolation.

PLEASURABLE STATES OF DISTANCE

Stimulus Reduction

Since closeness is mediated through the senses, the most complete form of distance is the reduction of sensory input. This is an unusual form of distance because it does not involve focusing upon the self. It is almost a state of nonbeing. The therapeutic procedure known as *stimulus reduction* involves putting the patient into a situation of silence and darkness, either in a chamber (Vernon, 1963) or in a tank of water (Lilly, 1956). Such a condition reduces the input from all sources, not only the input from other people. Particularly when it involves flotation, this has been shown, for some patients, to produce both psychological and psychophysiological signs of deep relaxation and tension reduction (Suedfeld, 1980; Suedfeld and Kristeller, 1982). Stimulus reduction is also available commercially. It is important to distinguish between stimulus reduction that is voluntarily accepted and that which is forcibly imposed (sensory deprivation; see subsequent discussion). As with all states of relatedness, that which is voluntarily accepted is a different and more pleasurable experience than that which is forcibly imposed.

Meditation

Meditation has been widely practised for a number of reasons. In recent times it has been adopted as a safe and effective way of combating stress. It is a process of sitting quietly in a detached state. Under such circumstances, it is difficult simply not to experience anything. When the input of sensations from outside is reduced, thoughts and memories flood into consciousness. These may be excluded, limited, or included. They can be excluded by focusing upon a visual object or a physical sensation or by repeating either silently or aloud a particular word or sound, sometimes called a *mantra*; they can be limited by concentrating only upon the here and now; or they can be included by letting them come and go while remaining detached from them and returning to the mantra when they become too intrusive (West, 1987). This is a form of escaping from self as well as escaping from others.

Solitude

Distinct from meditation, solitude involves dwelling upon and indulging in whatever comes into consciousness. It does therefore involve focusing upon the self. The poet Wordsworth was much concerned with seeking to attain a central peace by adopting a passive attitude and allowing thoughts to come (Spurgeon, 1970). In his poem about daffodils called "*I Wandered Lonely as a Cloud*" he wrote:

> *For oft, when on my couch I lie*
> *In vacant or in pensive mood,*
> *They flash upon that inward eye*
> *Which is the bliss of solitude;*

In solitude, as in sleep, thoughts and memories that have been put or pushed aside, because more immediate concerns press for attention, re-emerge. However, they may not always be pleasant and solitude therefore need not necessarily be blissful.

Relating to the Environment

It could be argued that, in most conditions of distance the need for closeness persists and has to be satisfied in indirect ways, some of which would merit the term "distant closeness." Many would also fall into the category of receiving closeness in the absence of a donor. One such way is feeling related to or united with the nonhuman environment. Freud (1939) used the term "*oceanic feeling*" to refer to the feeling of being at one with the universe, of being related to something limitless and unbounded. Relating to the environment need not involve the oceanic feeling. It also includes deriving pleasure (or security) from being in familiar surroundings. Being alone in one's own room, house, or garden, in a familiar street, or on a familiar walk is much easier and much more pleasant than being alone in a strange place.

In a lonely place, signs of life (e.g., a lighted window or smoke rising from a chimney), or evidence of others having been there before, (e.g., a ruin, a plowed field, fences and gates, discarded vehicles, or even litter), create distant kinds of closeness in providing evidence that people are around or have been around.

Relating to God

Many forms of meditation have a religious significance, and people commonly meditate in order to feel close to their particular deity (West, 1987). People usually pray in solitude. For some, the oceanic feeling is indistinguishable from feeling in the presence of God. The religious hermit chooses to live in solitude in order to be close to God. Despite the fact that God remains a profound source of closeness, it is difficult not to associate relating to God with distance - though this is not to deny that many religious ceremonies occur within a group setting. It could appropriately be described as a form of distant closeness.

SLEEP

Sleep is a form of distance adopted extensively throughout the animal kingdom. Hibernation is a period of sleep that extends over many months, during which the basal metabolic rate falls dramatically and the animal lives off its body's food stores. In sleep the animal is vulnerable to attack by predators, which is why many animal species sleep in herds, packs, or flocks, or sleep in inaccessible places. Since animals sleep despite being rendered vulnerable by it, sleep must serve important functions.

In sleep the body's response to sensory stimuli is reduced. This serves to diminish external closeness but to intensify internal closeness. Sleep can be an escape from environmental stresses; people sometimes fall asleep in unpleasant situations. When people attempt suicide by an overdose of tablets, particularly sleeping tablets, they are often unclear whether they wish to die or to sleep for a long period of time. They simply know they want to escape from present circumstances. Frankl (1967) observed that prisoners in Nazi concentration camps were reluctant to wake their sleeping companions because they knew that this was their only respite from the unpleasantness of camp life.

Sleep is confirmation, if confirmation is needed, of the existence of the psychic interior. In sleep people are confronted by their internal world, and the ideas and feelings they have tried to put aside during waking hours catch up with them. Internal objects can emerge with fearful intensity. In dreams people create imaginary scenes and events that incorporate their wishes and anxieties; these can be so disturbing that the person escapes from them by waking up. There are certain similarities between what normal people experience during dreams and what psychotic people experience during wakefulness, which reinforces the idea that psychosis is a form of distance.

In dreams there is a predominance of what Freud (1911a) called *primary process* thinking. He considered this to be ontogenetically and phylogenetically earlier than the more rational and logical *secondary process* thinking, which predominates during wakefulness. Although it probably does represent an earlier form of thinking (e.g., it is more common in young children and primitive people), it is not necessarily inferior. It is more a consequence of being cut off from external reality. In some respects it is a conceptual shorthand: ignores categories of space and time, sometimes fusing past with present; it condenses disparate ideas and images into one, as an expression of their interrelatedness; it displaces ideas from one object to another; it makes free use of metaphor and symbolism.

GIVING DISTANCE TO OTHERS

It is not always easy to determine whether distance is being given to someone or taken for oneself, for creating or maintaining space between oneself and another is doing both at the same time. In normal social interactions people are normally respectful of other people's need for distance. It is customary to leave a suitable space between oneself and a stranger when sitting in a public place (Mazur, 1977), not to speak to and to avoid staring at or touching a stranger. Goffman (1963) gave the term "*civil inattention*" to the tendency to avoid eye contact with strangers on buses and trains. These rules are also applied, though less rigorously, to friends and acquaintances.

The good relater is aware that anyone with whom s/he is involved needs distance and is prepared to allow the other to experience it. This involves (1) allowing her/him time to be alone, to go places alone, and to do things on her/his own; (2) allowing her/him to have a life of her/his own; (3) not encroaching upon her/his personal space; (4) allowing her/him the right to privacy and being willing for her/him to keep secrets; (5) respecting the value s/he might place upon certain personal possessions; (6) being prepared not to enter into her/his psychic interior without invitation; (7) acknowledging her/his need for autonomy, allowing her/him to be in charge of her/his life and to make her/his own choices; (8) respecting her/his need to be different and not feeling threatened by her/his differentness; (9) encouraging her/him to develop her/his own individuality and creativity; and (10) permitting her/him to direct some love and indulgence onto her/himself.

VARIABILITY IN THE TOLERANCE OF SENSORY INPUT

It is difficult to differentiate between the pure and simple input of sensory stimulation and the input of communications from others that, inevitably must be conveyed in the form of sensory stimulation. Just as stimulus reduction has powerful effects, so does what has been called *stimulus overload* (Baron and Byrne, 1991). People appear to vary in their tolerance of sensory input. This may be due to a variability in their overall tolerance of stimulation or in their capacity to selectively screen out unwanted stimulation. Introverts are less tolerant than extroverts (Eysenck, 1947), and autistic individuals (Ornitz, 1983) and schizophrenics (Tsuang, 1982) are the least tolerant of all. It is possible that some of the variation in the need for distance is accounted for by toleration of stimulation.

DISTANCE AND THE DEVELOPMENT OF THE SELF

Mahler (1961) correctly described the distancing process that begins between the first and third year of life as the process of *separation-individuation*. This implies that as the child becomes separate in a spatial sense it also becomes separate as an individual being. Kohut's (1971) description of identity development complements Mahler's. He conceived of mother and child as starting with a shared identity. Gradually the child selects out parts of the mother's identity and takes them into itself by the process of *transmuting internalization*. Blatt and Shichman (1983) wrote of the *introjective developmental line*, which was concerned with the attainment of a differentiated, consolidated, stable, realistic, and essentially positive identity. In relation to a later developmental stage, Bowen (1978) wrote of the *differentiation of self from the family of origin*. Much has been written on the issue of identity and the self (Yardley and Honess, 1987), all of which cannot be covered here. In the present context, the following questions are relevant:

1. To what extent is the person aware of having an identity that is different from that of other people?
2. How clearly can that identity be described?
3. How securely is it held?
4. How effectively can it be expressed?

The developing child acquires a separate identity by being permitted and encouraged to *have a mind of its own*, so that it can distinguish between what it likes, thinks, believes what other people do. To this end it needs to be asked questions such as: What would you like to eat, wear, do? What do you think of this, that, or the other? If it discovers that its ideas do not always correspond with those of other people, it needs to be reassured that different people like and think different things, and that its ideas are as important as those of anyone else. Parents and influential others can easily erode a developing sense of self by *putting ideas into the child's head*, by saying: You like this, don't you? or We like this, don't we? We don't want to do/believe things like that, do we? Social pressures are strong to conform to a majority view. Being accepted by the majority (closeness) may seem preferable to standing out as someone different (distance). Having the confidence to be different, *being true to oneself*, is the essence of having an individual identity. An extension of Descartes's proclamation "I think, therefore I am" would be "I think differently from other people, therefore I am a different person." It is easier for someone to experience her/himself as different if her/his ideas contrast markedly with those of the majority. The ontologically insecure person (e.g., the emerging adolescent) may try to stand out against the majority by adopting extremes of dress and behavior and by expressing outrageous opinions. As s/he becomes more secure, the contrast between her/himself and others need not be so great.

Originality versus Conformity

The propaganda of autocratic governmental regimes, as well as the persuasiveness of commercial advertisements, are directed toward reducing individual differences and imposing uniform opinions. Autocratic regimes consider nonconformists to be subversive. A degree of conformity to group norms is essential for the smooth running of any society. A society of individuals would be chaotic; at the same time, every society requires a proportion of its members to be individualistic. It is to such people that it looks for originality, inventiveness, and creativity. Change emanates from nonconformists who express dissatisfaction with the status quo.

Distance is associated with being idiosyncratic and original, with not taking for granted the existing order of things, and with thinking things out for oneself. Creative endeavor takes place within what Fromm-Reichman (1959) called *constructive aloneness.* Storr (1988) observed that many of the world's great thinkers never married. Originality, which is at the heart of all inventiveness and creativity, is not necessarily advantageous. As Millon (1981) expressed it, the more estranged an individual becomes from her/his social environment, the more out of touch s/he becomes with the conventions of reality and with the checks against irrational thought and behavior that are provided by reciprocal relationships. Originality can become eccentricity and eccentricity can deteriorate into sheer craziness. Ideally, the creative person needs to move between distance and closeness, thinking things out in isolation, and then returning to the real world to test them out. Constructive originality might be termed "*harnessed craziness.*" The harnessing comes less from interaction with others than from what Freud (1923) called the ego functions, namely thinking things out and making sense of things.

Autonomy

Autonomy involves being driven from within; it is the opposite of being controlled or directed from without. It involves being in charge of one's own existence, and destiny, generating one's own objectives, and setting one's own standards. A child will only develop a sense of autonomy if there have been times when it has been left to its own devices and if it has had opportunities for making up its own mind. Motivation from within moves in to fill the void left from the absence of direction from without. Autonomy is linked with freedom from restraint, freedom of choice, and freedom of will. It is also linked with self-confidence. A person will only behave in an autonomous way if s/he has been encouraged to feel that s/he has the right to do so, if s/he has been given her/his head. Existing definitions and measures of autonomy (e.g., those of Edwards, 1959; Beck et al., 1983) tend to be too broad and to embrace other aspects of distance. A person may possess the capability of being autonomous without being able to exercise it, that is s/he may be under the control of another or others.

PERSONAL BOUNDARIES AND PERSONAL SPACE

The Self and Its Boundaries

The word "define" is related to the French word "*définir*", which means to set bounds to. Part of the process of defining a person's identity involves determining what its boundaries are. At a rational level, it seems strange that there should be boundaries to something as abstract as identity, yet people sometimes use the phrase "It wouldn't be me" to act in such and such a way, meaning that it would be out of character for me to do so. Thus, there are characteristics that people consider are or are not included within the definition of themselves. Psychoanalysts use the term "*ego boundary*" to refer to the distinction between self and not self, but this is a metaphorical concept and no one is ever required to stipulate where such a boundary might lie. A person is said to have a weak ego boundary if her/his identity merges easily with that of someone else, as in fusion or identification. Insofar as fusion and identification are manifestations of closeness, a distant person would seem to have a strong ego boundary. The term "*permeable*" is sometimes applied to the ego boundary to imply a preparedness to identify with another person; so in this sense a distant person would have an impermeable ego boundary. In Chapter 4 this issue was discussed in relation to gender when the suggestion was made that women have more permeable ego boundaries than men.

Anzieu (1989), a French psychoanalyst, used the term "Le Moi-Peau", which translates as the *"skin ego,"* to refer to what he called a psychic envelope containing, defining, and protecting the psyche. He considered it to be more elaborate than the ego boundary and linked it more with the little-used Freudian (1895) concept of the *contact barrier*. He saw it as the interface between the psychic interior and the external world. He proposed similarities and analogies between the skin ego and the skin itself. He was preoccupied with the psychological significance of the skin, which, he considered, serves both as a container of the person and as shield against the physical and the human environment.

The Skin and the Clothes

People are acutely conscious of the skin as the outer boundary of the person (Montagu, 1986). In cold countries, but also in many hot countries, clothing serves not only to keep people warm but also to create protective barriers against other people. The removal of successive layers from outdoor clothes to indoor clothes to underclothes communicates a preparedness to allow others progressive access to the person within, which has particular significance as an invitation or permission to sexual closeness. Touching a person, even through layers of clothing, represents an encroachment upon her/his physical being. There are strict social rules that govern when and under what circumstances this may happen.

Personal Space

Even outside of the person there is an exclusion zone known as the *personal space*. Eibl-Eibesfeldt (1989) observed that our personal space is carried about with us like an invisible bubble. Hall (1966) gave the name *"proximics"* to the study of the conventions of distance regulation adopted within different cultural settings. McBride et al. (1965) were able to measure the anxiety generated by the intrusion upon people's personal space; and Altman (1975) observed that the more anxious a person is, the less close s/he will permit others to approach.

Privacy

Privacy is a major component of distance. It is something special and precious that people will go to great lengths to preserve. As with distance in general, it is valued more by some people than by others (Larson and Bell, 1988); but, as with closeness, its importance becomes most apparent when there is danger of it being lost. Altman (1979) considered the capability for privacy regulation to be generic to all cultures and described it as a multilevel behavioral process involving many different aspects of behavior. He wrote, "People who are relatively successful at regulating boundary openness-closedness not only come to know where they begin and end but are also able to develop an actual and perceived sense of competence to control their lives" (page 102).

The Psychic Interior

The psychic interior is a secret place where none may go save the person whose place it is. The phrase "keep it to yourself" means keep to some thought or piece of information in this secret place and not to reveal it to anyone. There is no direct way of gaining access to personal thoughts or personal information that are kept inside. No one can know what someone is thinking unless s/he chooses to tell. Keeping secrets reassures the person that others cannot get in. Though some secrets are shared with trusted others, other secrets are not told to anyone. Telling lies is a way of deceiving others into believing that access to the psychic interior has been granted, when really it has not. Keeping others out of one's psychic interior is an important means of maintaining a sense of separateness from others. Interrogators try to invade the psychic interior.

The psychic interior contains the internal representation of the self and the environment. It also contains the vast store of past memories and a large number of internalized others who continue to relate to the person with whom the person continues to relate.

Personal Property

Personal property is of two kinds: that which creates further shells around the self, and that which becomes an extension of the identity. Further shells are created by armor; an armored car; walls; barricades; one's own personal bed and room; a lockable door; a house with burglar alarms, bolts, and a lockable door; a garden or grounds; a hedge; a fence; a moat; a lockable gate; a drawbridge, and so on. Even that which creates shells around the self also serves as an extension of the identity. Beyond that, however, people accumulate property and possessions that become outward representations of their inner values.

Two other aspects of the accumulation of personal property are related to some extent. First, property can (and frequently does), represent power and is therefore a form of upperness. Second, people who are not good at establishing close relationships with others are inclined to relate more to things. Things which they accumulate therefore become substitutes for others.

INTEREST IN AND LOVE OF THE SELF

If closeness is concerned with interest in and love of others, at least one form of distance is concerned with interest in and love of the self. At its most fundamental, it is directed toward survival. It includes seeking and maintaining an optimal environment, attaining an adequate level of fitness, obtaining sufficient supplies of food and drink, and defending against predators, aggressors, or invaders. In a modern society it includes earning enough money to pay for others to provide these necessities. In our relating to others it is desirable to attain a position between the extremes of total selflessness and total self-centeredness, between self-neglect and self-preoccupation.

Relating to the Self

People who enjoy being alone are said to enjoy their own company; that is, in some way they are able to keep themselves company. Writers such as Foa (1961) and Benjamin (1974) have concerned themselves with the ability of humans to relate to themselves. It is equivalent to what Macdiarmid (1989) has called self-cathexis (see Chapter 3). But cathexis (see Chapter 1) involves directing psychic energy toward the *mental representation* of someone and not toward the actual person, so somewhere within the self there must be an internal representation of the self. It is strange that the self can relate to the self, but subjective experience bears out that this must indeed be so. People must be capable of being object to their own subject. The phenomenon may be the adult equivalent of the child's imaginary companion; since adults appear not to have imaginary companions, it may be a development out of this. It is that which enables people to be able to converse with themselves. Writing a diary often assumes the form of a communication with the self. Sometimes, when the diary is addressed as "Dear Diary," it becomes an imaginary companion.

Narcissism

The term "narcissism" is derived from the Greek myth of the young man, Narcissus, who fell in love with his reflection in a pool and pined away and died because he could not unite with the object of his love, but the Narcissus theme has also recurred in western literature (Vinge, 1967). The term was first used by Ellis (1898) in his description of auto-erotism. Freud (1914) believed that the major proportion of libido remained narcissistic, that is, self-directed, throughout life. This he called *normal* or *healthy narcissism*. He considered that normal self-regard resulted from the reservoir of self-love that was retained from the stage of primary narcissism. Secondary narcissism, he maintained, develops when libido is withdrawn from the mother, during the phase of psychic weaning, and is reinvested in the self (see Chapter 4).

Jacobson (1964) believed that Freud's thinking on narcissism lacked precision because it failed to distinguish clearly between the ego and the self or to acknowledge a need for the concept of *self-representations*. The term "ego," she believed, should be reserved for the compartment of the psyche that is concerned with the ego functions (e.g., perception, rational thought, and mechanisms of defense). The term "self" should be used to refer to the entire identity of the person, including both the body and the psyche. The term "self-representations" should refer to both conscious and unconscious endopsychic representations of both the physical and the psychic self. Having made these distinctions, she was able to define narcissism, or self-love, as the libidinal cathexis of the self-representations. By analogy, object-love is the libidinal cathexis of internalized objects (i.e. the internalized representations of others).

Self-Worth

Kohut (1977) maintained that the child develops a sense of self-worth through feeling merged with an idealized other, usually the mother, which he called a *self-object*. Gradually this merging is replaced by a sense of something separate that is lovable in its own right. The reinforcement of the child's emerging delight in self by the parents was discussed in Chapter 4. Kohut (1977) maintained that without these phase-appropriate narcissistic gratifications of childhood a mature and realistic sense of self-worth cannot develop.

Beyond childhood and throughout life, for all but the most autonomous, self-worth is very much influenced by the judgments of others. Parents, teachers, peers, and influential others become internalized and their judgments continue to play upon the individual, though these can be reinforced or neutralized by further judgments made by new others. The autonomous individual comes, over time, to set her/his own standards by which s/he is able to judge her/himself, but it is not always easy to throw off the accumulated effect of past and present judgments.

Self-Awareness, Self-Consciousness, Self-Approval, Self-Acceptance

Shibutani (1961) pointed out that people are not always aware of themselves: when reading a book or watching a film, or when indulging in something they have done many times before, they are not. People can become aware of themselves as objects, which makes self-criticism and self-control possible. They may or may not respond to themselves in the same way that others respond to them. Self-consciousness may be more likely to come about in settings of social participation, but particularly if there is an interference in an ongoing activity. Self-consciousness in this sense is more a concern about how others think of one.

To some extent, what parents think of themselves affects what they think of their children, since their children are an extension of themselves. If parents are accepting of themselves they are more likely to be accepting of their children, and, consequently their children are more likely to be accepting of themselves. The parental attitude of: whatever s/he has done, s/he will always be my child, and I will always love her/him, might apply equally to one's attitude toward oneself.

Curiosity about oneself and wanting to know oneself better are the distant equivalents of curiosity about the other and wanting to know the other better. They are positive forms of distance. Establishing a continuity between one's present and one's past, joining up with split-off parts of oneself, and integrating fragmented parts of oneself are constructive activities in many forms of psychotherapy. It is a principle of Gestalt therapy (Fagan and Shepherd, 1970), bioenergetics (Lowen, 1975) and other body-focused therapies (Fisher, 1973; Liss, 1974) that accepting and owning one's self, particularly one's body, is an important part of becoming a fully integrated person.

Self-Indulgence

Self-love may lead to self-indulgence, but self-indulgence can assume many forms. Lowen (1967) argued that the person who loves and respects her/his body treats it well. Self-gratification in the form of over-eating or the excessive consumption of alcohol may be self-indulgent in the short term but in the long term is not being self-respectful. Masturbation and other forms of auto-erotism create self-excitement and are therefore self-indulgent. Treating the self to pleasures such as getting up late, having long meal breaks, taking time off from work, visiting favorite places, and listening to favourite pieces of music are forms of self-indulgence. Bathing, using perfume, and adorning the body with clothes and jewelry are forms of self-love; but disfiguring the body to make it conform to a fashionable shape or using cosmetics that harm the skin are not, in the long term, self-respectful. Much self-beautification is directed toward being more attractive to others and is therefore aimed as much at closeness as at distance.

DISTANT CLOSENESS

Distant closeness is the most prevalent of the four paradoxical positions (see Chapter 3). It is so prevalent because closeness of any kind is so frightening that people are driven to devising strategies for gaining closeness from the safety of distance. Because it requires less commitment, sexual closeness is often easier to manage than amicable closeness and can itself therefore be a form of distant closeness. Young adults often pass through a series of transient sexual relationships before settling into a more committed relationship. Even within a committed relationship one partner, more often the man, expresses closeness predominantly through sexual behavior. Because even sexual closeness is frightening, there are many forms of distant sexual closeness. These include voyeurism, exhibitionism, making erotic telephone calls to strangers, frotteurism (sexual excitement from pressing against strangers in crowded places), fetishism (sexual excitement from objects or body parts) and masturbation with pornographic photographs, videotapes and films.

Having a range of nonintimate relationships, as does a shopkeeper, a postman, a parson, a warden, a doctor, or a schoolteacher, may provide a substitute for one single intimate relationship. This is linked with the concept of extroversion/affiliation/gregariousness considered in Chapter 5. Devoting oneself to one's work, deriving closeness not just from the workpeople but also from the work itself, is a common source of distant closeness. Relating to a pet, or to a number of pets, may provide an intense level of closeness, but it is not the same as relating to a person or to people. Finally, much distant closeness falls into the category of what was described as packaged closeness in Chapter 5. It is derived from radio, television, films, novels, magazines, and newspapers.

DISTANCE AND EXPLORATION

Movement away from others need not involve preoccupation with the self. It may involve a movement outward toward new places or new others. The advantages of exploration, for both the individual and the species, are considerable. There is a paradox about exploration, for although it involves moving away from one set of places or people, it involves at the same time moving towards another set. Thus, it combines distance seeking with closeness seeking. Part of the pleasure of exploration is the feeling of union with the universe, or oceanic feeling. In one sense, exploration is a consequence of closeness fatigue, for where closeness is associated with a preference for the familiar, exploration is associated with a seeking out of the unfamiliar.

RELATING TO THINGS AND RELATING TO DRUGS

In a scientific and technological age, there is a great need for experts in a range of subjects are not directly related to people. These include geology, chemistry, physics, electronics, computing, and engineering. People who are interested in such subjects are of great benefit to society. In the section on distant closeness, it was stated that those who wish to avoid close involvement with people involve themselves with things instead; by relating closely to things, they satisfy some of their closeness needs. It seems likely that those who are interested in technological subjects belong to this category of person. Developing a fondness for, or an attachment to, house plants, garden plants, machinery, motor cars, musical instruments, computers and the like is also a kind of closeness.

A particular form of relating to things involves relating to drugs. Sometimes drugs are taken to achieve a state of oblivion, and this is not relating at all; at other times they are taken at social gatherings to facilitate relating; but it is appropriate to consider that many drug addicts actually relate to the drugs they take (Levin, 1987). Part of the appeal of drugs may be that they mimic the pleasurable sensation generated in the brain when a state of relatedness is attained. Thus, the pleasure is achieved without the necessity of striving to attain the state of relatedness. This is reminiscent of the Olds and Milner (1954) experiment in which the rat was trained to stimulate its own hypothalamus and did so repeatedly.

The tendency to relate to things grows out of the young child's tendency to relate to transitional objects (Winnicott, 1953). Things are unemotional and nonrejecting and are easier to handle and control than people. They are logical and predictable and operate according to natural laws. Distant people prefer to be unemotional and logical. Suttie (1935) linked the interest in science (and presumably also in technology) to the taboo on tenderness (see Chapter 3).

ABSTRACTIONS, VERBOSITY, OBSESSIONALITY

The distancing tendency extends beyond simply relating to things. It includes a concern with theory and abstractions such as are involved in philosophy, music, mathematics, statistics, and economics. Beyond this, it extends to the excessive use of or preoccupation with words, as in making long speeches and writing long, theoretical books. Because the close person is spontaneous, s/he is direct and to the point. The distant person, in contrast, is circumlocutory and verbose. S/he is also obsessional. *Obsessionality* is, among other things, an inability to behave spontaneously. It involves a preoccupation with detail and correctness; a need to plan, prepare, and check carefully; and to proceed with caution.

DISTANT RELATING

The term *"distant relating"* (introduced in Chapter 3) may seem paradoxical, since much of the definition of distance involves directing attention away from others and toward the self. In fact, distant relating forms part of normal social interacting. Even well-adjusted people cannot relate closely toward everyone all of the time, though distant people are inclined to relate in a distant way toward most people most of the time. Distant relating, or *formal relating,* involves the way in which people relate to nonintimates such as tradespeople, professional people, or providers of services. It tends to concern things or abstractions or to refer to people as though they were things or abstractions (such as in a legal or medical consultation). It is the kind of relating adopted at conferences and official functions. It is the way in which the author of this book is relating to the reader. Personal disclosures are avoided. The wording is precise and to the point and is aimed at seeking or providing information. Statements are carefully prepared and spontaneity is suppressed.

In distant relating, the open show of emotion is minimal and if there is smiling or laughing it tends to be forced or restrained. Eibl-Eibesfeldt (1989) used the term *"expression masking"* to describe the exercising of self-control in order not to betray emotions "of which a stranger may take advantage." This, he claimed, can lead to habitual fixation in which the mask is worn continually, even in the company of friends.

Distant relating can occur between intimates when some formal issue needs to be settled, such as when a parent needs to discipline a child, or when marital partners need to negotiate a financial agreement. Difficulties arise when a person relates in a distant way in a situation in which closeness is appropriate. Such a person keeps things to her/himself, plays with her/his cards close to her/his chest, speaks with carefully thought out precision, avoids eye contact or physical contact, holds back emotion, and reveals little interest in or concern about the other or the other's ideas. Instead s/he may prefer to talk about her/himself or her/his own ideas, or better still about abstractions, generalizations, and things.

DISTANT PERSONALITIES

It is a principle of spatial theory that the well-adjusted person is competent in the entire range of forms of relating and demonstrates flexibility and versatility during the normal course of social exchanges. It follows, therefore, that a person who adopts a consistently distant form of relating is poorly adjusted. There are several possible explanations for this:

1. People might vary in their innate need for social involvement, just as different species do. Autistic individuals, and some who are described as being schizophrenic, give the impression that their tolerance of social involvement, or perhaps any form of sensory input, is limited, that closeness fatigue sets in very quickly.
2. People who have been the recipients of enforced closeness from possessive and intrusive others may experience a persistent or chronic closeness fatigue which causes them to be wary of the encroachment of others. This is the adult equivalent of the avoidance observed in abused toddlers (George and Main, 1979).
3. People with a poorly developed identity may avoid others for fear of losing themselves in the ensuing involvement.
4. People who have suffered the painful breakup of earlier close relationships may either avoid further close involvements or develop strategies for reducing the extent of their involvement in relationships.

The DSM III, Axis II, classification of disorders of personality (American Psychiatric Association, 1980) includes two categories of severity. Within the least severe category, the Basic Personality Disorders, is included the *socially detached pattern*. This is divisible into an active variant called the *avoidant* personality and a passive variant called the *schizoid* personality.

The Avoidant Personality

The active, avoidant personality was described by Millon (1981) as being "exquisitely sensitive to rejection, humiliation or shame" and "devastated by the slightest hint of disapproval." The reason for withdrawing from opportunities for developing close relationships is, he maintained, a fearful expectation of being belittled or humiliated. Millon likened this type of personality to Horney's (1945) "detached" or "moving away from people" type (see Chapter 3). She wrote of this type: "His goals are negative: he wants not to be involved, not to need anybody, not to allow others to intrude on or influence him. There is a general tendency to suppress all feeling, even to deny its existence" (pages 73-84). For both Millon and Horney, this type incorporates a degree of lowerness as well as distance, but only the distant features will be considered here. The basis of the avoidant personality appears to be a fear of close involvement with others for fear of being hurt should the relationship break down. It seems likely that s/he has had experience of close relationships that have broken down and, in consequence, has developed a "*once bitten twice shy*" attitude. S/he probably retains yearnings for closeness that s/he tries to suppress, and in so doing suppresses all other feelings as well.

Bartholomew (1990) distinguished between two types of distant individual. The first, the *fearful avoidant*, desires intimacy but fears rejection and is hypersensitive to social approval; the second, the *dismissive avoidant*, places value on independence and asserts that relationships are relatively unimportant. This indicates that there are two classes of avoidant personalities, those who continue to consider the possibility of closeness and those who try to do without it.

Kohut's (1971) narcissistic personality appears to correspond reasonably closely to the avoidant personality of the DSM III, Axis II, but appears to be a mixture of Bartholomew's two types. It is described as having an extreme sensitivity to slights and a defensive withdrawal into the self resulting from hurts experienced in childhood. Lasch (1984) considered what would be the equivalent of the avoidant personality to be prevalent in modern, western society and used the term "*narcissism*" to describe the superficiality, deep sense of emptiness, egocentricity, rampant individualism, and avoidance of intimacy that typify the consumerist culture. Lasch considered that narcissistic types thrive in a society that rewards those who manipulate others and punishes those who show genuine care. This is reminiscent of Suttie's (1935) taboo on tenderness (see Chapter 3).

Horney (1945) emphasized the *self-sufficiency* of the detached type, which she maintained assumes two forms: resourcefulness and the conscious or unconscious restricting of needs. By doing everything for her/himself and doing without things that s/he cannot do for her/himself, s/he does not need to ask anything of anyone and therefore avoids the risk of being turned down. This is reminiscent of the popular song that begins:

> *There was a jolly miller once,*
> *Lived by the River Dee*

and ends:

> *I care for nobody, no, not I,*
> *If no one cares for me.*

Parkes (1973) developed a measure of *compulsive self-reliance*, which he applied to amputees. He found that compulsively self-reliant people reacted badly to amputation. Bowlby (1980) developed the concept further and observed that compulsively self-reliant people chose not to utilize available sources of social support at times of crisis. Also, he maintained, they were at risk for pathological mourning following the death of a marital partner.

The Schizoid Personality

Psychoanalysts use the term "schizoid" to denote a splitting of the self from external reality. Fairbairn's (1940) schizoid personality type was considered to be someone with an attitude of isolation and detachment who is preoccupied with inner reality. S/he experiences her/himself as artificial in some way and feels as though s/he is separated from others by a sheet of glass. Deutsch (1942) wrote of the *"as if"* personality type who lacks any genuine emotional relationship to the outside world but outwardly behaves "as if" s/he does have. Winnicott (1956) described the process of creating what he called a *false self,* which is a pretended self, though which the person lives, in order not to truly be a part of what is going on. The function of the false self is to protect the real self, which hides behind it. Guntrip (1969a) described a similar split between what he called the *Central Ego* and the *Withdrawn Ego.* The Central Ego, which is the equivalent of Winnicott's false self, is left to cope with the stresses of everyday living while hiding the Withdrawn Ego, which is the equivalent of Winnicott's true self, which contains the person's vulnerability and feelings of needfulness. Only the Central Ego has contact with other people and things. Consequently the Withdrawn Ego becomes more and more isolated and therefore more and more in need of protection and concealment.

The passive schizoid personality is described by Millon (1981) as lacking the need to communicate with or relate affectionately to others, showing little or no desire for social involvement, preferring to be a loner, being clumsy, unresponsive, and boring in relationships, reserved, seclusive, cold, unfeeling, humourless, dull, aloof, and distant. S/he differs from the avoidant personality in being indifferent to either the praise or criticism of others. S/he works quietly and unobtrusively at her/his job. Suedfeld (1991) observed men who had spent many years working in Arctic weather stations. He called them *"deepeners"* because they appeared to have the capacity to "look for, find and examine complex aspects of a superficially monotonous setting" (page 139). They tended to have consuming hobbies - many to do with the Arctic, such as geology or archaeology - which they pursued avidly.

The Schizotypal Personality

The DSM III, Axis II personality disorder called *schizotypal* was considered by Millon (1981) to represent a form of distancing that was more extreme than the avoidant and schizoid patterns. It is included in the category of Severe Personality Disorders. He considered that the withdrawn and isolated existence of the schizotypal type causes her/him to develop oddities in behavior and thought such as circumstantial speech, suspiciousness, magical thinking, ideas of reference, and illusions. S/he remains on the edge of society, leading an idle, meaningless, and ineffectual existence, drifting from one aimless existence to another, rarely accepting enduring responsibilities or developing close involvements.

The Paranoid Personality

In the DSM III, Axis II, classification of personality disorders (American Psychiatric Association, 1980) the *paranoid personality: suspicious pattern* is included among the Severe Personality Disorders. The person with such a personality is cold, humorless, self-sufficient, guarded, secretive, devious, and scheming (distant qualities). Additionally s/he is hypersensitive, suspicious, and mistrustful. S/he finds it difficult to relax, is hypervigilant and concerned with hidden motives and special meanings, and takes precautions against any perceived threat. S/he tends to misinterpret the actions of others, to exaggerate minor slights and take offense where none is meant. S/he is inclined to respond with anger to what s/he frequently interprets as deception, deprecation, or betrayal and shows a tendency to counter-attack when s/he perceives any threat. S/he is liable to make a preemptive strike in the anticipation of hostility from others. She tends to avoid blame even when it is warranted.

The Psychopathic Personality

Also in the DSM III, Axis II, classification of personality disorders, is a category called the *antisocial personality: aggressive pattern.* This approximates what others would call the psychopathic or sociopathic personality. It has a vertical component, which will be considered in Chapter 7, and a horizontal component, which will be considered here. A salient feature of the antisocial personality is a feeling of bitterness that others have treated her/him badly, particularly in terms of affection and fairness. In consequence s/he is determined to get even with society and may be cruel, ruthless, and remorseless. S/he is prepared to resort to aggression more readily than most and is capable of experiencing relief from it. S/he may ward off a show of tenderness with aggression. S/he is frightened of sustained close involvement (because of the pain if it should fail) and will break up a relationship if it shows signs of becoming permanent. Unlike the schizoid individual, s/he needs involvement of sorts but prefers to develop a series of short-term relationships. S/he can be gregarious, but will form alliances mainly with other antisocial personalities, toward whom s/he may develop firm loyalties. S/he stays outside of conventional society, reluctant to accept its norms, but may conform to the norms of an outsider culture.

NEGATIVE FORMS OF DISTANCE

As with negative forms of closeness, some negative forms of distance involve upper distance and lower distance. These will be explored in Chapter 9 when the intermediate positions are considered.

Giving or Receiving Disrespectfully Imposed Distance

Some of these categories involve a degree of upper distance.

Avoidance, Ostracizing, and Marginalizing. Avoidance, ostracizing and marginalizing involve the imposition of distance in situations in which closeness would be appropriate, such as families, schools or places of work. The person avoided, ostracized or marginalized is considered, either temporarily or permanently, to have caused offense or to be constituting a threat, but s/he cannot, for some reason, be ejected. In an unresolved marital conflict, the partners may remain living together but avoid speaking to each other for hours, days, weeks, or even longer. Being the recipient of these forms of behavior can be extremely painful and may lead to suicide attempts, or even suicide.

Enforced Isolation. Because being deprived of involvement with others is painful, enforced isolation is sometimes adopted as a form of punishment. In ancient times, the person might have been marooned on an uninhabited island. In present times, *solitary confinement* is the most usual method. This is also used in penal institutions and some mental hospitals as a means of controlling disruptive behavior. Its effects vary according to the person's preferred level of sensory input. Psychotic patients, who have a low preferred level become less psychotic, but nonpsychotic patients can become grossly psychotic, with delusions and hallucinations (Suedfield and Roy, 1975).

Rejection. Rejection is shunning another's offer of, or invitation to, closeness or breaking away from an existing close relationship. The rejecter (1) may have no need for closeness at that time or for the closeness that is on offer; (2) may have sufficient closeness from other sources, may not like the person who is offering the closeness or with whom s/he has closeness, or may have made the decision to seek closeness from someone else; or (3) may be experiencing closeness fatigue.

Being the recipient of rejection is painful. If the relationship is well established or the rejection is unexpected, it is extremely painful. The pain of rejection is often intensified by its summation with the pain of previous rejections. A person who is afraid that a close relationship may come to an end, particularly if s/he has experienced previous painful rejections, may choose to give the rejection first in order to reduce the pain.

There is a close connection between rejection and suicidal behavior. Such behavior is often precipitated by rejection (Birtchnell, 1983) but is itself a form of rejection. It relieves the pain of rejection but also serves the function of punishing the rejecter. Draper (1976) wrote of the pain in living (from past and recent rejections) of the suicidal person.

Relating to Others as Things. Others *are* things in that they have substance and physical qualities, but at the same time they are people. A surgeon performing an operation on a human body, must be knowledgeable of the physical qualities of the body and, to some extent therefore, must relate to it as a thing, but s/he probably never ceases to be aware that it is also a person. The tendency of distant people to prefer to relate to things has already been discussed. If distant people prefer to relate to things, they may see people as things or choose to relate only to aspects of them that are things, such as their organs or their abstract thoughts.

Distance Making Cruelty Easier. Humans are capable of inflicting great cruelty upon each other. Although close people are sometimes cruel to each other, it is much easier to be cruel from a position of distance. In the famous Milgram (1974) studies, in which experimental subjects were deceived into believing that they were administering painful electric shocks to another person, the "victim" was usually kept in an adjoining room. It is easier to drop bombs on an entire population from a high altitude. It is easier to wage war upon a nation that has been identified as "the enemy." These are ways of depersonalizing people. Getting to know them as people and identifying with them as fellow humans makes it much more difficult to be cruel to them. Miller (1987) maintained that it was common in Hitler's generation for children to be reared harshly and that this was what made possible the cruelty of the Nazis during World War II.

Pathological Attitudes Toward the Self

Self-Disapproval, Self-Hate. Self-disapproval and self-hate are accompaniments of some forms of depression. It seems likely that such attitudes toward the self are the effects of disapproving internal objects. The person has taken on the attitudes that others have expressed toward her/him. In extreme form s/he may believe that s/he is rotten or decaying inside, that s/he is dying of a serious disease, or that an offensive smell is emanating from her/him. S/he may believe that s/he is a nuisance to other people, that s/he is the cause of their misfortune and that they, or the world, would be better off without her/him. Such attitudes sometimes lead to suicide.

Hypochondria. In hypochondria the person fears that s/he may be physically ill rather than believing that s/he is (Barsky & Klerman, 1983). It is linked more with anxiety than with depression. It has to do less with self-disapproval and more with a sense of insecurity. It may be accompanied by genuine physical pains in different parts of the body, which probably are due to muscular tension resulting from anxiety. The typical hypochondriac harbors an excessive concern about her/his body over a period of years, derives only temporary relief from the reassurance of doctors, and adopts various forms of self-treatment.

Dysmorphophobia. The person with dysmorphophobia is obsessed with the appearance of part of her/his body, commonly the nose, erroneously believing it to be unsightly and believing that others look at it and make unfavourable remarks about it (Birtchnell, S.A., 1988). S/he may avoid social contact and become housebound. S/he may make persistent attempts to have it altered by plastic surgery.

Transsexualism. The transsexual believes that her/his internal gender identity (i.e., the gender that s/he experiences her/himself as being), does not correspond with the gender of the body s/he has. S/he becomes obsessed with having her/his body changed, by hormones or plastic surgery, so that it can resemble the body of the opposite gender (Green and Money, 1969).

Anorexia Nervosa. In anorexia nervosa the person, usually a young woman, is obsessed with the erroneous belief that s/he is too fat (Crisp, 1980). Consequently s/he refuses to eat, vomits whatever s/he does eat, and takes purgatives. S/he admires others who are thin and spends much time looking at her/himself in the mirror, wishing that s/he could be thinner. Her/his fear of food may be so great that s/he may actually starve her/himself to death.

Flight from or Avoidance of the Self

It is possible not only to distance oneself from other people but also to distance oneself from oneself. This includes avoiding looking at and neglecting one's body; avoiding thinking about oneself, either in the past or the present; and avoiding responding to or attending to impulses or needs originating from within. This may involve keeping on the move and never sinking roots, getting lost in work (Oates, 1971) or distractions such as music and entertainment, becoming an anonymous member of a group or cult, or acting the part of another person. Extreme variants of this include developing a total amnesia for who one is, believing oneself to be someone else, experiencing oneself as unreal, and believing oneself to be nonexistent or dead (*depersonalization*).

Escape

Escape involves getting away from something or someone dangerous, threatening, or disturbing. In many animals escape is the most important form of distancing, but in man, apart from unusual situations, such as escaping from an enemy or an attacker, it is relatively unimportant. It is not just getting away from closeness: it may involve getting away from upperness or lowerness if either of these is experienced as unpleasant (e.g., when forcibly imposed). Escape may be a perfectly reasonable form of behavior. Only the more pathological forms of escape will be considered here. Escape may be transient or long-term. It need not involve movement: one's body may remain in the unpleasant situation while one's mind is "elsewhere."

Sleep. The issue of sleep as an escape from unpleasant circumstances was discussed earlier in the chapter.

Distant Depression. Price (1972) considered the possible biological advantages of depression, and drew a parallel between phasic depressive illnesses and hibernation. He would not have known about the recently described condition of seasonally related depression (Kasper and Rosenthal, 1989), which has its onset in the autumn and is characterized by overeating, decreased activity, and hypersomnia. The condition, which is quite rare, may have an evolutionary link with hibernation. Price would say that whereas hibernation is nature's way of surviving unfavorable climatic conditions, depression is nature's way of surviving unfavorable social conditions.

Morris (1979) produced evidence of a link between introversion (see Chapter 3) and depression. Such a link is apparent only in unipolar depression, that is when there are no manic swings (Akiskal et al., 1983). Seasonally related depression, on the other hand, is mainly of the bipolar variety. Depression commonly is associated with social withdrawal; upon recovery, communication with more than one person increases (Pedersen et al., 1988). Pilkonis and Frank (1988) found avoidant personality disorder to be the most common personality disorder in hospitalized depressives.

Fugues. In a fugue (Stengel, 1941, 1943), the person may wander, drive, or travel for a variable period of time, sometimes extending over hours, in a dissociated state and suddenly become aware that s/he is in a strange place and not know how s/he got there. S/he may remain in such a state over a period of days and, on recovery, have amnesia for where s/he has been and what s/he has been doing.

The Splitting of the Self from the Body. Laing (1965) believed that, in many schizophrenic patients there appears to be a splitting of the self from the body so that the disembodied self regards the body as though it were just another thing in the world. He wrote, "Such a scission cleaves the individual's own being in two, in such a way that the I-sense is disembodied, and the body becomes the centre of a false self system" (page 174). The self wishes to be wedded to and embedded in the body but is constantly afraid to lodge in the body for fear of the dangers that might befall it if it did.

Dissociative States. Attempts have been made to distinguish between the splitting of the self from the body of the schizoid personality or schizophrenic and that of the hysteric. Laing (1965) wrote, "The hysteric characteristically dissociates himself from much that he does." (page 95). Whether or not there is such a distinction, it is clear that, at moments of stress some people can dissociate themselves from what is happening as though they are watching themselves from outside, and this enables them to tolerate it.

Withdrawal

Withdrawal involves drawing away from others and turning in on the self. It is important to make a distinction between withdrawal and meditation. The decision to start or stop meditating occurs at a cortical level. The decision to enter into or emerge from a state of withdrawal occurs mainly at a subcortical level. Withdrawal is a feature of some advanced forms of schizophrenia. The person may walk about, and perhaps perform a few normal functions, but be totally self-preoccupied. S/he may mutter to her/himself, perhaps in response to auditory hallucinations, but her/his communication with others will be limited, selective, or nonexistent. The preoccupation may be entirely with the inner self and s/he may be quite neglectful of her/his physical condition or appearance. It is often said of such a person that s/he is *inaccessible,* but Freeman (1971) made the important point that the schizophrenic rarely gives up all contact with others, though such contact as s/he does have is always weak and fragile. Fromm-Reichmann (1959) quoted a patient who had recovered from such a condition as saying, "Hell is if you are frozen in isolation into a block of ice. That is where

I have been" (page 9).

Two conditions associated with withdrawal are *mutism* and *stupor*. Mutism is a condition in which the person, though perfectly capable of speaking, chooses not to speak. Quite normal people sometimes make a *vow of silence*, and mutism is sometimes part of religious rituals, but it also occurs in some psychiatric conditions. Stupor is a state in which the person, though remaining entirely conscious, neither speaks nor moves. It may occur in a setting of hysteria or severe depression but is most commonly a variant of schizophrenic withdrawal. Schizophrenic stupor is called catatonia. In the days before drug treatment this could persist for periods of weeks or months. It is sometimes accompanied by the assumption of strange postures.

Negative Effects of Isolation and Sensory Deprivation

Schachter (1959) observed a marked variation in people's capacity to survive in conditions of isolation. Even when voluntarily confined, some people become desperate to be released after as little as two hours, while others can endure periods of a week or more. Recent reports of hostages released from conditions of solitary confinement extending over periods of years indicate that humans can adapt to such conditions when forced to do so, though perhaps the regular though minimal contact the hostages had with their guards provided sufficient doses of closeness to enable them to remain stable. Harris (1959) observed that schizophrenics are particularly tolerant of isolation and may even experience a reduction in hallucinatory experiences.

Lilly (1956), reporting upon the experimental reduction of ordinary levels of physical stimuli, observed that the inner life becomes so vivid and intense that it takes time to readjust to living with people and to re-establish satisfactory criteria of sanity. After only a few days under such conditions, subjects sometimes experience fantastic dreams, become deluded, and hallucinate. Similar experiences have been reported by solitary sailors (Slocum, 1948) and prisoners subjected to long periods of solitary confinement (Burney, 1952; Grassian, 1983).

Suicidal Behavior. Suicidal behavior as a form of escape has been discussed earlier. Durkheim (1897) associated suicide with what he called *egoism*, that is, having an absence of group ties and carrying a responsibility for one's fate. Egoism is clearly a form of distance. He explained the low prevalence of suicide in certain religious groups as a result of such groups preventing the individual from being overly self-directed, and the low prevalence at times of war as a result of the nation being united by a common purpose. Sainsbury (1955) demonstrated a link between suicide and social isolation. Apart from suicide pacts, suicide always takes place under conditions of distance. It is an assault upon the self, when the person is alone with her/himself.

Negative Forms of Distance that Are Consequent upon Deficiencies of Closeness

Lack of Trust. People are inclined to believe that what has happened to them in the past is likely to continue to happen to them in the future. Those who have always experienced a satisfactory degree of closeness will continue to seek and accept it and to assume that if they allow themselves to get close to people they are not likely to pull away and cause hurt. If they are let down they may become mistrusting not only of the person who lets them down but of people in general. Nontrusting people need and want close involvement but are afraid to allow themselves to have it.

Lack of trust lies at the heart of many forms of negative distance, but it assumes different guises. It forms the basis of the avoidant personality, with its accompanying compulsive self-reliance and suppression of all emotion as a precaution against experiencing any kind of need for others. Millon (1969) described what he called the active or avoidant schizophrenic, who is characterized by chronic overactivity and interpersonal distrust. Bannister (1987) referred to the enormous distrust of certain schizophrenics; he observed that during psychotherapy trust continues to be tested time and time again. A patient recovering from a chronic schizophrenic illness, reported upon by Hayward and Taylor (1956), said, "The problem with schizophrenics is that they can't trust anyone. The doctor will usually have to fight to get in no matter how much the patient objects" (page 218). Millon (1981) observed that the aggressive personality has faith only in her/himself and is secure only when s/he is independent of those who s/he fears may undo, harm, or humiliate her/him.

Insecure Distance

Insecure distance can assume different forms, depending upon the aspect of distance the person feels insecure about.

Ontological Insecurity. The term "ontological insecurity," as used first by Laing (1965), incorporates poor identity formation, lack of autonomy, and ill-defined ego boundaries. Though these three deficiencies run into each other, it is better to consider them separately. The person with a poorly formed identity has no clear idea of who s/he is, what s/he likes or dislikes, or what things are and are not important to her/him. S/he is an insubstantial person who does not feel real and who is not experienced as real by others. The person who lacks autonomy is incapable of self-motivation, has no personal objectives or personal standards, and looks to others for direction and approval. The person with ill-defined ego boundaries has difficulty determining which are her/his own thoughts, ideas, or emotions and which are other people's. Chameleon-like, s/he takes on those of whomever s/he happens to be with.

Laing (1965) wrote, "The schizophrenic either does not know who or what he is or he has become something or someone other than himself" (page 172) and "To the schizophrenic, liking someone equals *being like* that person: being like a person is equated with being the same as that person, hence with losing identity" (page 174). Bowen (1978) has described schizophrenia as a failure of differentiation. Blatt and Wild (1976) conceptualized schizophrenia as involving malfunctioning self-other boundary processes, in that the self-other boundary seems to have an uncontrolled and inconsistent permeability. Schizophrenic states associated with ontological insecurity include believing that an alien force is taking over, penetrating or controlling one's mind or body; that thoughts are being put into one's head; that one's voice is speaking another person's words; that others can read one's thoughts; that another person is repeating or commenting upon them in the form of a running commentary; or that they are being broadcast over the radio (Wing et al., 1974).

Fear of Being Penetrated or Understood. Whereas wanting to be entered into or understood is a characteristic of closeness, fear of being entered into or understood may be a characteristic of distance. The insecurely distant person fears that people can see into her/him as if s/he is being X-rayed. This is a deficiency of being able to keep others out. Laing (1965) wrote, "in psychotic conditions the gaze or scrutiny of the other can be experienced as an actual penetration into the core of the `inner' self" (page 106). One way of avoiding such penetration is to present the body for others to look at but to withdraw the self from the body, so that the body is offered as an alternative to the self. It has sometimes been suggested that psychotics speak and write unintelligibly as a way of avoiding being understood, and that in the presence of a sympathetic listener they begin to talk intelligibly.

Fear of Being Touched. Some people extend and exaggerate the normal tendency to protect their personal boundaries and personal space to an acute fear of being touched, even by people they know well. Sometimes the fear applies specifically or predominantly to people of the opposite gender; in women, this is commonly associated with a fear of sexual assault.

Fear of Animals, Germs, Contamination. It is sensible for humans to be afraid of animals such as lions, tigers, sharks, snakes, and even ferocious dogs, which are capable of killing them or doing them serious harm. It is less sensible to be afraid of birds, rats, mice, bats, spiders, beetles, moths, wasps, and other small insects. To some extent these fears may emanate from generalizing from animals that are truly dangerous to similar ones that are not. They may also represent a fear of invasion or penetration.

It is sensible to take reasonable precautions against infection and infestation, but some people carry this to extreme lengths. Extremes include needing to wash after touching a person or after touching money, books and the like that other people have handled; and excessive washing, changing of clothes, bathing, and use of disinfectants. These fears tend to be more a feature of neurosis than psychosis.

Xenophobia. Eibl-Eibesfeldt (1989) observed that "Fear of others is one of the universals that decidedly influence our social life. It leads to xenophobia, a characteristic that undoubtedly has accelerated human cultural evolution" (page 175). The fear of strangers in children was mentioned in Chapter 4, but Kaltenbach et al. (1980) observed that stranger avoidance reactions were even stronger in mothers. For the greater part of their existence humans have lived in small, homogeneous groups, the members of which have been familiar to each other. When strangers were encountered they were responded to with suspicion and sometimes with hostility. Until recently the majority of people have lived in close, stable communities, in villages or small towns, in which facilities have been available for strangers to meet and become familiar with each other. In modern cities, high population density, greater mobility, increased anonymity, and the influx of immigrants from foreign cultures has resulted in greater fear and mistrust of others.

Xenophobia is closely linked with *racism* and *nationalism*. Feinman (1980) observed that white infants are more fearful of black strangers than white ones, which indicates that the fear of people of other races is established at an early age and may even be innate. The fear is reinforced by the fact that people from different racial groups have different customs, and this contributes to their unfamiliarity. The essence of racism and nationalism is the belief that people from other races and other nations are inferior and that therefore they should be exploited and denied certain rights and privileges.

Racism and nationalism are categories of xenophobia. All three are linked by a fear of the unfamiliar, and that fear is easily converted into aggression. Xenophobia both contributes to and is maintained by distance. When people become more acquainted with strangers and with people from different races and different countries, and when they recognize that they have much in common, they become less fearful of them and less aggressive toward them.

Suspiciousness and Defensiveness. A person is suspicious if s/he suspects the intention of the other. Suspiciousness is accompanied by lack of trust, but the lack of trust of the suspicious person is not the same as the lack of trust of the avoidant person. The avoidant person is afraid that the other will withhold or withdraw closeness. The suspicious person is afraid that the other will do her/him harm. Suspiciousness leads to defensiveness, which involves adopting an attitude of alert vigilance (similar to the agonic mode of relating described in Chapter 2). Defensiveness involves developing protective armor, shields, and barricades and accumulating weaponry for fighting off the assailant.

The threat from outside may be of two kinds: the threat of penetration and the threat of harm or destruction. Often the two are related, since the suspicion is that once the other has got inside s/he will do harm or be destructive. Harm or destruction have strong vertical implications and therefore should not extensively be considered here. They are relevant, however, since a person will remain distant to someone s/he fears will do her/him harm. An important consideration is what exactly is to be harmed or destroyed: the body or the self? The schizophrenic may find it difficult to distinguish between the two.

In normal relating may be the person's good name that is under threat. Gibb (1961) observed that speech is so frequently judgmental that the defensive attitude is commonly brought into play. The defensive person is constantly worried about how s/he might appear in the eyes of others and whether their remarks will put her/him in a favorable or an unfavorable light. Defensive arousal prevents the listener from fully concentrating upon what is being said to her/him; the more defensive s/he becomes, the less accurately is s/he able to perceive the motives of the speaker.

Denial, Projection, and Reversal. These three defensive processes, though first attributed by Freud (1911b) to certain paranoid patients, are considered to have more general application. Denial involves denying that one might have certain undesirable feelings; projection involves incorrectly asserting that someone else has them; and reversal involves maintaining that the feelings one might have toward another, the other has toward oneself. By these three devices, the paranoid individual is able to always conceive of her/himself as good and right.

Paranoid Delusions and Hallucinations. Paranoid delusions are a stage beyond the suspicions held by the individual with a paranoid personality. The person incorrectly believes that others are talking about her/him, that the remarks they make have double meanings, and that their gestures indicate that s/he has certain undesirable characteristics. S/he interprets remarks made in newspapers and on radio and television as referring to her/him. S/he may believe that someone, some force, or some organization is trying to damage her/his reputation, do her/him physical harm, drive her/him insane, or kill her/him. S/he may hear a voice or voices saying these various things (Wing et al., 1974).

SUMMARY

Distance should not be viewed as the absence of closeness: it is as much a positive state as closeness is. In distance, the self is built up and related to. Pleasurable states of distance are achieved by the reduction of sensory input in order to be alone with oneself, with the environment, and with God. Sleep is a natural form of distance in which there is a catching up with one's psychic interior. In normal social interaction it is important to respect other people's need for distance and to provide them with opportunities to be distant. In order to effectively be distant it is necessary to establish a firm sense of personal identity so that one can have a mind of one's own. Out of this develops the capacity to be autonomous, original, and creative. Around the self are the personal boundaries and a series of shells such as the skin, clothes, personal space, and personal property. Relating to the self is an essential feature of distance: it involves being aware of and curious about the self; accepting, valuing, and indulging the self.

Distant closeness involves deriving a degree of closeness from the relatively safe position of distance. Distance is not simply a focusing upon the self: it is also a way of relating to others. Everyone relates in a distant way to some people, but some people relate in a distant way to most people. These are called distant personalities; they include the avoidant, schizoid, schizotypal, paranoid, and psychopathic. Negative distance assumes the following forms: giving or receiving disrespectfully imposed distance; pathological attitudes toward the self; flight from or avoidance of the self; escape; withdrawal; the negative effects of isolation and sensory deprivation; negative forms of distance that are consequent upon deficiencies of closeness; and insecure distance.

7

Upperness

Upperness involves being in a position of advantage or superiority in relation to another or others. It can assume many forms, so when a person is said to be upper in relation to another, the respect in which this may be so should be made clear. Because it is a relative term, there should be some way of determining or demonstrating, even if only approximately, how much of a particular attribute the one person has in relation to the other.

Upperness often involves having the power to influence others. Such influence may be beneficial or harmful. An important distinction should be drawn therefore between what might be called *benevolent* upperness and *malevolent* upperness. Because the more securely upper person is inclined to use her/his upperness for the benefit of others, the more positive forms of upperness tend to be benevolent and the more negative forms, malevolent. Also benevolent upperness tends to be more associated with upper closeness and the malevolent forms with upper distance.

In contrast to animals, humans have a broad range of sources of upperness. This is important, since everyone needs to accumulate adequate supplies of it from somewhere in order to feel good about her/himself, be able to live with her/himself, hold her/his head up high, and feel that s/he is someone of importance. As with closeness, a person may derive small amounts of upperness from a variety of different sources or a large amount from one main source.

Upperness may concern how one person compares with another, or how s/he compares with her/his own group or community. The relative merit of one person compared with another can determine the nature of their relationship, irrespective of how either compares with other people. Because there are so many ways of being upper, in any particular relationship, one person may be upper in some respects and the other may be so in others. Thus there may be no absolute sense in which either is upper to the other. Even in professional relationships, in which levels of seniority often are clearly defined, the professionally lower person may recognize her/himself to be upper to his superior in various respects (e.g., s/he may be more physically attractive or better at sports).

When a person compares her/himself with the rest of a group, because upperness is a relative condition, her/his likelihood of experiencing it will depend upon her/his assessment of the distribution of any given attribute among the members of the group. In a small group s/he may experience her/himself as outstanding, but in a larger group, where there is a broader distribution of the attribute, her/his worth will fall into perspective and her/his former experience of upperness will disappear.

Either in a two-person relationship or in a group, whoever emerges as the upper one may depend upon the circumstances. In a two- person relationship, one person's competence may lie more in the practical sphere, and when fixing things about the house s/he will be upper; but the other's competence may lie more in the social sphere, and when entertaining friends s/he will come into her/his own. In a school, there may be one group of children whose academic skills put them in a position of prominence in the classroom, and another whose athletic abilities put them in a position of prominence on the playing field. These ideas are linked with the broader issue of *social comparison* theory and research, which have been reviewed by Wood (1989) and Suls and Wills (1991).

INTERNAL UPPERNESS AND EXTERNAL UPPERNESS

Internal upperness is the person's own assessment of his standing, qualities and so on, external upperness is the assessment of her/him by other people. A person with a reasonable degree of autonomy may, in certain areas at least, be capable of judging for her/himself what level of upperness s/he has achieved. For example, s/he would be able to tell if s/he could walk farther, run faster, jump higher, grow bigger vegetables, think faster, win more games of chess, or make more people laugh than certain other people. There are some areas however (e.g., cooking, singing, writing poetry, answering arithmetical problems, making love), in which s/he may be dependent upon the judgment of others; but even in these areas s/he may be sufficiently objective about her/himself to be able to fairly assess how good s/he is.

The judgment of others may not necessarily be reliable: praise may be withheld when it is due and given when it is not due. There can be a close interrelationship between internal and external upperness. A person whose parents/teachers/peers were parsimonious with their praise may grow up with an unjustified poor opinion of her/himself or her/his abilities, and one who was exposed to excessive and indiscriminate praise may grow up with an inflated opinion of her/himself or her/his abilities. A creative person in particular may be profoundly affected by the judgments of her/his critics.

ACHIEVEMENT

Achievement is the successful attainment of a goal by drawing upon one's personal resources or capabilities and overcoming difficulties. Although it is clearly related to upperness and frequently contributes to it, it is not necessarily the same thing. It is important to distinguish between *personal achievement* and *competitive achievement*. Personal achievement does not involve other people and therefore is not strictly a form of upperness. It can involve the mastery of a skill, such as walking, riding a bicycle, learning a language, or playing an instrument; or meeting an objective, such as sailing around the world, climbing a mountain, or living to be one hundred years old. Competitive achievement inevitably involves other people. It involves doing better than them in various respects and is therefore a form of upperness. The satisfaction, or elation, that accompanies achievement, can be the same for either personal or competitive achievement. Presumably, therefore, the brain interprets them as comparable. Certainly most forms of personal achievement provide the potential for attaining upperness; perhaps this is how they are experienced by the brain. When a person masters a particular skill or meets a particular objective s/he is aware that there are others who have not, and perhaps, at some level, s/he compares her/himself with these others.

There are three (related) forms of achievement that are attained by way of other people: *achievement through identity, enabling achievement* and *combined achievement*. Achievement through identity occurs is when someone (such as one's child) or some group (such as the football team one supports) with whom one identifies has achieved something; enabling achievement occurs when someone one has taught, coached, or helped achieves something; and combined achievement occurs when, with combined effort, a group or team to which one belongs has achieved something. All three experiences give rise to the same quality of emotional response.

THE MAIN SOURCES OF (POSITIVE) UPPERNESS IN HUMANS

Innate Attributes

Humans are born with certain natural advantages over other animals and other humans. It is not always easy to determine what these are, since early influences and early experiences play their part, but it must be acknowledged that they do exist. They are perhaps more potentialities than actualities, since in many instances they need to be realized. They include physical structure such as height, length of limb, and size of brain; physical capacity such as muscular power, speed, dexterity, and visual, olfactory, and auditory acuity; the capacity to resist and combat infection; physical attractiveness; and brain functions such as alertness, memory, and capacity to solve problems.

Personal Attractiveness

In the area of personal attractiveness, upperness and closeness overlap. People who are attractive because of their physical appearance or their personality are much liked by others, who want to know and be friends with them. At the same time, people who, by virtue of their attractiveness, are popular and much liked sometimes become famous and earn a great deal of money. This issue was discussed in Chapter 5.

It is not always easy to differentiate between physical attractiveness and having an attractive personality, because each can contribute to the other and one is never seen without the other. A successful person who feels good about her/himself may naturally smile a lot and adopt an attractive posture, gestures, and facial expressions. Because of this, people sometimes behave as though they are successful in order to look attractive.

In the film and entertainment industries, popular performers are called *stars*. Although stars may have outstanding ability or personal attractiveness, their appeal can be greatly enhanced by media experts who specialize in presentation and publicity. Increasingly, such experts are being employed by business people and politicians in order to enhance their public image.

Leadership Qualities

Leading is one of the characteristics of upper animals and upper people. People lead (and others follow) for a variety of reasons. Ironically autonomy, which is a distant quality, is an important component of leadership, since the leader must have a clear idea of where s/he wants to go; but s/he must be able to convey that s/he knows how to get there. Where s/he wants to go must be where others want to be taken; so the leader must be in tune with those s/he is leading. Yukl (1981) maintained that there is no list of key traits shared by all leaders, but Lord et al. (1986) observed that several traits appear to be related to leader emergence in many situations. Kets de Vries and Miller (1985) concluded that what most leaders appear to have in common is the ability to reawaken primitive emotions in their followers.

Taking an evolutionary stance, Crook (1986) suggested that leaders emerge if they have skills or capabilities that are advantageous to the group. A more psychodynamic view is that those who have the greatest need to lead come to assume the role of leader. Freud (1921) observed that a leader must be of a masterful nature, self-confident, independent, and absolutely narcissistic. Kernberg (1979) believed that those with narcissistic personalities often are driven by an intense need for power and prestige and that frequently they are found in positions of authority and leadership. Kets de Vries and Miller (1985) suggested that perhaps only strongly narcissistic individuals are willing to undertake the arduous process of attaining a position of power.

The effective leader has a definite sense of purpose and a strong conviction of her/his own rightness. S/he harbors no doubts about which is the right way. The more certain s/he appears to be that s/he knows where s/he is going, the more prepared people are to follow her/him. A leader needs to have a strong and easily recognizable identity. At times of major change, powerful and dramatic leaders emerge who are called *charismatic leaders* (Conger and Kanungo, 1988). They recognize the intolerable nature of present circumstances, have a vision of how such circumstances could be changed, and express a passion and determination to change them. Weber (1947) used the term *"charisma"* as meaning endowed with exceptional, supernatural, or superhuman powers, regarded as of divine origin.

Acquired Skills and Competencies

More than any other animal, humans can increase their potential for upperness by learning and training. This is especially so in industrial societies. They become capable of performing complex physical and mental tasks.

Acquired Experience and Knowledge

Experience and knowledge contribute to various capabilities. They are also commodities in themselves that can be passed on or sold to other people. For mankind as a whole, the accumulation of experience and knowledge has greatly enhanced man's power and influence. Science is discovering and understanding natural laws so that nature may be used to man's advantage. This includes harnessing and channeling natural sources of power.

Tools, Machinery and Weaponry

From earliest times man has been able to construct tools, machines, and weapons that have increased his effectiveness both constructively and destructively. They are, in effect, extensions of normal physical capabilities. They increase physical strength, dexterity, mobility, acuity of the senses, and with computers, mental ability. They create advantages for the individual and the nation. Industrialization and civilization are the consequences of their development, and the greater power of the developed nations is due almost entirely to them.

Whilst weapons may have positive uses, such as hunting for food and as a defense against attackers, they are mostly used in a negative way by criminals to threaten and kill. Many nations spend vast sums of money on weaponry and accumulate vast arms stores, often at the expense of the welfare of the people. For nations, more than for individuals, arms stores are used as a measure of upperness. In this sense, nations relate to each other in a more primitive way than do individuals.

Academic and Professional Qualifications

These give confirmation that certain skills, competencies, experience or knowledge have been acquired. They entitle their possessors to certain positions of occupational or professional status.

Earning Capacity

In Chapter 2 it was suggested that money represents a way of packaging power so that it may, like electricity, be stored or transported from place to place, and drawn upon when required to provide benefits for its possessor. In Chapter 2 the term "upperness" had not been introduced, but by now a more appropriate term for money would be "*packaged upperness*." In industrial societies a source of money is essential and most people obtain money by working. Just as certain ruminant animals need to eat for most of their waking day in order to obtain enough food to survive, so do many people need to work for the larger part of most of their waking days in order to obtain enough money to survive. In working they exchange what forms of upperness they have, such as fitness, physical strength, intelligence, skills, competencies, knowledge, physical or personal attractiveness, for the packaged upperness, money, that they then exchange for food, clothes, heat, transportation, services and so on.

Having a Salable Commodity

Beyond personal attributes and abilities, material possessions such as raw materials, food, fuel, manufactured goods, objects of art, land, and accommodation are sources of upperness becausee they may be sold for money.

Money

Money is a useful form of upperness because it can be exchanged for other forms. For many people in industrial societies it is envisaged as an end in itself, and their efforts are directed toward accumulating it and converting it into possessions. People are rated according to how much money or how many possessions they have. There are, however, forms of upperness that money cannot buy. These include physical strength, intelligence, knowledge, understanding, attractiveness, skills, competencies, and professional qualifications. Nations also accumulate money, but this is a more realistic activity for them since money can be used to improve the quality of life of their peoples.

STATUS

Status is an acknowledged social position within a group, community, or society.

People with high status adopt characteristic postures, gestures, forms of speech, and modes of dress that provide confirmation of their status to themselves and others. Those who do not have high status sometimes emulate them in order to gain respect. Their behavior and communication toward those they consider lower to them incorporate many subtle and not-so-subtle variants of Price's (1988) down-hierarchy catathetic signals (see Chapter 2), which are intended to put them and keep them in their place.

People with high status usually have more money and possessions (by inheritance, reward, or earnings) than people with low status and live in large houses in prestigious neighborhoods, drive large cars, and wear expensive clothes. Since people who have much money, however they may have obtained it, are able to adopt the same life-style as people with high status, having much money has become almost the equivalent of having high status.

People with high status enjoy certain rights, expectations, entitlements, and privileges, which are not necessarily related to their wealth. They are maintained in their position of high status by the attitude and behavior of those who experience themselves as lower. Such people tend not to openly criticize, contradict, or insult them; and they treat them with respect and deference. In Price's (1988) terminology (see Chapter 2), they convey up-hierarchy anathetic signals that may communicate admiration, adoration, exaltation, or gratitude.

ROUTES TO (POSITIVE) UPPERNESS

Ambition

Ambition is a need or determination to succeed. It is related to an awareness of potential, but not all who are aware of their potential are ambitious and not all who are ambitious have any obvious potential to succeed. The origins of ambition are complex. It may as easily spring from deprivation and bitterness as from the early experience of success. For some, success comes easily; for others, it is the outcome of prolonged struggle. However achieved, it is exhilarating; once achieved, it may become addictive. Part of the exhilaration of success is the praise and acclaim of others. This, more than anything, may contribute to its addictiveness, particularly for those who consider themselves to be unlikeable. A.S. Neil, the founder of the English progressive school Summerhill, used to maintain that few of his pupils ever became famous, because, he added, they had no need to. Certainly there is a sense in which ambition grows out of discontentment, and some ambitious people are forever discontented and unhappy. Some, however, are ambitious simply for the opportunity to do the kinds of things they know they are good at.

Victory in Open Competition

Following victory in open competition, the person comes to experience another or others as lower. Open conflict is the human equivalent of the ritual agonistic encounter (see Chapter 2). It may range in seriousness from victory in open warfare, lasting many years, during which millions of people are killed, to victory in a game of cards. It is because humans so enjoy the experience of victory that they engage in endless conflicts between individuals, groups, or nations. The best conflicts are those in which the participants are evenly matched so that each has a reasonable chance of winning. Many such conflicts, as in sports and games, are conducted in an atmosphere of fairness and mutual respect. The loser congratulates the winner and there is no ill feeling on either side.

Defiance

Defiance is an unpreparedness to accept the lower role that is imposed by upper others. The defiant person believes her/himself to be deserving or capable of higher status and resists the suppressive or oppressive behavior of those who try to keep her/him down. Defiance might be described as the hunger for upperness gaining expression in someone who is feeling deprived of it. Defiance frequently is experienced and expressed by children, since commonly they suffer suppression by parents, teachers, and others. It tends to be described as cheekiness, impertinence, insubordination, or disobedience. Clearly there are times when children are required to do what they are told; in the setting of a trusting relationship, they normally can be relied upon to do so. Defiance is usually the result of clumsily, unfairly, and disrespectfully imposed lowerness.

Adult versions of defiance include strikes, revolts, rebellions, uprisings, and mutiny. Such behavior often calls for bravery and a preparedness to make sacrifices for the ultimate benefit of others.

Gaining Social Status

Upperness (in the form of social status or wealth) may be passed by inheritance from one generation to another, as in an aristocracy or in the Indian caste system; bestowed, as promotion by a high ranking member of a hierarchy upon a lower ranking member (i.e., by being moved up within the hierarchy); gained through merit, as a result of fulfilling predetermined criteria such as passing examinations or demonstrating a level of competence in prescribed areas; or attained by popular acclaim, either by the democratic vote of peers or by emerging as someone with outstanding qualities.

Negotiation or Mutual Agreement

In the process of interrelating (see Chapter 1), two people might agree (either in a momentary interaction or over time) that in a particular respect one should be upper and the other lower. This might result from one proposing to behave in an upper way (e.g., "Shall I show you how to do it?" "Would you like me to teach you?") or one inviting the other to relate in an upper way (e.g., "Will you show me?" "Will you teach me?").

Experiencing Another or Others as Lower

Experiencing another or others as lower generates a feeling of upperness. How the person might respond to being in such a position depends upon how secure in her/his upperness s/he may feel at the time and how substantial her/his stores of it may be. Three responses are possible: simply indulging in it, taking advantage of the circumstances to push the other lower still, and helping the other up. People are sometimes drawn toward those whom they experience as lower (e.g., children, the poor, the needy, the disabled, the sick), because they want to help them and because helping them makes them feel good. However, people also try to push others into a position of lowerness because the lowerness of the others contributes to their upperness.

The Experience of Being Upper to Animals and Things

Most animals are less powerful than humans, and being in relation to them generates the experience of upperness. This accounts for the appeal of pets. Using animals for transport and for doing work also generates the experience of upperness, as does the control of certain powerful forms of machinery, particularly methods of transport.

Being Coerced into Upperness by Needful Others

When another asks for information, guidance, care, approval, protection, food, or the like, the person is immediately coerced into a position of upperness. Children coerce their parents into upperness, and people who idolize or adore others coerce them into upperness.

Upperness through Identification or Association

In the section on achievement, the possibility was mentioned of attaining a sense of achievement by identifying with a successful person or team. Gaining upperness not just through identification, but also through the looser process of association, is common, particularly for people of relatively low status. National pride and sharing in the successes of the nation and of prominent national figures are examples of this; but it also extends to civic pride, pride in one's place of work, school, political party, street, or family. People are excited by the success of their friends and family members and particularly of their children. The excitement of being a *fan* of a political leader, pop group, or football team comes from the vicarious upperness derived from the success of these.

POSITIVE UPPER FUNCTIONS

The organization of a complex industrial society depends upon groups and individuals within it performing specialist upper functions. Many positive upper functions (e.g., providing advice or information) have the effect of helping others up (i.e., reducing their lowerness and increasing their upperness). What is the advantage to the individual of giving upperness to someone else? The answer is that her/his overall store of upperness remains unchanged because s/he is rewarded for performing these functions by receiving an income. This income (i.e., money, or packaged upperness) may then be exchanged for other forms of upperness, which underlines the interdependence of members of a society.

Of course, many acts of helping others up are not rewarded financially and the rewards of helping others up are not strictly financial. A large part of parenting involves protecting and providing for children, who undoubtedly are lower. It also involves imparting information and teaching skills. Parents receive no financial rewards for their labors and in fact sometimes spend large sums of money on their children. Doctors, teachers, nurses, ambulance teams, aid workers, and others derive positive satisfaction from their work. At times of accidents and disasters, people work tirelessly and are excited by their successes. The satisfactions from these behaviors are multiple: parents identify with their children, as do care workers with those whom they help, and to a large extent the successes of the children and the helped people become their successes; being in the presence of needful others itself generates powerful experiences of upperness, and these are reinforced by the responses of gratitude.

Parenting

For most animal species, the most evident form of benevolent upperness is parenting. Many of the more positive forms of upperness in humans are extensions of parenting functions. Parents, and to a lesser extent teachers, need to perform the function of raising children from a position of relative lowerness to one of equality and then of relative upperness. Parents who are insecure in their state of upperness sometimes have difficulty allowing their children to draw level with them and ultimately to overtake them. They may abuse their position by trying to keep their children down.

Good parents ease their children up gradually, permitting them privileges and responsibilities as they appear capable of handling them. Childrens' progression upward may not be uniform: sometimes they may slip down and need to be consoled and reassured. Parents should encourage them within their capabilities and show obvious and appropriate delight at their successes. As the children draw level some form of ritual is desirable, during which the children are welcomed into the world of adults.

Protection

Human parents protect their young, but in humans the development of specialist defensive groups has been carried further. Humans, more than other species, attack each other; almost all defensive groups (e.g., the armed services and the police) are for the protection of humans against attack by other humans.

Provision of Food

The provision of food is another parental function that has been taken over by society as a whole. Man is the only species that has developed a policy for the large scale cultivation, production, and supply of food. Where this has been well developed it has resulted in massive population growth. Industrial communities are dependent upon the daily importation of vast quantities of food.

Provision of Other Material Needs

Having that which others need is a characteristic feature of upperness. S/he who has that which others need, whether it be strength, skills, knowledge, or provisions, has power. Individual humans, organizations, and nations gain wealth from possessing raw materials and manufactured items that others need.

Imparting of Information and Teaching of Skills

Humans progress by passing information and skills from person to person and from one generation to the next. A proportion of those who have knowledge and skills therefore need to serve as educators and trainers of others. Passing on information and skills are acts in which the donor reduces the gap between her/his upperness and the other's lowerness and brings the other up to her/his level. S/he is to some extent compensated for this by financial reward, but there remain additional motivations having to do with parenting, deriving pleasure from helping, and identifying with the person being helped.

Leadership

A group functions most effectively when it acts like a single organism, that is, when it has a small number of clear-cut objectives. Leaders are essential to determine what such objectives should be and ensure that group members work together to attain them. Leadership may range from an upper distant to an upper close perspective: from an upper distant perspective the leader decides what is best for the group and gives clear commands; from an upper close perspective s/he makes decisions on the basis of consultations with group members. There is a place for both. An upper distant approach is essential when harsh and unpopular decisions have to be made, as in times of war. An upper close approach is more appropriate when compromises have to be reached to accommodate conflicting interests and policies have to be revised to meet changing circumstances.

Adair (1987) wrote, "Leadership is of the spirit, compounded of personality and vision. Its practice is an art" (page 61). The leader stands out in front and inspires confidence. S/he needs to fire with enthusiasm those whom s/he leads, motivate them, and sustain their morale. S/he must generate excitement. Zaleznik (1977) observed that leaders often evoke strong emotions of love or hate. The leader should exemplify the qualities that are required in the group and bring out the best in people. A good leader helps each group member to realize her/his full potential and to believe in her/himself. This s/he does by pointing to and praising the group member's good qualities. Burns's (1978) description of the *transforming leader*, who looks for and brings out such qualities, is similar to that of the good parent.

Management

Management skills are not the same as leadership skills. Management is a more cerebral task. The manager, administrator, or controller is concerned with the efficient and effective use of resources, particularly financial resources. S/he needs to ensure the smooth running of a complex organization. This involves planning and coordinating, and setting and meeting objectives.

Responsibility

By taking care of the control side of an operation the manager frees the workers to concentrate on their appointed tasks. The workers assume that the manager knows what s/he is doing and put their trust in her/him. Because s/he is at the hub of the organization, any incorrect decision s/he may make can have far-reaching consequences. The conscientious manager remains forever aware of this and of the fact that s/he must accept the blame for whatever may go wrong.

Assuming responsibility for others is an important feature of many forms of upperness, and upper/lower relationships frequently require the lower person to entrust her/himself to the upper one. Passengers entrust themselves to the pilots of aircraft, and pilots entrust themselves to the air-traffic controllers. Parents entrust their children to teachers, and patients entrust their bodies to doctors.

Caring for Those Who Are Disadvantaged

The heightened capacity of humans for closeness, and the associated capacities for identification, sympathy, and empathy, results in humans being the species that cares most for its disadvantaged members. Although there appear to be no obvious evolutionary benefits to this, the more civilized the society, the more highly valued and completely developed its welfare services appear to be. An appropriate attitude toward the disadvantaged is *feeling sorry for* them, but this attitude easily can be abused. Being in the presence of the disadvantaged generates an experience of upperness, and it is likely that some insecurely upper people choose to work with the disadvantaged because it reinforces their experience of upperness. Unfortunately this has the effect of reinforcing the lowerness of the disadvantaged. As with the good parent, the correct attitude of the good welfare worker is to increase the state of upperness of the disadvantaged by enabling them to become more capable.

Rescuing Those in Distress

Although there are professional rescuers, such as fire-fighters, ambulance workers, and coast guards, there are also voluntary organizations, such as mountain rescue teams. Ordinary people often respond with immediate and selfless concern to people in distress and demonstrate outstanding bravery, sometimes involving personal sacrifice, to save people who may be complete strangers. Such behavior is best understood as an extension of normal parenting.

Treating and Nursing the Injured and the Sick

From an evolutionary point of view, there are advantages to the advancement of medical knowledge and the development of medical skills. Bacteria, viruses and parasites are man's most deadly predators; entire populations can be decimated by them. More generally, advances in health care contribute to survival and longevity. Although there are professions of medicine and nursing, doctors and nurses often are highly motivated to relieve suffering and save lives irrespective of how much they are paid to do so.

Issuing (Suitable or Acceptable) Commands

The person who issues the commands needs to have some hold over the person who is being commanded in order to ensure that s/he is obeyed. In a number of institutions and organizations, particularly in the armed forces, subordinates willingly submit to being commanded by their superiors in the interests of efficiency (i.e., they believe that their superiors are acting in their best interest). In order to be obeyed, people issuing commands should be seen to hold an acknowledged position of seniority and should speak with authority. Within a family, a respectful child will obey the command of a parent or even an older sibling.

Having (Reasonable) Expectations

Having expectations is a step beyond issuing commands in that the person of whom the behavior is expected has an understanding that s/he should act in a certain way without needing to be instructed. An example of this is Nelson's proclamation at the battle of Trafalgar that "England expects that every man this day shall do his duty." The expression "I trust that you will" behave in a particular way carries a similar connotation.

Setting Limits and Imposing Laws

Within a close relationship, people behave reasonably toward each other because they identify with and feel for each other and are able to appeal to each other's sense of fairness. People do not like to act in an unkind way toward those they feel close to. In some close communities this degree of mutual respect and understanding is maintained; even within societies, or around the world, people have humane feelings toward their fellow beings - but these are not sufficient to make them law-abiding.

When people are closely involved in intimate situations they act with consideration toward each other and difficulties are resolved by amicable discussion. The good parent or teacher can sometimes ensure the reasonable and fair behavior of children in this way, but sometimes they have to distance themselves in order to set and impose limits. As the degree of closeness between people is reduced, individuals become self-centered and disrespectful. Even in small groups it becomes an advantage, if not a necessity, for the group leader to draw up a set of rules that must be kept in order to ensure that group members behave fairly toward each other. Once groups extend beyond a certain size, the establishment and maintenance of laws of conduct becomes essential; within industrial societies, the laying down and enforcement of laws is an operation of some complexity. Governments introduce laws that the legal profession and the police enforce.

Reasonable Criticism

Criticism has both a vertical and a horizontal component. The vertical component implies an unfavorable comparison with others and has a putting-down effect. The horizontal component implies that the criticizer does not like the person being criticized and carries a possibility that s/he may not wish to continue to be her/his friend. The criticizing person inevitably is assuming a position of upperness in relation to the person being criticized, since s/he is conveying that s/he knows enough and is confident enough to be able to speak the way s/he does. A person's response to criticism is in direct relation to the respect s/he has for the criticizer. If the respect is high, the criticism is accepted, even though it may cause pain.

Passing Judgment

Passing judgment is a step beyond criticizing. The implication is that the person passing judgment is doing so with the backing of some higher authority. Such authority could be the state or a religious order, though sometimes these are impossible to separate. If it is the state, it is by an appointed judge and concerns whether a crime or an offense has been committed. If it is a religious order, it is by an appointed representative of that order and concerns whether a sin has been committed. In either case the judgment is likely to carry the disapproval of the community at large, and this may make the judged person feel ashamed or guilty. Adverse judgment incorporates a component of enforced distance since the judged person feels cast out and rejected.

Punishing

The most consistently effective means of law enforcement is punishment. Parents and teachers punish children; and groups, communities, and societies punish those who break their rules and laws. In certain religious orders punishments are imposed upon sinners, and in others the understanding is that they will be punished in an afterlife. Certain upper people are endowed with the authority to impose and administer punishments; and such punishments, even though they may involve humiliation, pain, torture, or death, are considered permissible by the community or society. Punishment may also involve enforced distance by expulsion or imprisonment.

Forgiving

Forgiving reverses the effects of passing judgment and punishment. The forgiven person is accepted back into a friendship or the community and her/his lost status is regained. Certain authorized, upper people have the power to grant pardon or forgiveness; again, it is usual for the forgiver to be an agent of a higher authority. In Roman Catholicism forgiveness is ritualized in the confessional, where the priest bestows God's forgiveness upon the confessor.

UPPER LOWERNESS

Upper lowerness is one of the four paradoxical positions. It involves being lower in, or from, a position of upperness. One form of upper lowerness is *humility*. The securely upper person is humble enough to appreciate the limitations of her/his upperness. There are two forms of humility: acknowledging (1) that even in ones own area of status or accomplishment there are others who are higher than oneself, and (2) that there are areas of status or accomplishment in which one may be lower to others. The upper lower person is able to maintain a sense of proportion about her/his position; is prepared to admit s/he is needful, makes mistakes, or has deficiencies in certain areas; and is willing to seek help, guidance, or correction from those who have knowledge or expertise in other areas. In an experimental setting, Gollwitzer et al. (1982) demonstrated that securely upper people were willing to engage in self-deprecation for the benefit of another. Insecurely upper people, on the other hand, could not readily bring themselves to be self-deprecating.

A quite different form of upper lowerness involves forcing or paying others to look after you (i.e., using upperness to gain lowerness). The person who has slaves or servants to attend upon her/him, to wash, feed, and dress her/him, is being upper lower, as is the person who pays to be waited upon in a restaurant, stays at an expensive hotel, or is indulged in a beauty salon.

UPPER PERSONALITIES

In the DSM III, Axis II, Classification of Personality Disorders (American Psychiatric Association, 1980) there are two personality disorders that are related to upperness. The first is the *antisocial personality: the aggressive pattern*. It was described in Chapter 6 as having both a horizontal and a vertical component, and only the horizontal component was discussed there. The second is the *narcissistic personality: the egotistic pattern*.

The Antisocial Personality

The person with the antisocial personality, also called the psychopath or sociopath, considers her/himself always to have been the victim of the vindictive behavior of others and has no reason to believe that things will change. In consequence s/he feels angry and vengeful; s/he is determined to seize, by fair means or foul, whatever power s/he can in order to prevent this state of affairs from continuing. Having gained such power, however, s/he is even more ruthless and vindictive than others were to her/him. S/he is set on retribution, striking back indiscriminately at society to make it pay for the wrongs s/he considers were done to her/him.

Millon (1981) considered that the DSM III definition of the antisocial personality was too restricted and added the following characteristics: an irascible temper that flares up quickly into argument and attack (reminiscent of Chance's (1984) agonic mode, described in Chapter 2); a rebellious and contemptuous attitude toward authority and tradition; a tendency to enjoy and gain satisfaction from derogating and humiliating others; and a fearless attitude toward danger and punishment.

The Narcissistic Personality

The concept of the narcissistic personality has its origins in psychoanalytic theory. Freud (1905) considered that the adult who has what he called a *phallic character* has been *fixated* at the *phallic stage* of psychosexual development, a stage at which the boy was preoccupied with his penis and the girl with the absence of a penis. The adult male with a phallic character was considered to overvalue his penis and to be vain and exhibitionistic; the adult female was said to be *castrating*, that is striving for superiority over men. The term "*phallic narcissism*" was first introduced by Reich (1933). Krohn (1978) considered it to be organized around wishes to exhibit and be admired in order to avoid feelings of shame and humiliation. Blatt and Shichman (1983) wrote, "The phallic narcissist struggles to demonstrate the power of his intellect and the attractiveness of his body and particularly his genitals in order to defend against the unconscious fears and apprehensions that he will be considered small, insignificant, weak, inadequate and unattractive" (page 232).

Kets de Vries and Miller (1985) considered there to be two types of maladaptive narcissist, which they called the *self-deceptive* and the *reactive*. They explained the origins of these in terms of Kohutian theory (see Chapter 4). The self-deceptive they considered never to have learned to modify their grandiose self-images or their idealized parental images (Kohut, 1978); the reactive they considered to have experienced their parents as being emotionally unresponsive and rejecting (Kohut and Wolf, 1978). The self-deceptive type are driven by a need to live up to unrealistic parental expectations; the reactive type care little about hurting and exploiting others in the pursuit of their own advancement.

Millon (1981) considered that narcissists believe themselves to be so superior that they are entitled to special rights and privileges. They view anyone who fails to respect them with contempt or scorn. They will not own up to having made any errors and react to criticism with rage. Blame is always placed on someone or something else. Solicitous subordinates are the only ones who are tolerated.

The interpersonal relationships of narcissists are generally assumed to be characterized by competitiveness and a callous disregard for the rights and feelings of others. This places them squarely in the position of upper distance. They do, however, become involved in close relationships. In such relationships they soak up the adoration of others and are prepared to love those who adore them. The closeness of the relationship between stars and their fans cannot be denied. Fans love their stars but stars also love their fans. In fact, stars become so addicted to their fans that they cannot give up performing, even when they have made large amounts of money; when stars cease to be popular and lose their fans, they can become extremely depressed.

The Authoritarian Personality

The "authoritarian personality" is a term introduced by Adorno et al. (1950) to explain the behavior of the Nazis during World War II. These authors developed the California F (fascism) Scale, which was intended to be a measure of such a personality (Titus and Hollander, 1957). The scale has been much criticized, particularly by Ray (1981), who pointed out that it incorporates a host of traits - including hostility, punitiveness, being dominant to subordinates and servile to superiors, rigidity, intolerance of ambiguity, ethnocentricity, and political conservatism - that have not experimentally been shown to covary. Ray (1976) also showed that test scores do not significantly correlate with authoritarian behavior.

NEGATIVE FORMS OF UPPERNESS

It is an interesting fact that few of the negative forms of upperness are viewed as forms of psychopathology; instead they are viewed as forms of antisocial or criminal behavior. We respond to psychopathology with concern and sympathy, but we respond to negative upperness with intolerance and anger. This is because we experience it as putting-down behavior.

Giving or Receiving Disrespectfully Imposed Upperness

People are forced into unwelcome and unwanted states of upperness by needful, helpless, and dependent others. Mothers sometimes cannot take to their newborn infants because they cannot bear to be pushed by them into an upper position. The young mother who is left all day and every day to care for small, demanding children comes to suffer from upperness fatigue. It may be the fear of upperness or upperness fatigue that drives some mothers to kill their children. The fatigue of schoolteachers, particularly of young children, is of a similar kind.

Those in relationships with dependent adults commonly, over a period of years, become exasperated and exhausted by their persistent clinging and helpless behavior. They become worn down by repeated requests for reassurances that they will not reject or abandon them. Doctors, nurses, and social workers become similarly exhausted by dependent patients and clients.

Some people who always need to be in control may find that they have maneuvered themselves into a relationship in which they become tired of making all the decisions and sometimes long to have decisions made for *them*, but they find that they have rendered their partners incapable of making such decisions.

People sometimes are pushed into positions of responsibility that they are not capable of handling. According to the *Peter principle*, people eventually become promoted to positions in which they are no longer able to perform competently. Whereas they might have been capable of functioning at the lower level of seniority, they are not capable of doing so at the next level. Gilbert (1992) has used the term *"success depression"* in describing the loss of a sense of belonging by being promoted out of one's in-group.

Insecure Upperness

A person who is insecurely upper will (1) make great show of whatever upperness s/he has by gloating, boasting, or being conceited, arrogant, or pompous; (2) try to confirm it by making suitable comparisons with others; (3) repeatedly test it out by giving commands, maintaining order, offering advice; (4) make (catathetic) taunting, down-putting remarks to rivals; (5) invite (anathetic) complementary remarks from admirers; (6) suppress criticism and surround her/himself with sycophants; (7) be constantly vigilant for rivals who may wish to displace or overthrow her/him; (8) employ spies and guards for protection; (9) avoid competition and eliminate rivals.

One particular form of insecure upperness is fear of failure (Birney et al., 1969). This is either the fear of not succeeding or the fear of losing whatever success has been achieved. It may be due to the fear of loss of approval in someone for whom approval depends upon being successful, or fear of not succeeding in an area that has become the person's primary source of upperness.

Upperness as a Defense against or Denial of Lowerness

Already it has been stated that aspects of both the antisocial and the narcissistic personality disorders can be seen as attempts to defend against or deny lowerness.

Feigned or Exaggerated Upperness. Because upper people are treated with respect, it is common for people to pretend to be more upper than they really are. This they do in a variety of ways, which include borrowing money and living beyond their means; telling lies about their capabilities and accomplishments; going where successful people go, dressing the way they dress, speaking the way they speak, walking the way they walk, and adopting the gestures and mannerisms that they commonly adopt.

Feigned upperness is particularly common in men, since in many cultures, upperness and masculinity are linked and upperness is considered to be a component of male attractiveness (Chapman and Rutherford, 1988). Tabachnick (1961) described how an insecurely upper person is able to gain strength by allowing a weaker person to become dependent upon her/him, and at the same time to gratify her/his own dependency needs by identifying with the dependent person.

Feigned Cheerfulness or Confidence. Since people who are successful appear to be cheerful and confident, assuming a facade of cheerfulness and confidence creates the impression of being successful. People are aware that looking unhappy and unconfident repels others. Thus, there is a universal tendency to present an appearance of cheerful confidence and to deny unhappiness and lack of confidence. Because of this, people feel they are expected always to be happy and confident and as a result, they lose touch with their true feelings.

Mania. Mania essentially is a pathological elevation of mood and as such is not a form of relating; but since delusions of upperness commonly accompany episodes of mania, it must have an association with upperness. Gardner (1982) wrote, "The manic plans, gives, or attempts to lead" (page 1438). Blackburn (1974), using the Hostility and Direction of Hostility Questionnaire (Foulds et al., 1960), observed that manic patients demonstrate high extrapunitive scores, that is, they blame others rather than themselves, though on recovery their extrapunitive scores return to normal. This suggests some kind of denial mechanism.

Manic Defense. Rycroft (1972) defined manic defense as a form of defensive behavior exhibited by persons who defend themselves against anxiety, guilt, and depression by (1) denial of these; (2) the operation of a fantasy of omnipotent control, by means of which they imagine themselves to be in control of all situations that might provoke anxiety or feelings of helplessness; (3) identification with objects (used in the psychoanalytic sense) from whom a sense of power can be borrowed; and (4) projection of bad aspects of the self onto others.

The idea of mania as an escape from or a denial of depression originated with Freud, but it was developed further by Deutsch (1933), Klein, (1934) and Fairbairn (1941). Segal (1964) considered the manic defenses to be of "overwhelming importance" and described them as having three components: (1) control, a denial of dependence; (2) triumph, linked with omnipotence, a denial of depressive feelings associated with the object; and (3) contempt, a denial of the value of the object and further justification for attacking it.

Delusions of Upperness. Wing et al. (1974) described four categories of delusions of upperness: (1) delusions of assistance in which an organization, force, or power is directing the person's life in some advantageous way; (2) delusions of grandiose identity, in which the person believes her/himself to be famous, rich, or titled, or related to a prominent person; (3) delusions of grandiose ability, in which s/he believes s/he has been chosen for a special mission or purpose because of her/his outstanding abilities, or simply that s/he has outstanding abilities; and (4) religious delusions, in which s/he believes her/himself to be Christ, God, a saint, or an angel.

Claiming to Have Extraordinary Powers. People who claim to have extraordinary powers such as telepathy, wizardry, clairvoyance, witchcraft or the power to heal, may be lying, may have convinced themselves on the basis of certain experiences they have had, or may be deluded.

Claiming to Have Had Extraordinary Experiences. People who claim to have had extraordinary experiences such as seeing ghosts or space-craft must also fit somewhere within this category. The motivation seems to be to create a false impression of upperness.

Upperness as a Means of Controlling the Behavior of Others

The upper person, unlike the close, distant, or lower person, is in a position to control the behavior of another or others. This s/he can do either because s/he is physically stronger or because s/he has some hold over them, that is, s/he has the potential for doing them good or doing them harm.

The Need to Be in Control. The person who needs to be in control is afraid to entrust her/himself to others or to allow others to decide how things should be done (fear of lowerness). Everything has to be done her/his way so that s/he knows exactly what is happening and how everything should turn out.

The Use of Upperness to Impose Identity. The person who is ontologically insecure (see Chapter 4) is afraid of the different identity of others. S/he uses her/his upperness to impose her/his own identity and to erode or suppress that of others. S/he cannot tolerate the possibility that s/he may be wrong and is too anxious to listen to what others have to say. If s/he goes along with someone else's opinion or way of doing things, s/he is afraid of losing her/himself in the identity of the other. The conflicts that take place between academic groups who hold contrasting theories arise from this kind of insecurity.

Constructing Upperness. An extension of the inclination to suppress or control the identity of another is the wish to construct an identity in another so that it will conform with that of oneself. Some parents do this to their children, but adults also do it to other adults. A fictional version of it occurs in George Bernard Shaw's play *Pygmalion*, in which a professor of languages tries to make a lady out of a flower seller. The constructer clearly has little respect for the existing identity of the person s/he is constructing and a belief that her/his own identity is superior.

Possessive Upperness. In possessive upperness the possessor uses her/his upperness as a means not only of imposing identity but also of enforcing closeness. S/he may control not only what the other thinks and believes but also what s/he does, what s/he wears, whether s/he goes out, how long s/he stays out, where s/he goes, and whom s/he visits. Although it may be natural for parents sometimes to behave in this way, particularly toward young children, it is an abuse of power for one adult to do so toward another. Such behavior is sometimes a feature of morbid jealousy (see Chapter 5). An extreme and fictional example of it, which is also a metaphor for it, is the man in John Fowles's novel *The Collector*, who captures and imprisons a young woman in a specially constructed house from which she cannot escape, in the hope that in time she may come to like him.

Intrusive Upperness. In intrusive upperness one person attempts to force her/his way into the personal space, body, or psychic interior of another. Breaking into another's property, rape, and the sexual abuse of children are examples of the first two of these. Examples of the third include denying the other a right to have secrets, trying to read her/his thoughts, or trying to put ideas into her/his head.

Overprotectiveness. All parents must be protective, but as the child becomes more capable the protection must be gradually withdrawn. Some parents, due either to their own anxieties or to an excessive need to hold on to the child, continue to be protective long after it is appropriate. This creates a child who cannot do anything for itself.

Compulsive Care Giving. This is a term introduced by Bowlby (1980) to describe the behavior of a person who is drawn to those who need to be helped. The compulsive caregiver only feels right when giving care and finds it hard to seek or receive help from others. Bowlby proposed that this is due to having been coerced during childhood into caring for an infirm or hypochondriacal parent. Compulsive caregiving may also be a means of denying one's own needfulness. Krell and Miles (1976), working with medical couples, observed that physicians commonly are able to dissociate themselves from any part they might play in the marital disturbance and are able to convince their partners that it is they who are ill and need treatment.

Abuse of Upperness for Personal Gain

Exploitation. Exploitation involves compelling others to work long and hard for minimal reward. This is possible because they have no other source of income and could not get other work. Slavery is a form of exploitation. Slaves can be made to work until they die of exhaustion or starvation. In well-developed industrial societies most forms of exploitation are illegal, though when levels of unemployment are high, the temptation for employer's to exploit those who work for them becomes considerable. People who are unaware of their rights are easily exploited. Altman (1979) pointed to an interconnectedness between the exploitation of man by man and the exploitation of nature.

Withholding Information. The negative activity of withholding information contrasts with the positive activity of imparting information. The withholder is aware that s/he has information that the other needs but deliberately chooses not to impart it as a means of maintaining power. Certain insecure teachers, who are reluctant to see their pupils prosper, may withhold some information, which makes it difficult for their pupils to understand. This they may do by not explaining what certain words mean or leaving out steps in an explanatory sequence. Employees may behave in a similar way toward a new work-mate: they may not reveal all the rules, not explain how things are done, where things are kept, how certain machines work. Professional jargon can provide a means of maintaining group cohesiveness, but it can also be used as a means of gaining an advantage over those who do not understand it.

Mystification. This is a term used by Laing and Esterson (1964) to describe what they considered the parents of certain schizophrenics did. Their opinion was that the parental behavior contributed to the schizophrenic breakdown. In their efforts to deny or conceal something they did not wish to admit, parents would tell the child that something was not true even though the child could see that it was. Because the child could not believe that her/his parents would lie to her/him, s/he began to doubt her/his own judgments. Whether or not this is a cause of schizophrenia, it is certainly a way that some parents and other upper people behave. It is similar to what has been called by Barton and Whitehead (1969) and Smith and Sinanan (1972) *the gaslight phenomenon*: one marital partner tries to convince the other that s/he is going mad by contriving to confuse her/him, by denying that certain things have been happening, which, in fact obviously have been happening. The phenomenon is named after Patrick Hamilton's play *Gaslight* (first performed in London in 1939, and later made into a film) in which a husband did this to his wife.

The process of mystification is featured in other works of fiction. In Kafka's sadistic play *The Trial* the central character is not told the nature of the offense for which he is to be tried. Pinter has introduced it into a number of his plays, notably *The Birthday Party*.

Megalomania. Children are attracted by stories of mad scientists who aspire to become master of the universe. Despite the fact that the mad scientists always get defeated, the stories may reflect a deep-seated power lust in us, which we repress as we assume the more responsible attitudes of adulthood. In some adults, the power lust resurfaces. To some extent power is an expansion of the identity. Certain megalomaniacs, like Napoleon and Hitler, expanded their empires to cover ever larger areas of the earth's surface. In industrial societies, megalomaniacs expand their business empires by taking over increasing numbers of companies and increasing their wealth.

Tyranny. Tyranny is the ruthless and remorseless control of another or others. The tyrant lacks any sense of fairness or justice and simply makes use of others to further her/his own ends. There is much in her/his behavior that is reminiscent of the omnipotent, grandiose infant (Kohut, 1971). Others are experienced as self-objects, that is extensions of her/his own self-system, like characters in her/his dreams. S/he has expectations that her/his every wish will be met and it is inconceivable to her/him that others will disobey her/him. If they do s/he may respond with what Kohut called *narcissistic rage*. This is a blind fury that knows no bounds. A tyrant may operate within a family system, in which all family members must learn to accommodate themselves to her/his will; within an organization; or within a country. A tyrant of a country has to construct a complex, controlling, hierarchical structure, with lesser tyrants imposing and enforcing her/his will and ensuring her/his safety.

Suppression. Suppression is an essential component of tyranny. It is as much a feature of a family controlled by a tyrannical member as of a totalitarian regime. There is only one truth: the official truth as proclaimed by the tyrant. Contrary opinion is disallowed. All publications are censored, and all who criticize the tyrant are punished.

Brainwashing. Brainwashing is another device of totalitarian regimes by which - through the process of humiliation, ridicule, and degradation - former beliefs, opinions, and values are discredited and the opinions of the regime are imposed and reinforced. Sargant (1957) has likened brainwashing to the processes of eliciting confessions and religious conversion and has pointed to similarities in the procedures used. It is a malign version of constructing upperness, described earlier.

Becoming Upper at the Expense of the Others's Lowerness

Gaining upperness at the expense of the lowerness of another or others would seem to be a a straightforward and satisfactory route to upperness. Animals are quick to take advantage of the deficiencies of others, and such behavior may be relatively common in certain primitive societies; but in civilized societies (1) it may be prohibited by law, (2) it may be strongly disapproved of, so that people are deterred from doing it by social pressures, and (3) people have an internal sense of morality, fairness, or decency, reinforced to varying extents by internalized authority figures, which prevents them from doing it or which causes them to feel guilty about doing it. Civilized people do find ways around such restraints and inhibitions; these will be discussed under the appropriate headings.

Undermining the Others's Confidence. There is a broad range of strategies, both obvious and subtle, for undermining the confidence of another. They include direct criticism, making unfavorable comparisons with others, ignoring her/his abilities and successes and pointing only to her/his shortcomings, praising others in her/his company, treating her/him in a condescending and patronizing manner, granting others favors and advantages, withholding vital information, and denying her/him necessary facilities.

Feldman (1976) described a strategy adopted by the marital partners of some depression-prone individuals. The partner makes an apparently innocent remark, which just happens to strike at a particularly sensitive spot in the other's shaky sense of self worth. This has the effect of precipitating the other into depression. In response to this the partner switches to the defensive role of protector and rescuer. Feldman speculates that the partners of such individuals are afraid of their success, and consequently, periodically resort to confidence-undermining strategies for keeping them weak.

Smugly Feeling Sorry For. Feeling sorry for has been included under caring as a positive form of upperness. It can however, tip into negative upperness if it assumes a smug and gloating quality. Pitying can be similarly abused.

Derision. Children more than adults laugh at the misfortune of others and, in their laughing, experience the state of upperness. In former times, adults would visit lunatic asylums to laugh at the inmates, but nowadays they do not so blatantly enjoy the misfortune of others. Ridicule and mocking are nonetheless ways of experiencing upperness at the expense of others, and many jokes and humorous stories relate accounts of other people in unfortunate circumstances.

Clowns and professional comics pretend to be stupid or in disastrous situations so that people will laugh at them. Perhaps it is because people know the clowns are only pretending that they are able to allow themselves to laugh at them. In general, laughter is generated by guilt; people laugh because they become aware of their wish to see others slipping into lowerness. They tend not to laugh when they perceive others to be in serious difficulties.

Humiliation. There is ample evidence that people derive pleasure from humiliating others, but, as with derision, they are inhibited from doing so by their consciences. Schoolteachers sometimes humiliate their pupils; nurses, particularly psychiatric nurses, sometimes humiliate their patients. Those in charge of prisoners feel justified in humiliating them because they are able to convince themselves that prisoners are inferior or that humiliation is part of the punishment. The more extreme forms of humiliation, include deprivation of privacy, forced stripping, denial of cleanliness, and being spat at and urinated upon. Humiliation is also an important component of rape (Groth et al. 1977).

Bullying. The term "bullying" is applied predominantly to children (Tattum, 1989). A child who experiences her/himself as relatively lower in certain respects discovers that s/he is physically stronger. By bullying s/he is able to gain valuable experiences of upperness which can quickly compensate for these deficiencies. When they are corrected, the bullying usually stops.

Intimidation. Intimidation is the adult version of bullying. In intimidation the normal upper to lower exchanges between adults break down and one adult elects to impose her/his will upon another by violence or the threat of violence. The intimidator experiences her/himself as deficient in bargaining resources and falls back upon the one resource of which s/he feels confident. The intimidator, like the exploiter or the manipulator, adopts a particularly distant form of relating and treats the other as though s/he were a thing. Relating by intimidation resembles that of animals in hierarchies (see Chapter 2) as the intimidator puts out periodic down-hierarchy catathetic signals.

Racism. Racism involves declaring or believing a particular racial group to be inferior, denying its members certain rights and privileges, persecuting them ,and in extreme instances, systematically exterminating them. Racism is linked with *eugenics* and, as such, is concerned with identity. It involves preserving and purifying one selected racial group. In Nazi Germany, propaganda was directed toward equating one particular racial group, the Jews, with a particularly feared and disliked animal, rats, which made it easier to hate and be cruel to them (Dawidowicz, 1975). In extreme instances racism leads to *genocide*. Lifton (1986) described how Nazi doctors justified carrying out genocide on the Jews by euphemistically referring to it as the "Final Solution."

Despising. Despising applies more to an individual than to a group. It is a conviction that the individual is vile or evil; such feeling may be based upon some unpleasant act or behavior committed by that individual. Despising is closely related to hating (though hating does not contain the same degree of upperness), and both kinds of feeling convey an element of anger. Many reasonable people are not prepared to despise anyone, and this confirms its negative quality.

Cruelty and Torture. Children, because their socialization process is less complete, are capable of great cruelty under certain circumstances. William Golding's novel *Lord of the Flies*, though a work of fiction, credibly illustrates this. Bandura et al. (1975) demonstrated that two effective means of making cruelty possible were diffusion of responsibility and dehumanization. They wrote, "By displacing responsibility elsewhere, people need not hold themselves accountable for what they do and are thus spared self-prohibiting reactions" (page 255). They found that experimental subjects meted out higher voltage electric shocks to those who had first been disparaged. In Milgram's (1974) experiments, subjects were prepared to administer what they believed to be fatal shocks when their experimenter told them to do so; Milgram maintained that most acts of inhumanity are carried out by ordinary people doing what they are told. Haney et al. (1973) showed that when students randomly were allocated the role of jailer, they readily devised ways of humiliating and intimidating the students who were allocated the role of prisoner. Haritos-Faroutos (1988) described how torturers sometimes are subjected to a process of gradual induction, by first acting as guards while others conduct the torture, then performing acts of moderate brutality, and finally being instructed to participate fully.

Sadism. As was made clear in Chapter 1, the satisfactory attainment of any state of relatedness should give rise to pleasure. Because of the various forms of social disapproval, it is difficult to accept that cruelty could give rise to pleasure. In sadism such pleasure is more openly acknowledged. It is important to distinguish between imposed and agreed sadism. Some forms of imposed sadism are extremely unpleasant and can be carried out only by very disturbed people. Agreed sadism is sometimes a feature of sexual behavior. Stoller (1979) expressed the extreme view that there is a sadistic element to all sexual excitement and that the absence of the desire to harm leads to sexual indifference. In the sexual encounter sadism and masochism are inextricably linked. It is normally understood that the cruelty will be contained within tolerable limits and commonly it is embellished by fantasy. For some the pleasure of cruelty is not sexual. Rarely the sexual arousal associated with sadism can lead to vicious crimes.

In the DSM-R, Axis II, Classification of Personality Disorders (American Psychiatric Association, 1987) there is a category called the *Sadistic Personality* which is characterised by a pervasive pattern of cruel, demeaning, and aggressive behavior directed toward other people.

Violence and Destructiveness. In order to be violent or destructive it is necessary first to have upperness (i.e., physical strength or weaponry), but violence and destructiveness are a means toward further upperness. Like bullying and intimidation, they are a way of cutting across conventional forms of upperness. A man with minimal status can shoot down the president with a gun or destroy a powerful computer with a bomb. Because these acts can upset the delicate balance of society's carefully constructed hierarchies, they are invariably illegal and carry heavy penalties.

A number of theories exist to explain how humans are able to behave in a violent or destructive manner. Freud (1933) believed that there were two classes of instinct: the *life instinct* and the *death instinct*. Both he considered to be initially directed toward the self, but later to be directed toward others. If, he maintained, the hostility generated by the death instinct is not periodically released, it results in dangerous acts of violence. Lorenz (1974) believed there to be a *fighting instinct*, common to all animal species; and Rushton (1988) believe that since aggressiveness carries such social advantages it has become an integral component of animal behavior. A number of social psychologists, notably Berkowitz (1989), have adopted what they call the *frustration-aggression hypothesis*. They believe that external frustrations lead to the arousal of a drive whose primary goal is the harming of some person or object. The drive leads particularly to attacks upon the source of the frustration. Acts of violence and destructiveness commonly occur under the influence of alcohol, which suggests that violent inclinations are constantly present but normally suppressed.

A distinction should be drawn between calculated and reactive violence. In *calculated violence*, a person, group, or nation chooses to use violence to achieve a particular end. In *reactive violence*, the violence is more likely to be a response to frustration. Violence may be directed toward one specific, person, group, or nation in order to attain a specific objective or it may be randomly directed, simply because the person is feeling angry.

Family Violence. Family violence is alarmingly common. Each year in the United States six million men, women, and children are the victims of severe physical attack by partners, parents, siblings, or children (Straus et al., 1980) and nearly one quarter of all murders are committed by family members (Curtis, 1974). Most family violence is inflicted by a physically strong family member upon a physically weaker one. Violence is a quick, though desperate, way of gaining upperness and is resorted to if the attacker cannot get her/his own way by any other means. Physically stronger family members are also able to exert control by the threat of violence, and physically weaker members comply in order to avoid violence.

Parent-to-child violence ranges from what might be called the calculated violence of using violence to impose and maintain order to the reactive violence that occurs when the parent becomes angry or frustrated by the child. Not infrequently the one merges into the other. The most frequently physically abused children are those between three months and three years of age (Galdston, 1965). Children, especially adolescents (Cornell-Pedrick and Gelles, 1982), are capable of being violent toward their parents. Husbands are violent toward their wives because they are bigger, stronger, and more aggressive and because their wives are prepared to stay with them despite their violence (Gelles, 1976). Some husbands are violent toward their wives because they believe they have a right to be (Straus, 1974); and some wives, incredibly, share this view (Gelles, 1974). Violence occurs toward the elderly because they are frail and defenseless; the older they are, the more likely they are to be violently abused (Bergman et al., 1980).

Hooliganism/Vandalism. Hooligans and vandals behave in a violent and destructive manner toward people and property for a variety of reasons (Gibbens, 1970). Their behavior enables them to feel effective and powerful when otherwise they may not. It is a way at getting back at society; therefore it contains an element of vengeance. It is also linked with envy. Berke (1987) referred to the *envious thief*, who breaks into a house predominantly to damage and defile it. Gilbert (1992) expressed the destructively envious attitude as "If I can't have it then I will destroy it so that others can't" (page 247).

Terrorism. Terrorists, like hooligans, resort to violent and destructive acts because they feel ineffective and powerless. Small and strategically placed acts of appalling horror draw attention to their cause and bring pressure to bear upon governments. Their use of detonated explosive devices enables them to remain distanced from the cruelty that they inflict.

Warfare. In warfare an entire nation behaves in a violent and destructive manner toward another. The normal restrictions on killing and violation are lifted, and quite ordinary people find themselves capable of behaving savagely toward their fellow men. This reveals how readily our violent propensities can be released. For an extensive review of this, see Durant (1981). As with racism and torture, approval to be violent and destructive is freely offered by the state; the enemy is devalued and dehumanized by state propaganda.

Criminal Behavior

Laws are imposed to ensure that people behave fairly toward each other, and those who behave unfairly are caught and punished. Criminals attempt to gain upperness by unfair, and therefore unlawful, means. This they do largely by obtaining money or possessions, which become a source of upperness for them. Like the bully, they compensate for any lack of conventional forms of upperness (e.g., earning capacity) by resorting to physical violence or use of weapons either to attack or intimidate others or to break into property. There are close associations between criminality and the paranoid and psychopathic personalities. Many criminals are sensitive to any suggestion of personal insult, to which they are liable to respond with destructive rage.

Reactions to the Absence or Loss of Upperness

Hopelessness. Hopelessness is to the vertical dimension what loneliness is to the horizontal dimension. The hopeless person aspires to upperness but sees no way of attaining it. As with loneliness, certain kinds of individual are considered to be more prone to hopelessness. These include those who either are (Schotte and Clum, 1982) or consider themselves to be (Bonner and Rich, 1988) poor problem solvers. Writers such as Alloy et al. (1988) and Abramson et al. (1989) have proposed a separate category of depression called *hopeless depression.* Hopelessness has been shown to be a powerful predictor of suicide behavior (Dyer and Kreitman, 1984; Beck et al., 1985).

Depression. The term *"ranking theory"* was introduced recently by Gilbert (1992) to cover the various explanations of depression in terms of holding low social status or losing social status. Price (1967) was one of the earliest to think in these terms. He (1968) proposed that "neurotic depression evolved as the behaviour appropriate to low ranking members of the hierarchy, while endogenous depression evolved as the behaviour appropriate to members falling in the hierarchy" (page 119). Although the first of his hypotheses has received little support, the second has been taken up by a number of writers (see Gilbert, 1992). Beck (1983) adopted the term *"autonomous depression"* to refer to the kind of depression developed by the autonomous personality type (see Chapter 3). He considered it to be more common in men than in women and to be permeated with the theme of defeat or failure. He likened it to the condition of *learned helplessness* as described by Seligman (1975). The patient, he claimed, believes that he has failed in his attempt to reach a crucial goal, blames himself for falling below his standards, and excoriates himself for his incompetence. He appears immobile, powerless, and devoid of initiative. Beck should have drawn a distinction between depression resulting from failure and that resulting from defeat. What he has described is the former, which is a lack, or loss, of personal achievement.

Depression resulting from defeat is a lack, or loss, of competitive achievement. The distinction between personal and competitive achievement was made at the beginning of the chapter. Price and Sloman (1987) were concerned more with depression resulting from defeat. They described it as losing in interpersonal conflict, strictly comparable with yielding in the ritual agonistic encounter (see Chapter 2). Later, Price (1991) described depression as the process of accommodating to an involuntary one-down position. His view of depression therefore is one of submission, which is in accord with the observation that aggression is suppressed in depression (Cochrane and Neilson, 1977; Riley et al., 1989). Since depression results from failure to attain any state of relatedness (see Chapter 1), there clearly is a causal connection between depression and failure to attain, or the denial of a state of upperness; but since vertical interactions are far more complex than the simple ritual agonistic encounters of animals, the mechanisms underlying what might be called *vertical depression* (in contrast to horizontal depression, which was described in Chapter 5) are also likely to be complex.

SUMMARY

Two important things to note about upperness are that (1) it assumes many forms, and (2) it is a relative term. When referring to upperness it is necessary to specify which form is being considered and with whom the person is being compared. The many forms of upperness ensure that everyone has ways of deriving the satisfactions of being upper. Whether in relation to another or to a group, a person may be upper in some respects and not in others. Therefore it is not always easy to say, in any absolute sense, who is upper to whom. Upperness frequently involves having the power to influence another or others, and such influence may be beneficial or harmful. Humans, far more than other animals, use their upperness for the benefit of others; most forms of positive upperness are beneficial. Such benefit is not necessarily one-way, however, and normally one form of upperness is exchanged for another. People's capacity for upperness is derived from personal attributes or from acquired skills and experience. Money has become a convenient way of packaging upperness. Status is the acknowledged social position of someone within a group or community. It is conveyed by certain forms of upper behavior and reinforced by the lower behavior of others. Upperness may be gained actively through ambitious striving or passively through the need, acclaim, or promotion of others. It assumes a broad range of functions reflecting the processes of a complex society.

Upper lowerness involves having the humility to acknowledge the limitations of ones upperness and be prepared to assume, when necessary, the lower position in relation to others. There are three main types of upper personality: the antisocial, the narcissistic, and the authoritarian. There is a broad range of negative forms of upperness. These are grouped under the following headings: giving or receiving disrespectfully imposed upperness; insecure upperness; upperness as a defense against or denial of lowerness; upperness as a means of controlling the behavior of others; the abuse of upperness for personal gain; criminal behavior; becoming upper at the expense of the other's lowerness; and reactions to the absence or loss of upperness.

8

Lowerness

Just as distance is not simply the absence of closeness, lowerness is not simply the absence of upperness. It is as important and as essential to well-being as the other three main positions, and it has its own benefits and satisfactions. In the rest of the animal kingdom, the advantages of lowerness are of two kinds: being fed, protected, and reared by parents; and gaining food, protection, and safety from occupying the lower ranks in a hierarchy. In animal species in which there is no parenting of young and there is no hierarchical structure, there are no advantages to lowerness at all. Lowerness has become much more extensively developed in humans than in any other species, but even in humans it has developed out of the two conditions of being parented and of occupying the lower ranks of the hierarchy.

In humans, being parented has assumed importance because the child remains within the parental home for so long that it becomes accustomed to having someone to look up to and rely upon. Mahler (1963) drew attention to Freud's aphorism that a lifelong, albeit diminishing, emotional dependence upon the mother is a universal truth of human existence. The same could be said of dependence upon the father; but whereas what we are seeking in a mother figure is more expressive, what we are seeking in a father figure is more instrumental (Parsons and Bales, 1955).

As was explained in Chapter 2, human hierarchies are far less rigid structures than animal ones and occupying the lower ranks is a far less easily definable condition. Because of the immense complexity of human societies, everyone is dependent upon a wide range of people for many provisions and services. The more complex the society, the greater the necessity for lowerness.

LOWERNESS AND NEEDFULNESS

One definition of lowerness is needing that which others have. The lower person is a needful person, but s/he should not be ashamed of being needful, for unless her/his needs are met s/he cannot function effectively. It is essential therefore that s/he recognize what her/his needs are and seek out ways of meeting them. This s/he can do only by entering into a lower-to-upper relationship with an appropriately upper person or organization. The excessively self-reliant individual (see Chapter 6) has needs but chooses not to have them met; in consequence, s/he is compelled to adopt a restricted life-style.

Accepting Welfare, Charity or Aid

In many western societies welfare or charity are made available for the poor or the disabled. Many underdeveloped countries accept aid from the more affluent countries. Most needful lower persons willingly and gratefully accept welfare or charity, and most underdeveloped countries accept aid. Some resist because it emphasizes their one-down position. They do not like to be felt sorry for. They resist because they have their pride. Pride is an important condition. It is a state of upperness within lowerness and is linked with self-reliance. Nations also have pride. A person may choose to swallow her/his pride in order to allow her/himself to accept her/his needfulness and accept charity.

THE RECEPTIVE QUALITY OF MUCH LOWER BEHAVIOR

In an earlier formulation of the present theory (Birtchnell, 1987), the lower pole of the vertical dimension was called *receptiveness*. This was derived from Fromm's (1947) *receptive orientation*, a character type who believed that "the source of all good" was outside and that the only way to get what s/he wants was to receive it from an outside source. Though the term "receptiveness" was abandoned in favor of the spatial term "lowerness," it is important to bear in mind that there is a markedly receptive quality to lowerness. Whereas upperness predominantly is an active form of relating (the upper person predominantly *relates to* others), lowerness predominantly is a passive form of relating (the lower person predominantly *is related to by* others). During the initiation phase of interrelating (see Chapter 1) in which the upper person predominantly (actively) *proposes* a form of relating, the lower person predominantly (passively) *invites* it.

Because of the receptive quality of lowerness, many of the characteristics of lowerness are the passive equivalents of the characteristics of upperness (i.e., being informed, taught, led, advised, helped, cared for, judged, punished, forgiven, etc). There would be little point in discussing each of these again. Instead, only those characteristics that have particular importance in their lower form will be considered.

THE PARADOX OF SOME FORMS OF LOWERNESS

In many positive upper-to-lower interactions (i.e., those in which neither person is relating in a negative way) the lower person is gaining from what the upper one is providing. That is, the differential between the upper and the lower person is diminishing, because the lower person is acquiring some of the upper person's upperness. This is particularly so in leading, guiding, imparting information, teaching skills, helping, rescuing, nursing, and helping to get better. An especially paradoxical form of lowerness occurs when, as is often the case, the lower person is promoted by the upper person. Sometimes the differential is restored by the lower person recompensing the upper person by the payment of money, but often it is not. Why is the upper person prepared to give away some of her/his upperness in this way? First, in interactions of this kind, what the upper person is giving is not so great as to seriously alter the differential, second, there is little likelihood of the lower person using what s/he has been given to turn the tables on the upper person (though occasionally this does occur), and third, the experience of giving serves to confirm the upper person in her/his upperness.

Examples of the lower person turning the tables on the upper one may occur during chronic feuding in some marital relationships. A tyrannical partner may go through a difficult patch, which evokes the sympathetic and caring response of the other. When restored to her/his former strength, s/he may revert to her/his tyrannical behavior. The parable is sometimes told of the woman who finds an ailing poisonous snake. She takes it home and warms it by her fire. When it is well she clutches it to her bosom and it bites her. As she lies dying she asks it why it bit her and it replies, "But you knew I was a poisonous snake."

THE VULNERABILITY OF THE LOWER PERSON

In an upper-to-lower interaction the upper person often is, to use Bowlby's (1977) term, stronger and/or wiser, and is therefore in a position to do harm to the lower one. The parent can kill the child, the informer can give incorrect information, the guide can lead the person astray, the pilot can crash the plane, the commanding officer can direct his troops into an enemy ambush, the bank manager can make unwise investments and lose the client's money, the rescue worker can let go of the rope, the motor mechanic can make the engine even more unreliable than before, the doctor can make the patient sicker. Therefore, adopting a lower position in relation to an upper one frequently carries an element of risk. Because the benefits of lowerness are so great, that risk usually is considered to be worth taking; in fact, such risk may sometimes contribute to the excitement of lowerness. It will be recalled (see Chapter 5) that there is also an element of risk in entering into a close relationship. Just as people who have been let down (betrayed) in earlier close relationships are reluctant to allow themselves to get close to others, so people who have been let down in earlier lower relationships are reluctant to allow themselves to be in a lower position in relation to others. Bowlby (1973b) concluded that the mature adult needs, at times, to have the capacity to rely trustingly on others, and at other times to be able to allow others to rely trustingly upon her/him.

TRUST

Although trust plays an important part in close relating, it plays a fundamental part in lower relating. A person will not adopt a (positive) lower attitude toward another without feeling trustful, but humans are quite attuned to being trustful. In a sense, in common with all other animals, we have a lower (trusting) relationship with nature. We take it on trust that the laws of nature will hold; that apples, for example, always will fall off trees. This provides us with a sense of security. In fact, nature is not entirely trustworthy. We trust that the ground will not give way beneath our feet, but when there is an earthquake it does. We trust that the rain will fall and the plants will grow, but when there is a drought it does not and the plants die. It is the sense of lowerness in relation to nature that forms the basis of many primitive religions.

In a complex, modern society we have similar trusts. We trust that water and gas will flow from our taps; electricity will flow when we turn the switch; our telephones will work; there will be radio and television programs; there will be food in the shops; the garbage will be collected; the repair man will come and fix the elevator, the air conditioning, or the refrigerator when they break down; an ambulance will come when we phone for one. We trust that the government will run the country responsibly, the financiers will control the economy, the armed forces will defend us when we are attacked, the judges will make sound judgments, the police will maintain order, the doctors will make us better. There are countries, and times at which, these things cannot be taken on trust.

ASCERTAINMENT OF TRUSTWORTHINESS

The ascertainment of the trustworthiness of the upper person can be a matter of importance to the lower person. It may be based upon sound criteria such as professional qualifications, position in society, belonging to an organization that guarantees the reliability of its members, reputation, or recommendation by friends; or upon uncertain cues such as appearance, gestures, or way of talking. Confidence tricksters make a living out of intentionally deceiving others, and the intentional deceit of tradespeople and repairpeople is well acknowledged. Hence the old cliche: "Would you buy a second-hand car from this man?" There must be an assessment of trustworthiness of the other, similar to the assessment of RHP in the ritual agonistic encounter, or an assessment of relative dominance (Kalma, 1991), as described in Chapter 2. There must be cues or signals of trustworthiness put out by the potential trustee conveying that the truster can safely to entrust her/himself to her/him.

RELYING UPON

The lower person frequently needs to *rely upon* someone who, in some important respect, is upper to her/him. It must be emphasized that needing to rely upon someone, however great the reliance may be, is not a maladaptive form of behavior. People who write about dependence imply that moderate degrees of dependence are acceptable but that extreme degrees are pathological. The difference between adaptive and maladaptive behavior is qualitative not quantitative; being pathological is not synonymous with being extreme (Birtchnell, 1991a). Because dependence is so linked with maladaptiveness (see subsequent discussion of the dependent personality) it is preferable to use the term "being reliant upon" when considering positive forms of relating. The newly born infant is reliant upon its parents. A person on a life support system is reliant upon the team of people who are operating it. A pilot in dense fog is reliant upon the radar system that is guiding her/him. A person who cannot speak the language is reliant upon an interpreter. The person who is reliant upon another person has to be trusting of that person, who therefore carries a heavy responsibility.

LOWERNESS AND THE NEED TO BE LIKED

Upper people do things for lower people for a variety of reasons. Toward the distant end of lowerness they do them because they have been made to by someone higher still (a higher authority) or because the lower person has paid them to do so. Toward the close end they do them because they feel well disposed toward the lower person. The need to keep on the right side of the upper person is therefore often an important consideration for the lower person. S/he has to be careful not to offend the upper person; if s/he does, s/he has to apologize in order to regain the upper person's favor. The picture is complicated further by the fact that closeness may be the commodity that the lower person needs of the upper person, and one of the greatest fears of the lower close person can therefore be fear of rejection (see subsequent discussion).

LOWERNESS IN PSYCHOTHERAPY

In Chapter 5 the closeness component of psychotherapy was discussed, but in most forms of psychotherapy there is also an important lowerness component. The patient is lower anyway because of her/his needfulness, but beyond this, in many psychotherapeutic procedures, with varying degrees of intentionality, the therapist imposes a state of lowerness upon the patient. In classical psychoanalysis, this is facilitated by requiring the patient to lie on a couch. The therapist conveys the message, "You may relax; you are safe with me." Because there are few opportunities in society for adults to unashamedly adopt such a complete state of lowerness, and because lowerness is so gratifying, this is beneficial in itself; but it is also the setting within which many forms of psychotherapy are conducted.

A particularly important form of lowerness is called *regression*. This involves reversion to an earlier state or mode of functioning. Freud (1915b) maintained that early stages of development persist and are imbricated in later developmental phases. They remain available as alternative modes of functioning. Giovacchini (1990) observed that "Regression regularly occurs during analysis and is an essential feature of the treatment process" (page 261). The argument goes that it enables the analyst to gain access to early phases and levels of development in order to facilitate reorganization of the personality in a new pattern. Regression occurs only because the analyst is able to hold and support the patient within the security of the analytic session. There are two possible forms of regression: (1) the patient returns to the blissful state in infancy of being soothingly held by the parent; or (2) the patient who never had such an experience is able to experience something approaching it in relation to the analyst. Whichever it is, the danger remains that the patient may come to like it so much that s/he will keep coming back for more.

Regression is also included by Anna Freud (1949) as one of the ego's mechanisms of defense. This can be understood only in terms of Sigmund Freud's (1905) psychosexual stages of development. In the face of conflicts over wishes of the phallic stage, the individual may give up her/his phallic wishes and regress, say, to the anal stage and remain fixated there.

RELAXATION

Relaxation is a technique developed by behavior therapists (Poppen, 1988) for reducing anxiety and muscular tension. It could be suggested that what it amounts to is a highly simplified form of regression (therefore of positive lowerness). The patient is invited to lie on a bed or sit in a chair; at the suggestion of the therapist who speaks to her/him in a soothing voice, the patient contracts and relaxes the muscles in different parts of her/his body. Sometimes, additionally, s/he is invited to imagine her/himself walking through a beautiful landscape or entering a peaceful garden.

HYPNOSIS

Hypnosis is related to relaxation, and sometimes relaxation extends into hypnosis, but it is much more obviously a state of lowerness. Hypnosis occurs more readily in a state of relaxation. French (1984), a skilled and experienced hypnotist, maintained that hypnosis is contributed to as much by the person who is hypnotiZed as by the hypnotist, and that what the person expects will happen does happen. The subject is entirely aware of what is taking place and has the capacity to resist, but somehow chooses not to. Hypnosis seems to have a direct influence upon the subcortex. This is particularly apparent with what is called *post hypnotic suggestion*. In this, an instruction is given to perform a particular action hours, or sometimes days, later. A the appointed time, the subject finds her/himself, at a cortical level, needing to concoct a reason for performing the action. This closely ties in with Groddeck's (1923) concept of man feeling that he is being lived by the It (see Chapter 1). The general consensus is that hypnotic induction procedures do not enable subjects to transcend their normal capabilities, and all tasks carried out under hypnosis have been shown to be performable by nonhypnotized subjects, given appropriate instructions (Wagstaff, 1986).

BEING PARENTED

Since lowerness in humans appears to have developed out of the condition of being parented, it is helpful to describe the main characteristics of lowerness in terms of those parenting experiences out of which they might have developed. Many parenting experiences also form part of the religious experience.

The Security of a Roof

It is disturbing to conceive of there being nothing but space above us. Although there are sound practical reasons for putting roofs on buildings, roofs also have a reassuring psychological effect. The expression "a roof over one's head" means more than having something to keep out the rain.

Being Protected

Having the protection of the armed forces and the police already has been mentioned. The young animal and the child looks (up) to the parent as a source of protection against predators and attackers. Older siblings commonly assume the role of protector to the younger ones. In some primate colonies a female will position herself in front of a high-ranking male, from which vantage point she will threaten a subordinate. This was called by Kummer (1987) *protected threat*. In a number of cultures the husband, being physically stronger, serves as a protector of his wife. In human relating people sometimes stay close to stronger others for protecting them or have hired protectors called *bodyguards*. Feeling protected is profoundly reassuring. Edna O'Brien, the Irish novelist, when asked for her idea of perfect happiness, replied, "Someone to watch over me" (*Weekend Guardian*, August 29-30, 1992).

Being Sheltered from Responsibility

The child is not concerned about how the family came to have a house, furniture, or other possessions, or where the clothes or the food come from, and does not need to know about family finance and insurance. It gets taken to and picked up from school, and holidays simply happen. Though it does not realize it at the time, this is part of the bliss of being a child. In human society there are many parallels to this. Governments, local councils, and boards of management take care of organizational matters. Only a small number of experts need know about how cities are planned, buildings are built, transport services are organized, mail is delivered, sewage is disposed of, computers, machines, automobiles, television, and telephones work. In the workplace the bosses take control and make the decisions, the workforce simply do their job and draw their wages.

Being relieved of responsibility has such appeal that many commercial organizations offer it as a positive incentive in the services they offer. They use expressions such as "Leave everything to us," "Let us do the worrying for you," or "Everything will be taken care of."

Being Told What To Do

The small child, who has a close and trusting relationship with its parents will, to a considerable extent, do what it is told. This is because (1) it has no clearly developed ideas about what it wants to do, and (2) it assumes that the parents know best and are not likely to tell it to do something that would cause it harm. As it grows older it may come to like doing certain things (the beginnings of autonomy) and may disobey if its parents tell it not to do them or tell it to do different things. Thereafter the parents may, as far as is safe and reasonable, begin to encourage it to do the things it likes doing (building up its sense of autonomy). Alternatively, they may continue to give commands and reinforce them, either by threatening punishment if it disobeys or being loving if it obeys and showing disappointment if it disobeys. In later life the child who has been encouraged to be autonomous will be disinclined to obey instructions unless they correspond with what it wants to do, and the child trained to be obedient will be lost and confused unless given clear instructions about what it should and should not do.

Beyond these general tendencies, the responsible citizen is willing to obey commands given by people who are recognized as having authority in their respective fields, . This s/he does because s/he assumes that they know what they are doing and that what they are telling her/him to do is sensible, useful, or necessary. Milgram's (1974) experiments have shown that under the right circumstances, people are capable of being extraordinarily and unquestioningly obedient. Orne (1962) showed that some people will agree to continue to perform absolutely pointless tasks when instructed to do so. One group of subjects was given a large stack of sheets of paper covered with random digits and told to perform additions. The experimenter went away for over five hours and found the work still in progress upon his return. Obeying commands can at times be a pleasurable experience (e.g., soldiers on parade) and people join highly disciplined organizations (e.g., the armed services) because they prefer to do what they are told rather than make up their own minds and take responsibility for their decisions.

The satisfaction and sense of security of being obedient to a powerful authority figure contributes to the appeal of religion, religious orders, and religious sects. Jesus instructed His disciples to "Follow me." The terms "follower" and "a following" are applied to groups that are led by a charismatic leader. The passive obedience of members of religious sects sometimes can be extreme, as was evidenced by the mass suicide in Jonestown, Guyana.

Having Things Done for You

The newborn infant is helpless and has to have everything done for it. As the child matures it becomes capable of doing more for itself; as its capabilities increase, it is encouraged to become more self-reliant. Some parents continue to do things for their children far beyond a time when it is appropriate to do so and their children grow up requiring or expecting things to be done for them. In a sense, the child that has things done for it has a kind of power; this is a version of *lower upperness*, one of the four paradoxical positions. It is reminiscent of Freud's (1914) phrase "His Majesty the Baby" and the writings of Ferenczi (1916) and Kohut (1971) discussed in Chapter 4. It may be the basis of the adult condition of *entitlement*, which is experienced by royal personages and members of the aristocracy but also by overindulged ordinary people. The opposite of this, *upper lowerness*, in which the adult forces or pays others to indulge her/him or treat her/him like a child, was described in Chapter 7. That adults are prepared to have themselves pampered in this way indicates the appeal of this form of lowerness. Restaurants and hotels play upon it in seductive invitations such as "Let us spoil you."

Being Fussed Over

Beyond doing things for their children parents make a great fuss over them: do nice things for them, take them on outings, buy them presents, give them treats. They do this partly because they identify with them and, in a sense, in indulging them are indulging themselves; and partly because they like to see the joy on their faces. Adults generally are deprived of this kind of treatment. They may receive it on their birthdays and sometimes during courtship. Some birds give presents as part of courtship. Some birds (also chimpanzees), indulge in mutual feeding during courtship, which may be the origin of kissing (Eibl-Eibesfeldt, 1970). Mutual indulging may also be part of foreplay.

Being Soothed and Reassured

Because of the vulnerability of the lower position, anxiety is an important aspect of negative lowerness (see subsequent discussion). Being soothed and reassured therefore are important aspects of positive lowerness. Children in distress run to their parents, who hold them and tell them that everything is going to be alright. If they hurt themselves their parents kiss it better. They say "There there," which is a powerfully reassuring expression. People cannot go to sleep if they are worried, presumably because in the wild if there is danger it is unsafe to sleep. Parents soothe their infants by cooing, holding, stroking, rocking, and singing to them which helps them to go to sleep. They tuck them in bed, which makes them feel safe.

Being Cared for at Times of Illness or Injury

When children are ill or injured their lowerness needs increase and, in response to this, parental care intensifies. Many adults have fond memories of being cared for by their parents through periods of illness. When adults are ill or injured their lowerness needs intensify too. They are tucked up in bed, just like they were as children, and they are ministered unto by doctors and nurses. Their friends and relatives respond by sending them get-well cards, visiting them, and bringing them presents. Adults sometimes believe that being ill is one of the surest ways of obtaining lowerness; in cultures in which religion is in decline, people turn to their doctors when they feel in need of help, and various forms of distress and despair have been given medical labels to enable them to do so.

SOCIAL SUPPORT

A great deal has been written about social support (the book edited by Duck (1990), provides a useful overview) and different writers have used it to mean different things. The idea is that involvement with others provides strength at times of crisis. For some writers it simply means closeness, but for most it involves being the recipient of help, advice, comfort, or consolation. Thus, giving social support is a form of upper closeness and receiving social support is a form of lower closeness. The term "*supportive psychotherapy*" is sometimes used to imply that the psychotherapist is doing nothing more than providing this commodity called support.

LOWER ATTITUDES

There is a cluster of lower attitudes that merge into each other. Trust, which already has been discussed, is perhaps the most central lower attitude, but this is linked with a number of related attitudes.

Humility/Modesty

Humility and modesty are generally considered to be admirable qualities. They are considered to be Christian virtues. They are associated with politeness and good manners and probably have their origin in the appeasement behavior and submissive gestures of animals (Eibl-Ebesfeldt, 1970). They are the opposite of flamboyance and assertiveness. They place an emphasis upon being nonthreatening in order to put others at their ease. They avoid accusing or blaming people, considering that no one is free from blame and therefore has no right to blame others. This improves the smooth running of social interactions. Modest people intentionally play down any upper-to-lower differential. When thanked for their help, which may have been considerable, they will reply, "It was nothing" or "Don't mention it."

Accepting One's Place

In a well-organised society, enough good things come the way of the lower person that life can be satisfactory for her/him. Occupying a lower position need not be stressful. This is because (1) in human societies, unlike many animal groups, upper people provide and perform services for lower ones, (2) there are many sources of upperness for the person of low social status (i.e., it is possible to be a happy peasant), and (3) humans, unlike animals, have a sense of fairness and will accept a lower position if they believe that they have been treated fairly. In some human societies, restrictions are placed upon moving up and down within the social order. Knowing that social mobility is not possible, creates complacency in the upper person and inhibits the lower person from aspiring to move upward. This can create a kind of stability. In a meritocracy, in which both upward and downward movement are possible, there is competition for places and the fear of failure. Even so, the person who has tried and failed may be willing to settle for what s/he has and feel no bitterness about it.

Honorably Accepting Defeat

Honorably accepting defeat (being a good loser) is a positive form of lowerness and is not accompanied by what Beck (1983) called defeat depression (see Chapter 7). By her/his own autonomous judgment, the person acknowledges that the other deserves victory and is willing to praise her/him for her/his superior ability. In games such as chess, it is possible to avoid the humiliation of losing by resigning at a stage when it looks as though the other is in a more advantageous position. The person who resigns, under circumstances such as this, is able to retain her/his dignity by offering the other victory rather than having defeat thrust upon her/him. In terms of evolution, this must be linked with the yielding subroutine of ritual agonistic behavior (Price and Sloman, 1987) described in Chapter 2, but because the loser introduces her/his judgment of the victor's superior qualities, s/he is able to retain a degree of (judgmental) upperness in a situation that threatens her/his loss of (performance) upperness.

Respectfulness

Respectfulness is the acknowledgement and acceptance that another person is upper in at least one important respect. It includes a certain fearfulness, due to an awareness that the upper person is capable of doing harm (as with a violent criminal), imposing punishment (as with a policeman), or expressing disapproval (as with the judgmental parent). The person who is respected would normally be considered honest, fair, and scrupulous and therefore expected to relate in a positively upper way. For these reasons, s/he is said to command respect. A person may be respected for some things (e.g., professional competence) but not for others (e.g., morality). The respectful person adopts certain forms of behavior toward the respected person; this is called treating her/him with respect.

Loyalty

Loyalty is a more emotional form of relating than respectfulness. It involves devotion, which is a mixture of love and admiration, and usually lasts forever. The loyal subject has a strong sense of allegiance and is faithful and true. S/he would serve her/his master to the extent that s/he would do unquestioningly whatever her/his master asked of her/him, would never deceive or betray her/him, and would die for her/him if necessary. In a sense s/he is a part of or an extension of her/him, perhaps even parasitic on her/him. Loyalty is similar to what Laing (1965) called ontological dependence (see Chapter 5) in that the loyal subject lives off or through her/his master.

It is possible to be loyal to a group: consider the *Three Musketeers* (in the novel by Alexandre Dumas), who had as their motto "All for one and one for all." It is possible to be loyal to a cause or even to a nation. Such loyalty is based upon firmly held, shared beliefs. It generates a feeling of solidarity: that if all members stick together and remain true to their cause, they will win. There are times, however, when the autonomous individual finds that her/his beliefs differ from those of the group and s/he experiences a *conflict of loyalties*, realizing that expressing or acting upon those beliefs will be damaging to the group.

Obedience

Some aspects of obedience already have been discussed. It is a complex phenomenon that is contributed to both by the person who gives the commands and the person who obeys. The person who gives the commands is more likely to be obeyed if s/he is of high status, is known to have the power to enforce her/his will, speaks as though s/he expects to be obeyed, is respected, and is commanding the other to do something that is reasonable and fair. The person who obeys is more likely to do so if s/he is of low status, either fears or has respect for the person giving the commands, has low autonomy, is of a conforming disposition, or considers the command to be reasonable and fair, but even if it is not, is too timid to resist. Witnessing others obeying will induce her/him to obey, but witnessing others resisting will induce her/him to resist. As the number of resisters increases (as in the Tiananman Square uprising or when the Romanian people rose up against Nicolae Ceausescu), the upperness-to-lowerness ratio becomes reduced and a revolt takes place.

Acquiescence

Acquiescence involves preparedness to go along with what is proposed. Although excessive acquiescence clearly is a negative quality and presumably is related to having a poorly developed identity, a reasonable degree of acquiescence should be a characteristic of the securely lower person. An excessive unpreparedness to go along with what is proposed would be an indication of untrustfulness. Research on acquiescence is complicated by the fact that authoritarian individuals score highly on measures of acquiescence. As Zuckerman and Eisen (1962) observed, "The authoritarian is a believer and a yes man" (page 98).

Compliance

Compliance has been defined as behaving in a manner that is contrary to one's beliefs or personal convictions in order to achieve accord with the views, wishes, and expectations of others (Tedeschi et al., 1985). Clear evidence of compliance was provided by Asch (1951), who showed that experimental subjects were prepared to say that lines were nearer to the length that others (primed to give incorrect responses) said they were than to how long they saw them as being. Some people are prepared to lie rather than be seen as the odd one out. Such behavior is linked with conformity.

Suggestibility

Suggestibility is closely linked with obedience and therefore with hypnotizability (Eysenck, 1989). Much of what was said about obedience applies to suggestibility. Suggestibility is not, as is obedience, doing what someone says, but believing what someone says; this is a common feature of hypnotism. When the hypnotist tells the subject that s/he cannot feel pain, s/he does not feel pain. Major surgical operations have been carried out under hypnosis. When a group of boys, known to be allergic to certain plants, were told untruthfully that they were being touched by a poisonous plant, they developed allergic skin reactions whether they were hypnotized or not (Barber, 1984). In fact, Wagstaff (1991) maintained that the only difference between hypnotic and waking suggestibility is that the former is "dressed up in extra social ritual." A fuller account of the subject of suggestibility can be found in Schumaker (1991).

Deference

Deference incorporates both obedience and respectfulness. Like reverence, it involves a more overt acknowledgment of lower status than respectfulness. As with acquiescence, in excess it would be regarded as a negative quality, but there are times and occasions (e.g., in the presence of a person of great authority) when it is a reasonable and appropriate form of behavior. There are a number of gestures of deference such as bowing, curtsying, touching, or lifting the hat (developed from removal of the helmet). These may have their origins in the appeasement gestures of animals (see Chapter 2).

Gratitude

Although it is possible for an upper person to experience and express gratitude in relation to a lower person, it is probable that when s/he is doing so it is from a position of upper lowerness. Gratitude is what the lower person experiences in response to what the upper person has given her/him.

Being Apologetic

As with gratitude, an upper person can be apologetic toward a lower person, but again, s/he is likely to be doing so from a position of upper lowerness. Usually it is a lower person who is apologetic toward an upper one. The apologetic person is acknowledging that s/he has caused offense (by being negatively upper, such as critical or insulting) and is trying to adopt a more lower posture in order to regain the favor of the upper person.

Guilt

This will be dealt with subsequently under the heading of the internalized upper parent. It has also been extensively reviewed by Gilbert (1988, 1989, 1992), who observed that it can deliberately be manipulated by the powerful upon the weak. It is an experience of discomfort that alerts the individual to her/his having wronged or caused distress to another. The lower person is more conscious of this than the upper person since s/he may be in danger of being disapproved of or punished for it.

Shame

Shame is often co-existent with guilt, and the two experiences run into each other. An important distinction between them is that guilt is primarily generated from within while shame is primarily generated from without (Lewis, 1986). Shame is a consciousness of what others think and represents a concern with reputation. Scheff (1988) suggested that shame is part of a bipolar affective system with shame at one end and pride at the other. One bows one's head in shame but holds it up with pride. He linked it with Goffman's (1968) concept of stigma.

Confessing and Seeking Forgiveness

Confessing and seeking forgiveness are more extreme versions of the apologizing process. The offense and the hurt caused are greater, and it is more difficult for the upper person to resist resorting to revenge or punishment. The confessor has to convey that s/he disapproves of her/himself and attempt to pre-empt the other's punishment by indulging in some form of self-accusing or self-punishing behavior or offer some kind of sacrifice in order to redress the upper/lower balance. Mowrer (1964) pointed to the therapeutic effect of confessing misdeeds and transgressions. Jones and Archer (1976) observed, in an experimental setting, that a person who has been selected as a confessor comes to like the person who confesses because, it was thought, it put her/him in a *command position*.

Deference, gratitude, being apologetic, confessing, and seeking forgiveness are all forms of what Price (1988) has called up-hierarchy anathetic signals and, when directed towards God, form part of prayer (see subsequent discussion).

Conformity

The horizontal component of conformity was discussed in Chapter 5. Conformity also has an important vertical component. In this respect, it is a form of obedience. The obedient child conforms to the expectations of its parents. These expectations may include being well behaved, clean and tidy, kind, modest, polite, reasonable, honest, conscientious, and industrious. If the parents are conforming, their expectations may be an extension of society's expectations of them. Conformity incorporates cultural norms and values.

Being Law-Abiding

A law-abiding person does not entirely abide by the law out of a fear of being found out, caught, or punished. Law abidingness has much in common with wishing to be part of an efficiently working system, and therefore with conformity. It also stems from a feeling of common decency. The good citizen enjoys being straight and fair with others and expects them to be fair and straight with her/him. More likely than not, her/his experience of others, particularly parents and teachers, has been of this kind. Nevertheless s/he does experience the law as being that which is above her/him.

LOWERNESS AND RELIGION

God as a source of closeness was discussed in Chapters 5 and 6. Here God will be discussed as a source of lowerness. Since, due to the prolonged period of parenting in humans, the child (and subsequently the adult), is accustomed to having someone to look up to and rely upon, it is conceivable that religious belief is an expression of man's continuing need for an upwardly directed relationship. Gods often are believed to reside in the heavens; the Christian God is referred to as "our Heavenly Father" or, more vulgarly, simply as "someone up there." The qualities of gods are upper ones and the attitudes of religious people are lower ones. Reference in this chapter will be made specifically to the Christian God, but the ideas expressed apply to gods in general.

Essential to the Christian belief are that God created the world; life is God's gift; God has a plan and a purpose and man has a place in each of these; God has laws that must be obeyed; God sees everything and knows when His laws have been broken; man has a responsibility not to offend God, but God is forgiving; God cares and provides; God is compassionate and comforting. The trusting element of lowerness is very important in religion. Those who are prepared to put their trust in God will have the experience of being looked after by Him.

Freud (1927) described religion as a regression to infantile dependence and the projection of the parent image onto the universe, but Guntrip (1969b) objected that this described only what he called *neurotic religion*. For Freud, religious belief was a response to a recognition of human helplessness. For Guntrip, it was something mysterious and incomprehensible.

The association of humility and modesty with Christianity already has been mentioned. Lowerness features prominently in Christian thinking (e.g., "Blessed are the meek: for they shall inherit the earth"). Jesus shunned possessions and said that it was easier for a camel to go through the eye of a needle than for a rich man to enter the kingdom of God. He urged people to give their money to the poor. The members of many religious orders live frugally and ascetically. Christianity is also associated with nonaggression and nonretaliation.

Worship and Prayer

Various forms of prayer and worship are common to all religions. In these, man experiences himself as being in the presence of God and speaks to Him; acknowledges his lowliness in relation to Him; seeks His forgiveness for transgressions; expresses his love for Him; sings His praises and adores Him; expresses his gratitude to Him; and seeks His protection, comfort, and help. In Price's (1988) terminology, these are up-hierarchy anathetic communications. Worship is a group activity led by a member of the church who is seen as a representative of God and serves as intermediary between God and the congregation. In some forms of worship emotive shouting, music, and dancing are used to stimulate the congregation into a state of high excitement. Such states are equivalent to being hypnotized and induce high submission and suggestibility (Sargant, 1957). French (1984) considered that many of the people attending even the more subdued high church service are in a hypnotic state.

DEIFICATION

In Chapter 3, Buber's (1937) distinction between the I-It and the I-Thou attitude was discussed. Buber's discourse was concerned with man's relation to God, whom he referred to as the *"eternal Thou"*. It might have been preferable for Buber to include a third attitude called I-God, for although man clearly adopts an I-Thou attitude when he relates to God, the nature of his relationship to God is qualitatively different from that of his relationship to ordinary people. Man is capable of adopting an I-God attitude toward ordinary people, but when he does, the nature of his relationship to them changes. They become *deified*. They may be kings, high priests, or both kings and high priests, and they are considered to wield supernatural powers. Deified people are held in awe: they are both marveled at and feared. It is also possible to adopt an I-God relationship to a thing, as in tree and plant worship (Jevrons, 1927). The tree or plant is figured as the body of a god, and eating part of it may cause divine possession or confer supernatural protection.

ADORATION AND IDOLIZATION

Adoration and idolization involve an amplification of the gap between the upper and the lower person. The adorer experiences the adored person as being the most high and her/himself as being the most low. Large and ornate edifices are built as places in which the adorer feels in the presence of the adored person, and large and beautiful statues are made in her/his likeness. An altar is built upon which sacrifices are offered to the adored person. Presumably the killing of animals is the adorer's substitute for the killing of her/himself, since being dead is the equivalent of being the most low. Presumably, too, the spirit of the sacrificed animal rises up to heaven. Statues and the altar serve as focal points toward which adoration may be directed.

Adoration is directed not only toward gods. Throughout history, kings and national leaders have been treated in this way. Buildings and statues have been built in honor of them; they have been made the focal point of highly elaborate and carefully orchestrated mass gatherings in which there has been much organized excitement. In recent years, similar treatment has been afforded to pop idols, sports teams and sports stars. Idolizers in this context are called *fans*. That the phenomenon is so common indicates the human need for such behavior, which amounts to ecstatic lowerness.

Adoration can also occur at an individual level. A child or a student may develop an adoring relationship toward a teacher. Something akin to adoration commonly occurs between lovers, though not necessarily symmetrically. A reciprocal relationship may develop between an adorer and someone who has a narcissistic personality (see Chapter 7). The narcissist loves the adorer for adoring her/him and the adorer loves the narcissist for providing a focus for her/his adoring behavior. Relationships in which there is adoration can never be truly intimate, for neither the adorer nor the adored person ever gets to relate to the real person.

The adoring relationship is satisfying for a number of reasons. Being in the presence of someone who is imagined as mighty creates a sense of security. Adoration involves a degree of identification with the adored person; if not identification, then affiliation: God the Father is everybody's father and the British Queen Mother is a kind of mother to the entire nation. There is a fantasy that the intense love directed toward the adored person is reflected onto the adorer and that everyone who adores God or some public figure has a personal relationship with Him or with that figure.

LOWER UPPERNESS

This is an appropriate place to discuss the position of lower upperness, the fourth of the paradoxical positions. Lower upperness involves gaining upperness from the position of lowerness. The lower upperness of the adored child already has been mentioned. A similar condition obtains when there is a sick or invalid individual, particularly a parent, who has everyone at her/his beck and call, running in circles around her/him. When the person feigns or exaggerates her/his disability for this purpose, it becomes negative relating. This will be considered later.

A different form of lower upperness is upperness through association, which has been discussed to some extent in relation to adoration. The employees of a successful organization, the doorman at a prestigious hotel, the chauffeur of an important person, the servants of a rich household, the workers of a wealthy farmer enjoy a certain status through association. People try to become associated with famous people in however humble a capacity they can. There are a number of pejorative terms for them, one of the least offensive being *"hangers on."* There are young women called *groupies* who offer sexual favors to members of pop groups, but more generally both women and men offer themselves as sexual partners to important people. The sycophant is another kind of hanger-on who praises, flatters, and emulates, as does a loyal disciple.

Yet another form of lower upperness is pride. This was discussed under the heading of welfare, charity, and aid. Pride assumes a number of forms, but it is largely a defense against being defeated or forced into submission. It is a defiance or pluckiness, but it is also linked with group unity. A group or nation under heavy attack may survive by adopting an attitude of pride or may be defeated but go down fighting. In former years, in Japan, a person who was insulted might have committed suicide at the doorstep of the insulter as an expression of pride.

THE INFLUENCE OF THE INTERNALIZED UPPER PARENT

In Chapter 4 it was explained that the internalized upper parent, which becomes established during childhood, continues to exert its influence throughout life. This influence imposes an attitude of lowerness upon the individual, which remains irrespective of any external relationships with which s/he is involved. This *background of lowerness* can have both positive and negative effects, but only the positive ones will be considered at this stage. It disposes the individual to be prepared to conform, obey, and generally fit into society, to be a decent, law-abiding citizen who works hard and conscientiously. It generates the emotional state of *guilt* an internal reprimand that comes into play when the person is aware that s/he is being unfair. Crook (1980) maintained that guilt evolved as an internalized behavior control system that prevents the animal/person from cheating. It seems unlikely that animals other than man experience guilt or are capable of comprehending the concept of cheating. Their behavior is probably controlled by expectations of reward and punishment. The internalized upper parent is, in many respects, the equivalent of the *conscience*. It is also the basis of the *superego* (see Chapter 4). It is underdeveloped in the antisocial personality (see Chapters 6 and 7) and overdeveloped in what Blatt and Shichman (1983) called the *introjective personality* (see subsequent discussion). To the nonbeliever, the experience of God is derived from a combination of the internalized close parent and the internalized upper parent.

It is not easy to accept that man's decent and humane behavior is due entirely to the constraints of the internalized upper figure. It seems probable that the principle "do as you would be done by" is a consequence of the individual identifying with and modeling her/himself upon other decent and humane people and also of perceiving through identification or empathy the effects that her/his behavior has upon other people (Eisenberg, 1986). Closeness seems to be an important factor here, for people who love one another are inclined to behave in a decent and humane way toward each other, irrespective of what they believe they are supposed to do.

WAYS OF ATTAINING (POSITIVE) LOWERNESS

Lowerness May Be Simply Available

For the infant born into a family, or for the child within a family, lowerness is simply there. Normally, parents respond to the presence of the infant or the child by wanting to protect, make a fuss over, care for, feed, clothe, and teach it. Providing that good relationships are maintained, throughout life there remains an understanding that parents or the parental home are always there to return to. Most children, however old they become, continue to have an upwardly directed attitude toward their parents. The best parents convey the message that "Whatever you do, you will always be my child," which creates a feeling of security. For many adults, the death of their own parents gives rise to an experience of there being nothing above them, and life is never the same again for them.

Beyond the family, within society there are so many institutions that give rise, in the individual, to an overall experience of positive lowerness. Society organizes, protects, nourishes, provides knowledge, and so on. For the religious person, God and the Church are an additional source of positive lowerness.

Lowerness That Is Offered or Given by an Upper Person

Another may offer to be upper in a helpful or constructive way. S/he may offer protection, nourishment, information, guidance, care and the like. In accepting the offer the person is putting her/himself in a lower position. The offer may not necessarily be unconditional and the recipient may be required or expected to give something in return. Alternatively, the lowerness may simply be given: another may rush in and protect or save someone from making a fool of her/himself, tell her/him the answer to a question, or rescue her/him from danger.

Assuming a Lower Position in Relation to Another

In being respectful, adoring, idolizing, or flattering toward another, the person is placing her/himself in a lower position in relation to the other. This provokes the other into responding in an upper way.

Asking/Pleading/Imploring/Begging

The act of asking is a characteristic of the lower position. It involves the person acknowledging her/his needfulness for something and placing her/himself in the position of requesting it from another. This is a position of vulnerability because the other has the option of declining to give it. The asking may be for something practical (distant) such as information, instruction, or guidance, or for something more emotional (close) such as help, reassurance, or rescue. The asker is in a stronger position if s/he is able to offer something (e.g., money) in return. If the other considers the offer a reasonable one, s/he will enter freely into the transaction. If the asker asks for a little, s/he is more likely to be given it than if s/he asks for a lot.

Depending upon what is asked for, the asker may need to increase the intensity of her/his asking in order to evoke a sympathetic response in the giver. The more desperate s/he is or can appear to be, the more likely s/he is to be given that which is asked for. Her/his desperation is brought out by her/his emphasizing the extent of the gap between her/his lowerness and the other's upperness. Because of the link between giving and closeness, it is in her/his interest to maintain as close a degree of involvement as possible between her/himself and the other. Similarly, the other finds it easier to decline to give if s/he can increase the distance between her/himself and the asker - as, for example, by walking by on the other side.

As was mentioned in Chapter 2, animals in the wild never beg but domesticated animals and animals kept in captivity have learned to do so. People respond to beggars, either animal or human, partly because they sympathize or even identify with them, and partly because their consciences (internal upper figures) prompt them to feel that that's what decent people do. That is, someone who is higher prompts them to respond in a certain way toward someone who is lower.

Care-Eliciting or Sympathy-Seeking Behavior

Care-eliciting behavior is directed toward the specific goal of being cared for and looked after (Henderson, 1974). It may include asking/ pleading/imploring/begging but is likely also to include various forms of nonverbal behavior. It has its origins in the care-eliciting behavior of infants. As Gilbert (1989) observed, "the advantage of being able to activate maternal care, rather than relying on the parent to dispense it, is enormous" (page 121). When distressed the infant emits a plaintive shrieking sound which as Konner (1972) observed the parent wants to hear stopped immediately. To this end, s/he normally picks up the infant and consoles it but occasionally may attack it violently. The adult who weeps or simply sheds a tear evokes a sympathetic response in others (Buss and Craik, 1986). There are other care-eliciting gestures such as appearing to be weak, lost or helpless, pouting, and looking appealingly into the other's eyes. An important care-eliciting strategy is inducing guilt in the other, sometimes called guilt tripping. The message conveyed is, "How can you leave me like this?" This is a strategy often adopted by beggars.

LOWER PERSONALITIES

The Dependent Personality

The only lower personality in the DSM III, Axis II, classification of personality disorders (American Psychiatric Association, 1980) is that which is called the *dependent personality: the submissive pattern*. Its characteristics are so broad-ranging that it probably incorporates a number of different styles of relating. Millon (1981) observed that dependent personalities are distinguished from other pathological patterns by their marked need for social approval and affection and by their willingness to live in accord with the desires of others. It is unfortunate that the need for affection is included since this places the condition astride the horizontal and vertical axes. It cannot be denied that most definitions of dependence do incorporate this affection-seeking component (Parens & Saul, 1971; Birtchnell, 1984, 1988, 1991b; Pilkonis, 1988; Livesley et al., 1990), and for this reason it is necessary to distinguish between what might be called horizontal and vertical dependence. In this Chapter the emphasis will be on vertical dependence.

In the DSM IIIR (revised), Axis II, classification (American Psychiatric Association, 1987) three of the nine diagnostic criteria concern horizontal dependence. The six vertical criteria are as follows: (1) is unable to make everyday decisions without an excessive amount of advice or reassurance from others; (2) allows others to make most of her/his important decisions; (3) agrees with people even when s/he believes they are wrong, because of fear of being rejected; (4) has difficulty initiating projects or doing things on her/his own; (5) volunteers to do things that are unpleasant or demeaning in order to get other people to like her/him; and (6) is easily hurt by criticism or disapproval. In the tenth edition of the ICD or International Classification of Diseases (World Health Organization, 1989), two of the seven diagnostic criteria concern horizontal dependence. The five vertical criteria are as follows: (1) encourages or allows others to assume responsibility for major areas of her/his life; (2) subordinates her/his needs to those of others upon whom s/he is dependent and is unduly compliant with their wishes; (3) is unwilling to make even reasonable demands on those s/he depends on; (4) perceives her/himself to be helpless, incompetent, and lacking stamina; and (5) tends to react to adversity by transferring responsibility to others. These characteristics combine what in an earlier analysis were called ontological and deferential dependence (Birtchnell, 1984).

Millon (1981) described how many dependent individuals search for a single all-powerful *magical helper*, "a partner in whom they can place their trust and depend on to protect them from having to assume responsibilities or face the competitive struggles of life alone. Deprived of this support, they withdraw into themselves and become tense, despondent and forlorn" (page 108). Bemporad (1980) used the term "*dominant other*" to describe a similar kind of upper figure who gives meaning to the dependent person's life. The dependent person, he maintained, lives not for her/himself but only in order to gain the approval of the dominant other. S/he enters into what Bemporad (1980) called a *bargain relationship* in which s/he abandons all personal pleasures (called *autonomous gratifications*) and avoids doing or saying anything that may cause the other offense. Millon (1981) agrees that the dependent person denies her/his individuality and subordinates her/his desires.

The Self-Deprecating Personality

The two major diagnostic classification systems, the DSM III and the ICD, do not include the kind of personality that appears to result from the incorporation of an excessively harsh and judgmental internalized upper parent. This was intended to be the basis of what was called deferential dependence (Birtchnell, 1984). Within their much broader construct of the introjective personality, Blatt and Shichman (1983) included the person who has intense fears of loss of approval and a disposition to feel worthless and guilty. The self-deprecatory personality tends to have a keen sense of morality; to subject her/himself to constant self-scrutiny; to consider her/himself to be stupid and incompetent; to be inclined, when things go wrong, to believe it was her/his fault; and to be excessively apologetic for her/himself. S/he will blame her/himself rather than consider blaming or feeling angry toward others. This corresponds with what Murray (1938) called abasement; it includes feeling timid in the presence of superiors, feeling inferior to others in most respects, feeling the need to confess to errors, and needing to be punished for wrong-doing. In order to win approval and recognition and to compensate for feelings of weakness and worthlessness, a person with such qualities may make insistent demands upon her/himself for perfection, drive her/himself toward high ideals and overachievement, but be incapable of enjoying her/his accomplishments or experiencing satisfaction from her/his successes.

Millon (1981) included self-deprecation in his description of the DSM III dependent personality. He said that dependent people have marked feelings of personal inadequacy; are disposed to downgrade themselves, claiming to lack abilities and attractiveness; magnify their failures and defects; minimize their attainments; underplay their attributes; and assume personal blame for problems they feel they have brought upon others. He stressed that much of this belittling has little basis in reality.

The Masochistic Personality

This is included in the DSM III, Axis II as a single word under the heading *"other personality disorders,"* which Simons (1987) believed reveals the tendency of psychiatrists to deny what is in fact a common, serious, and sometimes life-threatening disorder. It refers to the kind of person who persistently finds ways to spoil and take no satisfaction in any good that happens to her/him. S/he is a chronic and perpetual *victim* who provokes others to retaliate and do her/him down. S/he repeatedly seeks out her/his tormentors or places her/himself in situations of suffering and humiliation from which s/he could extricate her/himself should s/he choose to do so. Simons believed that in this kind of person the link between pleasure and pain has become unconscious, that the inner struggle has become externalized and acted out with the external world. In psychotherapy such a person provokes the therapist to sadistically abuse her/him or to give up on her/him; thus it is essential for the therapist to diagnose the unconscious masochistic motivation.

NEGATIVE FORMS OF LOWERNESS

Giving or Receiving Disrespectfully Imposed Lowerness

Lowerness Resulting from Malevolent Upperness. The section in Chapter 7 on becoming upper at the expense of the other's lowerness was concerned with giving disrespectfully imposed lowerness; it need not be repeated here. However, it is important to emphasize how extremely hurtful and damaging being the recipient of malevolent upperness can be. Being the recipient of such behavior does not simply involve being pushed into a lower position. It involves being insulted and humiliated to an extent that threatens to destroy the spirit. The malevolently upper person aims to break the will of the lower person, to weaken and incapacitate her/him so that s/he no longer represents a threat or a challenge. It is this kind of *forcing the person into submission* to which writers such as Price (1991), Price and Sloman (1987), and Gilbert (1992) refer when they consider depression to be a form of losing or yielding behavior. There are those who sometimes incorrectly assume that lowerness simply involves this kind of submission.

When disrespectfully forced into lowerness, the person may protest or submit. This is reminiscent of the stages of grief (Bowlby, 1961) and points to a connection between loss of upperness and loss of closeness. If the protester feels confident enough s/he may seek to retaliate or seek revenge. If not, the anger may remain but have no outlet. Hatred is largely an emotion of lowerness. The person who hates is angry about what has been done to her/him but feels powerless to do anything about it. The good thing about hatred is that it is directed outward where it can do no harm to the person who experiences it. The lower person who is still fearful of the upper person may be resentful or bitter but lacks the courage to be hateful. Unlike hatred, resentfulness and bitterness hurt because they are more inward- turning. When being angry seems pointless, despair and resignation set in.

Omega Humans. This term was introduced by Gardner (1982) to describe the most downtrodden members of a social group or society. He cited two examples. The first was the Chicago hobo of the 1920s (Anderson, 1923), who typically was ashamed, demoralized, gloomy, fearful, restless, fidgety, reckless, self-derogating, and self-destructive. He was isolated, talked little to others, and had little zest for life. The second was "Lomani," a person of the lowest social rank on the East Indian island of Alor (Dubois, 1944), who spoke in an expressionless monotone, seldom initiated conversation, and was distant and fearful. She never expressed aggressive feelings or exhibited aggressive acts and feared retaliation if she acted on her own initiative.

There are many societies in which entire racial or social groups are, or have been, suppressed and victimized. This happened to the Jews in Nazi Germany and Russia, the Negroes in America and South Africa, the American Indians in Canada, and the Aborigines in Australia. It is a feature of the Indian caste system. In a number of western cities there is what has come to be called an *underclass* of individuals who become eased out of the social system because they have no means of obtaining employment or accommodation and no access to social benefits.

Insecure Lowerness

A person may be insecurely lower as a result of (1) being abused or let down by untrustworthy upper people in the past, and subsequently not being able to trust any upper people, or (2) presently being in a lower/upper relationship in which the upper person is showing signs of not being trustworthy. It is important to differentiate between these, since in the former case, the person is projecting upon the present upper other an untrustworthiness that s/he does not deserve. The predominant emotion of the insecurely lower person is anxiety, which is the very opposite of the feeling of assured safety is experienced by the securely lower person.

Ontological Insecurity. Ontological insecurity was considered as a negative form of distance (see Chapter 6). It also manifests itself as a form of negative lowerness. Some lower people are insecure because they have no clear idea about who they are, what they want to do, how they ought to behave, or what values they should have. They therefore copy or blindly follow other people, conform to group norms, are gullible, and are easily influenced by advertisements or what other people say to them.

The Need for Approval of the Insecurely Lower Person. One form of insecure lowerness is the inability to make an accurate assessment of self-worth. This presumably is the result of unsustained assurance of self-worth from parents, teachers and other influential upper figures. Chodoff (1972) went so far as to define dependency as "that degree to which a person's self-esteem is maintained more or less exclusively by the approval and support of other persons or their surrogates" (page 670). Clearly this is only one aspect of dependency, but it indicates how important Chodoff considered it to be. Nemiah (1975) referred to the dependent person's relative absence of *inner resources* and her/his frequent need of a constant supply of *externally derived strengths*. Such a person, he said, is unable to put her/his setbacks into proper perspective and balance failure in one direction with success in another. Millon (1981) observed that whatever self-esteem the dependent person may possess is determined largely by the support and encouragement of others.

The Fear of Rejection. There is an obvious connection between being approved of and being liked, though within a spatial context the former is a vertical concept and the latter is a horizontal one. The picture is complicated by the fact that people with desirable qualities (forms of upperness) are more likely to be liked. A person who has, or believes her/himself to have, few desirable qualities will have to work harder at being liked than one who has, or believes her/himself to have, many. The insecurely lower person may be prepared to demean her/himself; submit to abuse or intimidation; avoid contradicting, speaking her/his mind, or starting an argument in order to maintain the other's favor. Although such obsequious behavior may work if the other is insecurely upper, it is likely to lose the favor of most other people.

The Fear of Upperness

A person may remain in a position of lowerness because s/he fears assuming a position of upperness. In developmental terms, this may be because s/he was never given permission, particularly by her/his parents, to enter the world of adults and be treated by them as an equal (see Chapter 4). Attempts to attain upperness therefore are always accompanied by feelings of guilt about doing better than her/his parents. The person may be frightened of having power over other people or of carrying responsibility for their well-being. S/he may fear that by gaining upperness s/he will lose lowerness and have no one to look after her/him. Thus, consciously or unconsciously, s/he may sabotage movements toward promotion and behave irresponsibly when placed in a position of responsibility. Schafer (1984) provided examples of people who spend their lives in pursuit of failure, the avoidance of success, and the idealization of unhappiness. Alcoholics who drink away their money may be indulging in this kind of behavior.

Falsely Assuming a Lower Position for Personal Gain

Already it has been said that for the adult being ill is one of the surest ways of getting lowerness. Szasz (1972) observed that "Like the infant's cry, the message 'I am sick' is exceedingly effective in mobilising others to some kind of helpful action" (page 172), but Parsons (1951) cautioned that the adoption of the sick role is permissible only when the disability is considered to be genuine and when the individual cooperates in efforts to return her/himself to health. To assume the sick role in the absence of demonstrable or understandable disability is an infringement of the code relating to illness behavior. Because of this, people have devised various strategies for feigning illness; these have been called *illness behavior* by Mechanic (1966) and *abnormal illness behavior* by Pilowsky (1969).

Malingering. This term is used when the person consciously strives to appear ill or to exaggerate the symptoms of minor illness in order to gain sympathy or to be exempt from strenuous or unpleasant work. Szasz (1956) pointed to the diagnostic confusion that the condition sometimes creates among physicians and psychiatrists.

Hospital Addiction. This is a condition, sometimes called *Munchausen's syndrome,* in which the person falsely claims to have abdominal pains or to be bleeding from various parts of the body in order to be admitted to the hospital and operated upon (Barker, 1962). S/he sometimes travels from hospital to hospital, succeeding in having many surgical operations.

The Patient Who Does Not Get Better. So gratifying may be the attention that the physically or mentally ill patient receives from doctors, nurses, or relatives that s/he becomes reluctant to relinquish her/his symptoms. Thus, what starts as a genuine illness turns into a chronically feigned one. An alternative strategy is that the patient recovers from the initial illness but at times of future stress feigns relapses. Such behavior gave rise to the expression "enjoying poor health."

The Chronically Suicidal Person. This is the person who, through genuine distress, attempts suicide and is impressed by the attention s/he receives. Schwartz et al. (1974) wrote, "Because of medicolegal factors as well as for other reasons, hospitals are expected to behave in nurturing ways in the interests of preventing suicide. The more suicidally the patient behaves, the more parental will the hospital staff become" (page 199). The patient rapidly learns that when there is danger of being sent home or discharged from treatment, a modest suicide attempt will regain the attention of those in charge of her/him.

Hysteria. Hysteria was briefly discussed (see Chapter 6) as a form of dissociation. This is because the part of the brain (subcortical) that is involved in choosing to adopt a sickness strategy in order to resolve a particular interpersonal conflict needs to effect a dissociation from that part of the brain (cortical) that would consider such a strategy morally unacceptable. Szasz (1972) explained that in hysteria the person may wish to avoid a particular line of action but cannot admit this to her/himself or to others for fear of personal or social condemnation. Instead, one part of her/him (subcortical), unbeknown to the other part (cortical), adopts a form of disability that prevents her/him from doing it. At a cortical level s/he protests and truly believes that "If it were not for this malady I could do it." Thus, instead of being condemned, s/he gets cared for. S/he will not relinquish the disability unless a solution is found to her/his predicament.

Feigned or Exaggerated Helplessness. Helplessness can be rewarding and sometimes is similar to hysteria. A person may discover that certain upper people derive satisfaction from helping them. In consequence they feign or exaggerate their helplessness or incompetence in order to increase the other's experience of upperness. Some men like to feel upper in relation to women (whom they may refer to as "the little woman") and some women are happy to play along with this. Millon (1981) wrote, "By acting weak, expressing self-doubt, communicating a need for assurance, and displaying a willingness to comply and submit, dependents are likely to elicit the nurture and protection they seek" (page 114).

Seligman (1975) and others have described a condition called *learned helplessness* which they have linked with certain kinds of depression. The condition was first observed in experimental animals who were being subjected to electric shocks from which they could not escape. Even when released from their harnesses and given the opportunity to learn how to avoid the shocks, some animals passively allowed them to continue without trying to escape. Seligman drew parallels with how certain humans become depressed when they believe they have no control over their destinies.

Induced Helplessness. The child whose parent has always done things for it grows up incapable of doing things for itself. It may come to adopt helpless gestures and attitudes that seduce others to behave in a helping way toward it; failing this, it may become idle, self-neglecting and unproductive. This type has been called *weak-willed* by Schneider (1950), *oral receptive* by Abraham (1924), and *inadequate* by Sullivan (1947).

Institutionalization. People who have spent long periods of time in institutions, such as prisons and mental hospitals, lose much of their sense of autonomy and find it difficult to fend for themselves or make decisions about what they want to do (Barton, 1959). If they are released into society they may become hopeless drifters.

Fawning. The voluntary assumption of an inferior position in order to gain the favor, or even the reward, of an upper person is an underhand practice that normally is frowned upon. It works because people fall easy prey to flattery, particularly if they are narcissistic.

Effects of a Harshly Judgmental Internalized Upper Parent

When parents and influential others have made harsh judgments and threatened the child with severe punishments, or when the child repeatedly has been told it is bad or evil or that it has offended or displeased God, the normal tendencies to experience guilt or shame are likely to be intensified. The child will grow up to be an adult who has an expectation that others will disapprove of her/him, that s/he is unworthy of their attention, and that s/he deserves to be punished. S/he will feel that s/he has no right to enjoyment and that nothing that s/he does is worthy of praise. Kleinians would argue that such states result from being too greedy for the breast and Freudians would argue that they result from being too desirous of the parent of the opposite sex. Whatever the origin, it undoubtedly is true that some adults carry around with them the unshakable belief that they are not as good as other people, and this is the basis of the introjective personality.

Introjective Depression. This is the kind of depression to which the introjective personality is prone. It is a condition considered by Blatt and Shichman (1983) to be a consequence of the incorporation of an overly harsh superego. It tends to be the most profound of all depressions and is accompanied by guilt over temptations or thoughts of transgressions, and feelings of shame at having failed to live up to excessively high ideals. The person expects to be disapproved of and criticized and is overly inclined to disapprove of and criticize her/himself. Self-harming and self-punitive behavior are common, and the person is capable of serious and brutal acts of suicide. People are not normally in such states continuously. Rather they are subject to one or more episodes that may come out of the blue or be precipitated by a relatively minor event that keys into this self-depreciatory system.

Introjective Delusions. In states of introjective depression the person may believe her/himself to be rotten or decayed inside, to have a serious illness, particularly cancer, or to be dead or dying. S/he may believe her/himself to give off an unpleasant smell and, because of this, will avoid people and avoid touching them. S/he may blame her/himself excessively for some minor misdemeanor; believe that s/he has committed a terrible crime, sinned greatly, or brought ruin to her/his family or to the world; and deserves punishment or death (Wing et al., 1974).

Making False Confessions. So strong may be the conviction of guilt and so great may be the need for punishment that a person may voluntarily confess to a crime s/he did not commit. This is a not uncommon occurrence when the commitment of a major crime has been publicized. Beyond this, there are many instances of innocent people making false confessions under interrogation. In witchcraft trials and in the treason trials conducted in Russia under Stalin's rule, false confessions were made by many thousands of people - though commonly in states of fatigue and weakness, and not infrequently after torture (Sargant, 1957).

Lowerness Experienced as a Lack of Upperness

Many forms of negative lowerness are equivalent to the denial of upperness, just as many forms of negative distance are equivalent to the denial of closeness. Moving into lowerness because that is where one wants to be is not depressing, just as moving into distance because that is where one wants to be is not depressing. The lower person's mood largely depends upon how the upper person behaves toward her/him. Benevolent upperness is gratifying; malevolent upperness is depressing.

In the section on accepting one's place it was pointed out that occupying a position of lowerness can be accompanied by the experience of contentment. It is necessary now to specify those circumstances under which it is depressing. First, the contrast between the lower and the upper person, on any particular parameter, needs to be made apparent. Being poor among other poor people, even when aware that rich people exist, need not be depressing; but being brought face to face with, or even outnumbered by, rich people may become depressing. Second, the lower person needs to witness how s/he loses out, in comparison with the upper person. Being incapable need not be depressing, even when aware that more capable people exist; but witnessing a capable person being successful may be depressing. Third, the lower person needs to witness the upper person being praised and rewarded by others for her/his successes. Fourth, and most important, the lower person needs to have his lowerness driven home by the insulting and derisive remarks of others.

Envy. Envy is a painful emotion experienced by a lower person who would like the particular form of upperness that another has but lacks the capacity to attain it. Gilbert (1992) observed that the envious person begrudges the attributes, success, rank, status, and attention accorded to the other; perhaps this is because s/he believes it to be unfair. Envy is generally regarded as a sin, and Klein (1957) linked it with guilt. Envy is sometimes resolved by the adoption of a sour grapes attitude (from Aesop's fable of the fox and the grapes), by which the lower person is able to convince her/himself that the upperness is not worth attaining anyway.

Responses to the Loss of Lowerness

The normal person experiences the loss of lowerness when those in whom s/he has placed her/his trust leave or let her/him down. This may happen with the collapse of a government, bank, or insurance company, the desertion of a parent, or when an employer, doctor, teacher, or parent reveals her/himself to be untrustworthy.

Lorenz (1966) described how, when a goose realizes its partner is missing, it loses all courage and flees (even from the youngest and weakest geese), and sinks to the lowest position in the ranking order. The goose appears to be reacting to the loss of a backer and a protector. As in this instance, loss of lowerness often is linked with loss of closeness. Millon (1981) described how the dependent person's demands for approval and reassurance may become so persistent as to exasperate and alienate the person upon whom s/he leans most heavily. Such exasperation and alienation serve only to increase the dependent's neediness. S/he may become so desperate, ingratiating, urgently pleading, and clinging as to be a millstone around the other's neck, which may provoke the other to express annoyance, disapproval, and finally rejection. Fearful of expressing hostility, lest this result in further rebuff, the dependent is likely to turn her/his feelings inward, first reproaching her/himself for her/his shortcomings and then promising to be more self-reliant. The other may temporarily relent, but once the cycle of decompensation has begun it is likely to generate a vicious circle that culminates in the dissolution of the relationship and the increasing despair of the dependent person.

SUMMARY

The positive forms of lowerness are more difficult to comprehend than the positive forms of the other three main positions, because man is the only species to have a well-developed range of lower functions. Lowerness is possible because humans are so much more able to use their upper position for the benefit of others. In lowerness the person is being receptive to this; by taking that which the upper person provides, s/he moves toward upperness. The lower person needs to rely upon the upper person and therefore is vulnerable to being abused by her/him; so trust of the upper person is essential to lowerness. Lowerness has evolved out of the condition of being parented; many of its features, like being protected, cared for, told what to do, soothed, and reassured, are what children receive from their parents. The internalized upper parent plays an important part in many aspects of lowerness. It provides a sense of fairness and justice and is an integral part of the religious experience.

Society would not function if people did not accept their lower position. They need to be suitably respectful, obedient, conforming, compliant, and deferential. They also need to have adequate skills for gaining the attention and assistance of upper people. The condition of lower upperness involves gaining upperness by being lower in relation to important upper people or organizations. Because the management of the lower position is so delicate it can easily spill into the more negative forms of lowerness, which are characterized by fear of being let down by the upper person and feeling excessively and harshly judged. The negatively lower person may therefore be self-blaming and self-punishing. Some lower people have learned to gain care and attention from upper people by feigning or exaggerating their needfulness.

9

The Interpersonal Octagon

The interpersonal octagon is represented by Figure 3 in Chapter 3. It comprises eight segments of a circle organized around the horizontal closeness-distance axis and the vertical upperness-lowerness axis. Historically it is linked with Lichtenberg's *compass of motives,* which was referred to by Freud (1950); the *interpersonal circle* (Figure 2 in Chapter 3) first published by Freedman et al. (1951), which will be considered further in Chapter 10; and the *circumplex,* which was first described by Guttman (1954) and is examined here in Chapter 3. Each octant of the octagon has a two-word name, the first word applying to the vertical axis and the second word applying to the horizontal axis. The words indicate the contribution made to the characteristic of the octant by the respective axes. Where an axis makes no contribution, the word "neutral" is used.

In order for characteristics to be arranged in a circular ordering, or circumplex, the two axes around which the circumplex is constructed must be *orthogonal,* that is, they must represent independent constructs that bear no relation to each other at all. It is not entirely certain that the closeness-distance and the upperness-lowerness axes are completely orthogonal. It may be that upper people are more inclined to be distant and lower people are more inclined to be close. A further condition is that the two axes represent bipolar variables, that is, that one end of each axis be construed as the opposite of the other end. Although in many respects distance can be construed as the opposite of closeness, lowerness is more the reciprocal than the opposite of upperness. Whenever there is a circular ordering, the understanding is that the characteristics of each octant represent the bipolar opposite of the characteristics of the octant immediately opposite it across the circle; that is, the octagon comprises four bipolar variables. It will become clear during the course of this chapter that although there is some usefulness in construing the two main axes in this way, there seems to be little usefulness in construing the two intermediate axes in this way. For example, how does it help to conceive of upper closeness as being the bipolar opposite of lower distance?

In the original interpersonal circle published by Freedman et al. in 1951, the idea was expressed that the characteristics of each segment of the circle should be conceived of as a blending of the characteristics of the segments on either side of it. In the interpersonal octagon - which, to a degree, is being put forward as an alternative to the interpersonal circle (Birtchnell, 1993a) - it will be shown to be useful to conceive of each of the four *intermediate* positions as a blending of the two main positions on either side of it, but not useful to conceive of each of the four *main* positions as a blending of the two intermediate positions on either side of it. There is, however, a difference between the horizontal main positions and the vertical ones. On the horizontal axis it is relatively easy to define neutral closeness and neutral distance without reference to any vertical considerations. On the vertical axis it is more difficult to define the extent of the behaviors covered by the upper neutral and lower neutral positions, and there does appear to be a continuum ranging from upper distant through upper neutral to upper close, and from lower distant through lower neutral to lower close; and the outer limits of the upper neutral and lower neutral positions have to be fairly arbitrarily drawn.

There are serious methodological objections to constructing an interpersonal octagon. As is clear from Chapters 5, 6, 7, and 8, the concepts of closeness, distance, upperness, and lowerness are extremely complex. Each is multifaceted. It would be difficult to describe, in a sentence or two, what might be considered each concept's essential characteristics. Each involves relating and being related to, and there would need to be a "relating" octagon and a "being related to" octagon. It would also be necessary to keep positive relating separate from negative relating. Beyond this, there are different forms of negative relating; these ought to be treated separately, especially disrespectful and insecure relating (though admittedly these sometimes merge). The differences between positive and negative relating have to be applied to relating and being related to. People relate differently to different people; ideally, who is being related to ought to be specified. It is possible and meaningful, however, particularly in regard to negative forms of relating, to refer to someone's general relating tendencies.

Despite these objections, there remains some justification for defining the characteristics of each octant. Whether for clinical or research purposes, whether describing long-term personality characteristics or short-term relating episodes, it is possible to have a system of classification that all can agree upon. Reaching agreement on such definitions and developing reliable and valid methods of measurement are formidable tasks for the future. In this chapter a preliminary basis for a set of definitions will be presented. Obviously, since entire chapters were written about the main positions, descriptions of the individual octants are going to be much briefer, but sufficient detail will be provided to present an overall picture.

PROPOSED CHARACTERISTICS OF THE EIGHT OCTANTS

The descriptions begin at the neutral close position, rotate in a clockwise direction, and end at the upper close position (which then becomes continuous with the neutral close position). The reader is invited to compare the descriptions of each position with those that precede and follow it, remembering that the upper close position precedes the neutral close one.

Neutral Close

Positive Characteristics. The neutral close position is characterized by seeking, attaining, and maintaining close involvement with another person. This involves the process of other-cathexis, which is the investment of libido in an internalized representation of her/him. Thoughts of her/him evoke good feelings. Being with her/him is pleasant and being separated becomes increasingly unpleasant. Inevitably there is an emotional dependence. It matters what s/he thinks and does. Threats to the close involvement are frightening and actual severance is painful. Closeness involves liking the other; wanting to be kind to her/him; wanting to know about her/him; identifying with her/him; sympathizing with her/him to the extent that it matters what happens to her/him; empathizing with her/him to the extent of being happy when s/he is happy and sad when s/he is sad. Two important characteristics of closeness are openness and sharing. Openness is being happy to make revelations and disclosures to her/him and willing to let her/him inside; sharing is liking to spend time with her/him, talk to her/him, and do things with her/him. Positively close interchanges are companionable, cooperative, and collaborative.

Negative Characteristics. (1) Insecure neutral closeness. The insecurely close person clings excessively to the other because of a poorly established internalization of her/him; finds even short periods of separation hard to tolerate; resists letting her/him go; and waits anxiously for her/his return. S/he may resort to extreme measures to attract or maintain the other's attention and react with anger or aggression to being ignored or rejected. S/he is afraid that the other will find other people more interesting or more attractive. S/he does not enjoy her/his own company; feels panicky and desperate when alone; and may be compelled to make telephone calls so as to make contact with somebody. She may read or leave on the radio or television for distraction or rely heavily upon pets. (2) Imposed neutral closeness. The negatively close person may develop strategies for keeping the other close. S/he does not respect the other's need for distance; s/he forces her/his company on the other and talks to her/him when she wants to be quiet; s/he is intrusive and inquisitive and cannot tolerate the other having secrets. S/he does not like the other to have friends or interests of her/his own and may make efforts to sabotage these. (3) Misperceived neutral closeness. S/he may make incorrect assumptions about the interest that others have in her/him or create fantasy close relationships.

Lower Close

Positive Characteristics. The lower close position is a blending of the lower neutral and the neutral close positions. It is characterized by seeking, attaining, and maintaining closeness from a position of relative lowerness or lowerness from a position of relative closeness. Since lowerness is part of the definition of the lower close position, the lower close person inevitably places the other in a position of upper closeness. S/he is needful of the closeness that the upper/close person can provide and relies upon the upper person to provide it. Such needfulness can have great appeal to the upper person because it means that the lower person is unlikely to reject her/him. By being weak and vulnerable the lower person is nonthreatening, and s/he may use this as a form of seduction. S/he can be assured that should the upper person choose to destroy her/him, the upper person would lose her/his source of closeness.

The lower close person (literally or metaphorically) snuggles up against the upper close person, feeling safe, protected, and looked after. S/he entrusts her/himself to the care of the upper person, placing her/himself in her/his safe hands. She also admires, adores, idolizes, or worships the upper person, and there are obvious links between lower closeness and certain aspects of religion. Lower closeness approximates what Murray (1938) called *succorance*, including being made a fuss over, particularly when hurt, and what Bowlby (1969) called attachment. Because the lower close person often is fed by the upper close person, this mode of relating links up with the psychoanalytic concept of orality (Abraham, 1924).

Negative Characteristics. (1) Insecure lower closeness. The insecurely lower close person lacks what Erickson (1963) has called basic trust (see Chapter 4). S/he needs closeness from the upper close person but fears that it may not be available or may be withdrawn. S/he experiences what Rochlin (1961) has called *the dread of abandonment.* Fenichel (1968) referred to the *orally fixated character*, that is, the person who is fixated at the oral phase of psychosexual development, who craves love and nurturance. Such a person lacks the confidence to be seductive and instead resorts to repeated requests for assurances that the other still cares and will not desert her/him. Bowlby (1973) described a young girl who was suffering from what he called *anxious attachment*; she repeatedly said, "Do you love me? You won't leave me, Mummy, will you?" (page 214). The lower close person may also feel insecure because the upper close person may rape or sexually abuse her/him. This is particularly so if it has happened already. (2) Ontological dependence. Laing (1965) explained that the person with an ill formed identity has the option total isolation (for fear of losing her/himself in another's identity) or of total fusion with another. The ontologically dependent individual simply assumes the identity of a selected upper other and lives through her/him. (3) Seductive lower closeness. The negatively lower close person may resort to ways of increasing the interest (or perhaps the guilt) of the upper close person, such as openly weeping, maintaining that s/he cannot live without her/him, feigning illness, or making suicidal gestures. (4) Self-accusation. Some feelings of badness may also be associated with the lower close position, since the person may conclude that s/he is not loveable because s/he is bad. Fast (1967) wrote of a form of depression "involving rejection by the powerful other" and of the depressive being "helplessly dependent on the other to reinstate him as good, acceptable, loved and part of meaningful life" (page 262).

Lower Neutral

Positive Characteristics. Lowerness is characterized by the person recognizing that s/he has certain needs, seeking to meet these needs through involvement with an appropriate upper person, and being receptive to the upper person's meeting of them. Needing and receiving closeness (including care and the more caring forms of protection) were fitted into the lower close position. A cluster of needs toward the close end of the lower neutral range concern being helped, guided, encouraged and advised. More centrally, the needs include being protected (as by the law or the police), being given instruction or information, and being judged or approved of. Toward the distant end of the range are the more impersonal needs such as being told what to do, being managed or being organized. Some of these needs are simply made available by the upper person or upper people; others, the lower person has to ask for. Various degrees of asking, the most intense of which is begging, are the principal strategies of the lower neutral person, though many positive lower-to-upper interchanges are cooperative and mutually advantageous. The lower person is appreciative toward the upper person for meeting her/his needs.

Negative Characteristics. (1) Insecure lower neutral. The lower neutral person may feel insecure because of the possibility that the upper person will take advantage of her/his position to exploit or harm her/him; ignore her/him; adversely judge her/him or punish her/him; withdraw that which s/he is offering;

or perform her/his upper function unreliably or incompetently (e.g., make matters worse rather than better, give bad advice or incorrect information, or lead her/him astray). S/he may therefore seek repeated assurances that the upper person will not let her/him down and approves of him. (2) <u>Seductive lower neutral</u>. The lower neutral person is able to coerce the upper person into responding to her/his needs by making the upper person feel either sorry for her/him or guilty about not helping her/him. This s/he may do by presenting her/himself, rightly or wrongly, as incompetent, lost, helpless, confused or irresponsible. (3) <u>Self-accusation, self-punishment.</u> The badness of the lower close person is more completely developed as guilt in the lower neutral position. Guilt exists in four forms: (1) as an actuality, that is, the person undoubtedly has done something wrong; (2) as determined by an appointed judge; (3) as communicated to the person by her/his internalized upper parent; and (4) as assessed by the person according to her/his own internal standards. Commonly all four correspond and reinforce each other. A person with an excessively harsh internalized upper parent will feel extremely guilty when any of the other three obtain; but s/he may also feel guilty if the offense is relatively minor, if an external judge would not be inclined to take it seriously, and if the person would not, by her/his own internal standards, consider it serious. It is therefore the internalized upper parent's judgment that may contribute most to the tendency toward self-accusation and self-punishment.

Lower Distant

Positive Characteristics. The lower distant position is a blending of the lower neutral and neutral distant positions. It is characterized by seeking, attaining, and maintaining distance from a position of relative lowerness or lowerness from a position of relative distance. The lower distant person accepts her/his place in the order of things and asks little of others. S/he does not aspire to high position but is humble and contented. S/he is compliant and noncomplaining and does what is asked of her/him. S/he is deferential toward, though not necessarily fearful of, upper people; out of respect for them s/he is careful not to offend them. S/he conforms to regulations and obeys the law. In fact, obedience, conformity, and respect are the principal components of the lower distant position. Although the lower distant person will obey others, she is not prepared to identify with them, for this would be a manifestation of closeness. S/he may, however, identify with an organization, town, or country, for these are more remote attachment objects. S/he may therefore be a loyal follower, a devoted citizen, and a patriot.

Negative Characteristics. (1) <u>Insecure lower distance.</u> The insecurely lower distant person is afraid of being either lower neutral or lower close because that places her/him in a position of vulnerability. S/he is shy and timid and maintains a low profile in the hope that others will not notice her/him. Even though s/he may be needful of the help and guidance of others, s/he avoids seeking it and restricts her/his activity in order that s/he can manage without it. (2) <u>Withdrawal.</u> When the lower distant person is threatened by the encroachment of others s/he will retreat or go into hiding. Becoming inaccessible and retreating into a shell may be her/his most effective form of defense. (3) <u>Blind obedience.</u> The lower distant person who has a poorly developed identity and a fear of assuming responsibility for her/himself may passively offer her/himself to be led, controlled, and directed by an upper distant person or organization. S/he may join a cult or become a member of the armed services and simply live according to others' instructions. (4) <u>Masochism.</u> The lower distant person may derive satisfaction from being downtrodden and humiliated. The masochism of the lower distant position is the reciprocal of the sadism of the upper distant position.

Neutral Distant

Positive Characteristics. An important aspect of positive neutral distance is having the capacity to derive pleasure from being alone and having a good relationship with oneself. As was explained in Chapter 6, totally distant behavior would involve not relating to others at all. Distant relating is actually relatively distant relating, which is called formal relating. In keeping with the principle that there must be positive advantages to the relating of all four positions, it must be acknowledged that there are times when formal relating is appropriate and necessary. Most people are involved in much distant relating every day. Most relating with strangers is distant, but so is much relating with friends. The positively distant person maintains a respectful distance from others and respects the need of others to have space for and time to themselves. S/he avoids being inquisitive or intrusive. S/he accepts that the other would not wish her/him to make personal revelations about her/himself and refrains from seeking personal information about the other. S/he restricts communication to that which is necessary for whatever transaction needs to take place. S/he is cautious and precise in what s/he says, and her/his remarks are more likely to be carefully prepared and rehearsed.

The neutral distant person has a strong sense of who s/he is, knows what s/he wants, and where s/he is going. S/he is capable of being self-sufficient and self-reliant. S/he may be an original and creative thinker but does not impose her/his ideas upon other people. S/he seeks and provides her/his own satisfactions.

Negative Characteristics. (1) <u>Insecure neutral distance.</u> The insecurely neutral distant person has a limited capacity for involvement with others. S/he feels uncomfortable, or frankly panicky, if others encroach too near to her/him and is embarrassed if people make personal revelations to her/him or want to know personal things about her/himself. S/he tries to restrict contact with others to a minimum, says little, and reveals as little as possible about her/himself. When people approach too closely or make too penetrating remarks, s/he may tighten up, fight them off, or try to escape the situation. (2) <u>Defensive distance</u>. The neutral distant person protects her/himself from intrusion or invasion by shields or barricades. S/he may literally build strong fences, high walls, and locked gates, construct a moat with a drawbridge, have heavily locked and bolted doors and install burglar alarms, or simply convey by her/his manner that others are not welcome. In a relationship s/he may indulge in avoidant behavoir such as going out and staying out a lot, threatening to leave permanently, ignoring the other, not touching or looking at the other, reading or watching television, refusing to talk or listen to what the other is saying, and keeping things to her/himself.

Upper Distant

Positive Characteristics. The upper distant position is a blending of the upper neutral and neutral distant positions. It is characterized by seeking, attaining, and maintaining upperness from a position of distance and distance from a position of upperness. Being in control is the principal objective of the upper distant person. S/he expects to be obeyed and treated with respect. S/he is an upholder of strong principles and a rigid disciplinarian. S/he is good at setting rules and maintaining order. S/he can be strict but fair and is capable of taking command when harsh decisions have to be made. S/he does not mind being disliked, providing s/he knows that what s/he is imposing upon or requiring of people is right and for the good of the organization or the community. S/he may find it necessary to impose punishments, and order is sometimes maintained through fear of punishment.

Negative Characteristics. (1) <u>Insecure upper distance.</u> The insecurely upper distant person may be afraid of losing upperness and afraid of losing distance. Since distance makes cruelty easier (see Chapters 6 and 7), when s/he is threatened the upper distant person is capable of cruel and ruthless behavior. S/he responds to insults with angry indignation. S/he can be ruthlessly suppressive. When her/his distance is under threat s/he can be cruelly rejecting. The most extreme form of upper distance is tyranny, and tyrants sometimes need to surround themselves with spies and armed guards. (2) <u>Imposed upper distance.</u>

One aspect of upper distance concerns the self. The upper distant person may use her/his power to ensure s/he gets her/his way and has things done her/his way. Actual or threatened violence is a common feature of negative upper distant behavior. This can result in brutal domination. Within a tyrannical regime it may extend to creation of a police state involving the elimination of rivals and threatening factions, the suppression of contrary opinion, and the imposition of censorship. (3) Exploitation. The upper distant person is inclined to relate to others as though they were things to be manipulated. S/he may have no scruples in exploiting them for her/his selfish ends. (4) Narcissism. It is difficult to locate narcissism within the octagonal system. The form that was called reactive narcissism by Kets de Vries and Miller (1985) clearly belongs in the upper distant position. The upper distant narcissist loves only her/himself and has a disregard for the rights of others. S/he is unable to recognize how others feel and is capable of great cruelty and ruthlessness. Another form will be considered in the upper close position. (5) Megalomania. The upper neutral person may become obsessed by power and the wish to rule, influence, and control others. (6) Sadism. The upper distant person derives satisfaction from seeing others suffer, for this confirms her/him in her/his lowerness.

Upper Neutral

Positive Characteristics. The upper neutral person has certain assets (knowledge, skills) and strengths (leadership, powers of judgment) that enable her/him to be of service to others. Her/his attitude falls somewhere between the discipline imposing of upper distance and the caregiving of upper closeness. The upper neutral position is very much the reciprocal of the lower neutral one, and the services the upper neutral person can provide correspond with the needs described in the lower neutral section. The upper neutral person can be an inspirational leader, an efficient manager, and an effective teacher. S/he feels important; this sense of importance is reinforced by experiencing the needfulness, admiration, and gratitude of the lower neutral person. The upper neutral person is also expected to give or withhold approval and to make judgments about rightness and wrongness, innocence and guilt.

Negative Characteristics. (1) Insecure upper neutral. The characteristics of insecure upperness were listed in Chapter 7. The insecurely upper neutral person is anxious lest the upperness that s/he has is not acknowledged or respected and may resort to bullying, self-assertion, arrogance, pomposity, boasting, pointing to others' weaknesses, ridicule, insult, and humiliation. S/he is also anxious lest through competition with others s/he be overtaken and pushed into relative obscurity. The failing politician, sportsperson, or public performer may be

anxious that s/he is no longer able to maintain her/his previous standards and will
begin to lose public acclaim. (2) Imposed upper neutral. The upper neutral person
may find it preferable to manage the lower person as a means of keeping her/him
helpless and nonassertive. S/he may offer to take responsibility for making
decisions and take on all the difficult tasks, so that the lower person becomes
irresponsible and incompetent. The lower person initially may find this
arrangement appealing but in time may make a plea for assuming more
responsibility. This is the last thing the upper person wants. S/he will therefore
try to subdue the lower person with remarks such as, "Why don't you leave it
all to me? You know you're no good at that sort of thing." (3) Overriding
ambition. The neutral upper person may become driven to attain ever higher
levels of importance, seniority, or wealth. S/he may become intoxicated by the
acclaim and recognition that this brings and work ceaselessly to this end. Each
achievement simply serves to provoke further striving.

Upper Close

Positive Characteristics. The upper close position is a blending of the upper
neutral and neutral close positions. It is characterized by seeking, attaining, and
maintaining upperness from a position of closeness and closeness from a position
of upperness. The upper close person responds to the needfulness of the lower
close person and feels protective and caring toward her/him. One aspect of upper
closeness approximates what Murray (1938) called *nurturance.* It includes being
generous toward others, feeling sorry for those who are less fortunate, and
wanting to help those who are in trouble. The upper close person is kind,
supportive, praising, encouraging, and sympathetic; listens to the other's troubles;
and is consoling and comforting. S/he is rewarded by the other's gratitude. The
upper close person may also be the object of the lower person's adoration,
idolization, deification, and worship.

Negative Characteristics. (1) Insecure upper closeness. An upper close
person may fear that the lower person is no longer needful of the closeness s/he
is offering and is losing interest in her/him. A parent may fear that her/his child
is trying to break free in order to form close relationships with peers. A doctor,
particularly a psychotherapist, may fear that her/his patient can manage without
her/him. When the upper close person is the object of adoration' s/he may fear
that lower others will cease to consider her/him worthy of such treatment, or
come to see through her/him. (2) Imposed upper closeness. The upper close
person is able to use her/his upperness to impose closeness. A young parent may
keep her/his children away from school or take them shopping with her/him in
order to avoid being alone. A feature of negative upper closeness is

possessiveness, or even imprisonment. An elderly parent may try to prevent her/his children leaving home or getting married or insist that they live close to her/him and visit regularly. One marital partner may prohibit the other from going out where s/he may meet people, having separate interests, spending time with friends, or dancing with other people. (3) Narcissism.. The narcissist of the upper close position is exhibitionistic and requires constant attention and admiration. S/he loves to be loved and loves those who love her/him; but s/he loves them only because they love her/him. S/he accumulates fans and loves her/his fans, but the love is primarily adoration and flows from them to her/him. (4) Using upperness to gain closeness. An upper person may force closeness upon a lower person. A grandparent may try to take over the care of her/his grandchildren, or lavish attention on them, because it makes her/him feel good, irrespective of the effect this may have upon the children or their parents. A man may rape a woman; one marital partner may compel the other to have sex; or a parent may sexually abuse a child. Some may argue that there is nothing close about enforced sex, but this confuses closeness with respectfulness. The enforcer does experience closeness even though the victim does not. It must be acknowledged that respectfulness of the other's feelings is a component of positive closeness; and from this point of view, to enforce closeness might seem a contradiction in terms. The person who enforces closeness steals closeness in a self-centered way, just as the voyeur or the frotteur does. (5) Housebreaking. Although most housebreakers are intent on stealing money and possessions, there is an aspect of housebreaking that has to do with penetration, that is, breaking into someone's private property. Some rapists first break into the victim's house or apartment.

RESEARCH APPLICATIONS OF THE INTERPERSONAL OCTAGON

A self-administered questionnaire, called the Person's Relating to Others Questionnaire (PROQ), was constructed by which a person could rate her/his general relating tendencies to others within each of the eight octants. This showed that the relating characteristics of depressed subjects were significantly worse than those of nondepressed subjects; but whereas the relating of the fully recovered depressives showed a significant improvement, that of the partially recovered depressives remained poor (Birtchnell et al., 1992). A set of four questionnaires was constructed, called the Couple's Relating to Each Other Questionnaire (CREOQ), by which each marital partner could rate her/his relating to the other and the other's relating to her/him within each of the eight octants. The unique features of the CREOQ were that (1) they applied to one specified other person, and (2) they measured both relating and being related to. These questionnaires showed that the relating of couples who were seeking marital therapy was significantly worse than that of couples whose marriages

FIGURE 4
A Graphical Representation of Scores on the Person's Relating to Others Questionnaire (PROQ)

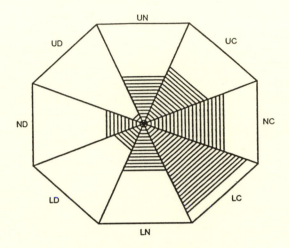

A typical patient's octant scores

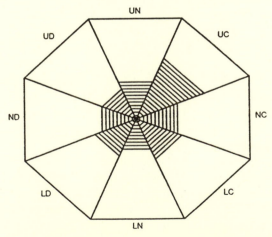

Mean octant scores from a general population sample

Here the pre-treatment scores of a typical psychotherapy patient are compared with the mean scores from a general population sample.

226

FIGURE 5
A Graphical Representation of Scores on the Couple's Relating to Each Other Questionnaire (CREOQ)

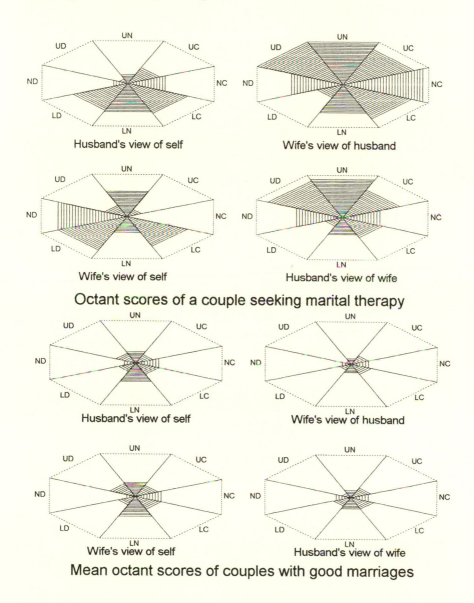

Octant scores of a couple seeking marital therapy

Mean octant scores of couples with good marriages

Here the pre-treatment scores of a couple seeking marital therapy are compared with the mean scores from a sample of couples with good marriages.

were considered to be stable (Birtchnell, 1993b). In both the PROQ and the CREOQ there were ten negative items and two positive items for each octant, so they were predominantly measures of negative relating. The positive items were included mainly to break up the negative orientation of the questionnaires, but even with these small numbers of positive items, it has appeared that high negative scores are not always accompanied by low positive ones. Thus, there is a case for measuring positive relating and negative relating separately.

Beyond the development of questionnaire measures of relating, there is a need for development of (1) interview-based measures, and (2) observational measures. Gardner (1992) proposed a technique, which he called LUCD plotting, by which the minute-by-minute actions, or changes in relating behavior over long periods of time, of one or more individuals could be plotted, on a computer monitor, around the intersecting horizontal and vertical axes. Such an approach could be adopted only after strict criteria for the coding of rating behavior were established.

CLINICAL APPLICATIONS OF THE INTERPERSONAL OCTAGON

In both individual psychotherapy and marital therapy it is possible - without asking specific questions, on the basis of patients' reports and behavior - to formulate people's interpersonal circumstances in terms of their relating to others and others' relating to them, both generally and as applied to specified other people. It is also possible to observe their relating tendencies within the therapy session. Therapeutic strategies can be planned in terms of improving patients' negative relating behavior and enabling them to cope with the negative relating of others.

More formally, the PROQ can be administered at the commencement of individual psychotherapy and the CREOQ at the commencement of marital therapy as a means of providing numerical scores, which can be converted into graphical representations (see Figures 4 and 5), that which give a clear indication of the principal areas of relating difficulties. Therapeutic strategies can then be devised for correcting these difficulties, and at the end of therapy the measures can be repeated to determine whether the changes the therapy was directed toward have actually taken place.

One of the most fundamental contributions spatial theory can make to clinical psychology and psychiatry is the creation of a logical framework within which it is possible to fit most of the major forms of personality disorder and mental illness. This contributes to a clearer understanding of the nature of these conditions and points to new ways of considering how they might be interrelated. For example, there may be advantages for example, to viewing the conditions of distance as belonging to one particular class with certain common characteristics. This raises intriguing questions about how one distant condition might be distinguishable from another.

SUMMARY

Once the characteristics of the four main positions within the spatial system have been described, it becomes possible to examine how they might be related. It also becomes possible to separate out the four intermediate positions and determine what their characteristics might be. This gives rise to what will be called the interpersonal octagon. In order to accommodate the full complexity of human relating, it becomes necessary, for each of the eight positions in the octagon, to differentiate between relating and being related to and between positive relating and the various kinds of negative relating. In addition to this, a person may relate differently to different people, so the person related to may have to be specified. Finally, the distinction has to be made between a relating tendency that extends over time (which also may extend across relationships) and isolate episodes of relating.

Two types of questionnaire measure are described; the PROQ, which measures the person's general relating tendency, and the CREOQ, by which marital partners rate how each relates to the other and how the other relates to her/him. There also is a need for interview-based measures and observational measures. Individual psychotherapists and marital therapists may use the spatial system for identifying the nature of patients' relating difficulties and for devising intervention strategies. The questionnaires may be used as a means of monitoring changes in relating brought about by therapy. Finally, the spatial system has value as a conceptual framework within which to classify personality disorders and mental illnesses.

10

The Interpersonal Circle

The basic format of the interpersonal circle was described in Chapter 3 and illustrated in Figure 2. The reader is advised to re-read the relevant section of Chapter 3 before proceeding with the present chapter. Although the first written account of the interpersonal circle was by Freedman (1950), its detailed development was the work of Leary (1957). Like the interpersonal octagon, the interpersonal circle was constructed around two axes that were assumed to be orthogonal. Although Leary may have gotten the names of the axes wrong, he seems to have gotten many of the underlying principles right. He referred to the sixteen segments of the circle as *generic interpersonal themes*, implying that they could be interpreted in a variety of ways. As the title of his book suggests, his main preoccupation was with the classification of personality types. He considered that the personality of most people could be categorized according to one of the sixteen segments, which he called the *preferred interpersonal style*. He acknowledged that the psychologically healthy person would be able to call upon a range of styles to suit various situations, but that the maladaptive person would tend to rely upon a very rigid and intensely expressed style, regardless of the situation, that would force others to respond to her/him in the same narrow way.

He proposed that people express their interpersonal styles "reflexively," that is, in an automatic, spontaneous, and involuntary fashion (which is similar to the principles of relating set down in Chapter 1 of this book). He also proposed that interpersonal reflexes tend to initiate or invite complementary interpersonal responses from others in such a way as to lead to a repetition of the original reflex action. In Figure 6, which has been modified from one of Leary's original diagrams, the reflexes are represented by the sixteen outer segments and the corresponding responses are represented by the sixteen inner segments. This has come to be called the *complementarity hypothesis*; Paddock and Nowicki (1986) considered that it may be the most theoretically important and clinically useful

FIGURE 6
Leary's Interpersonal Circle

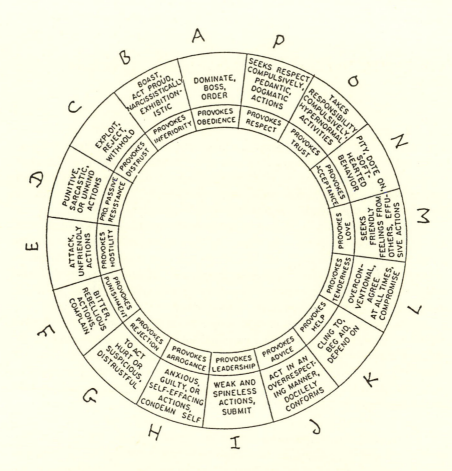

This is a simplified version of Figure 1 which appeared on page 65 of Leary's (1957) book. Reprinted with permission of the author.

idea to arise from the Leary model, because it articulates how disordered behavior may be maintained interpersonally. A number of scholars (Carson, 1969; Kiesler, 1983; Duke and Nowicki, 1987; Wiggins, 1982) have tried to develop the hypothesis further. Orford (1986) maintained that it remains largely unsupported by the evidence and needs to be modified and retested, but this view has been challenged by Kiesler (1987, 1990; Strong et al., 1988). As it stands, the hypothesis is too simplistic. It takes no account of whether the initial act of relating was positive or negative, proposed or invited, accepted or declined.

COMPARING THE AXES OF THE CIRCLE WITH THE AXES OF THE OCTAGON

The axes of the interpersonal circle, laid down by Freedman in 1950, were not challenged until forty years later (Birtchnell, 1990). They have become enshrined within the area of study known as interpersonal psychology, and they form the basis of a number of measures and methods of assessment (Kiesler, 1990, 1992). This has had the effect of preserving them in their original form and rendering any form of revision extremely difficult. They can, however, be found wanting on a number of counts.

1. They do not easily fit into an evolutionary model. The horizontal axis, concerning love versus hate, refers essentially to human interaction, and the terms "loving" and "hating" are not appropriate for the majority of animal species. Benjamin et al. (1986) maintained that Benjamin's version of the interpersonal circle (see subsequent discussion) does have its roots in evolutionary processes but carried their argument no further.

2. Nowhere in the interpersonal psychology literature is the theoretical basis for the two axes discussed. It is difficult to establish links between the axes and other theoretical systems (as was done for the present system in Chapter 3). Both Freedman et al. (1951) and Leary (1957) proposed that the theory be regarded as an extension of the work of Sullivan (1947, 1953), but Sullivan did not refer to these axes.

3. The characteristics attributable to each of the two axes should belong to the same class of phenomenon. Whereas loving and hating are feelings, dominating and submitting are forms of behavior. Much of the interpersonal literature is concerned with personality, but loving and hating are not personality characteristics.

4. Although Leary used the term "generic" to describe the categories of the circle, the axes are not generic in the way that the axes of the octagon are. The lack of applicability of the love-hate axis to all animal species already has been mentioned. Although dominating and submitting behavior has been observed in a broad range of animal species (Lorenz, 1981), it is not universal; and it is only one aspect of the interactions that occur between more powerful and less

powerful animals. Parenting is not a form of dominating. As was demonstrated in Chapters 7 and 8, the range of upper-to-lower interactions that are observable between humans extends far beyond the simple and primitive processes of dominating and submitting.

5. Even when the circle is expanded to its full complement of sixteen segments, there is a great paucity of description of the types of behavior that might be subsumed under each of the main headings, as is provided in Chapters 5 through 8. This is because the circle has been used mainly as the basis for various measuring instruments, which rely on brief statements.

6. Freedman, Leary, and most other interpersonal psychologists have failed to distinguish between relating and being related to. Benjamin (1974), whose work will be mentioned later, is the notable exception to this.

7. In line with evolutionary theory, it should be possible to describe the positive advantages and the well-adjusted and constructive forms of behavior that are associated with each position, to the extent that no position could be construed as being better or worse than any other position. Loving is the only well-adjusted and constructive form of behavior of the four positions of the circle. Hating, dominating, and submitting are essentially maladjusted and nonconstructive forms. Furthermore, loving is clearly preferable to hating, as dominating is to submitting.

8. No clear-cut objective is spelled out for any of the main positions, and there is no emotional link-up with the attainment or lack of attainment of any of them. There is no concept of need or hunger for a position or experience of satiety when a need is met, or fatigue when there has been overexposure to a position. It would make no sense to say that hate, for example, is an objective or that one should feel hunger for hatred and experience satiety when an adequate amount of it has been attained.

9. Consequently it is not possible to describe competencies for each position. Leary had difficulty defining constructive forms of hating and submitting and was able to define positive forms of dominating only by assuming it to have the broader meaning of being in a position of authority. Interpersonal psychology has survived, despite its deficiencies, because implicitly it is a theory of pathology. This is in keeping with Leary's stated objective of developing an interpersonal system that would supplant the existing classification system of psychiatric illnesses (see Leary, 1957, page 10). The interpersonal classification presented here was based upon patients attending a psychiatric clinic.

10. Without a clear definition of positive relating or competence, Leary had no means of determining what negative relating or incompetence might be. He was thrown back upon the principle that Sullivan (who was a psychiatrist) had propounded, that there is a continuity from mental normality to mental illness. This led him to introduce the concept of intensity: low intensity equals normality and high intensity equals pathology. Laforge and Suczek (1955) incorporated this into their Interpersonal Check List. Items endorsed by 90 percent of respondents

were considered to be of low intensity, and those endorsed by only 10 percent of respondents were considered to be of high intensity. As will be clear from what has gone before, negativity within the interpersonal octagon is not a matter of intensity. The fact that mental illness is less common than mental normality, even though there are all stages between normality and illness, does not mean that it is an extreme version of normality.

COMPARING THE LEARY OCTANTS WITH THE SPATIAL OCTANTS

Leary sometimes compressed the sixteen segments of the interpersonal circle to eight octants by combining neighboring segments and using a combination of their code letters to identify them. Each octant was given a two- word appellation, the first word (described as a form of adjustment) representing a moderate version and the second (described as a form of personality) a more extreme version of the form of interpersonal behavior represented by the octant. He devoted a short chapter of his book to each of them. It is easier to work with these octants than with the original sixteen sections because they permit comparison with the octants of the circles of subsequent other workers and with those of the interpersonal octagon.

Working around the circle in a clockwise direction, and starting in the same position as for the interpersonal octagon (due east), I will give brief summaries of each of the octants (as far as possible in Leary's own words) and make comparisons with the equivalent octants of the interpersonal octagon. It ought to be emphasized that the characteristics of the octants of the interpersonal octagon were determined according to the principles of spatial theory as laid down in this book, without any reference to Leary's book.

The LM Position (Corresponds in Place to Neutral Close)

Called adjustment through cooperation. The typical LM person aims to establish harmonious, amicable relations with others. S/he is extroverted, popular, and well liked and is happy to go along with the conventional pattern. S/he is disinclined to express a unique, original, or highly controversial point of view.

The maladaptive form is called the overconventional personality. Such a person strives to please and to be accepted. S/he is extroverted and outgoing to an intense degree. S/he smiles, agrees, collaborates, and conciliates.

The correspondence between this and the neutral close position is reasonably good, though insufficient attention is paid to involvement with a single other. Extroversion may be a defense against such involvement. The maladaptive form veers too much toward lower closeness and the issue of separation anxiety is totally ignored.

The JK Position (Corresponds in Place to Lower Close)

Called adjustment through docility. The typical JK person outwardly relies upon or looks up to others. S/he trains others to assume a strong, friendly role and to offer help, advice, and direction. S/he is dutiful and conforming. S/he conveys the message, "I am a meek, admiring person in need of your help and advice."

The maladaptive form is called the dependent personality. Such a person uses her/his symptoms to communicate a helpless, painful, uncertain, frightened, hopeful, dependent passivity. S/he easily lapses into fearful, tearful behavior.

The correspondence between this and the lower close position is good, though the term "docility" is unnecessarily pejorative, and seeking advice and direction would fit more appropriately in the lower neutral position.

The HI Position (Corresponds in Place to Lower Neutral)

Called adjustment through self-effacement. The typical HI person wards off anxiety by self-deprecation. S/he trains others to look down upon her/him with various intensities of derogation and superiority. S/he is mobilized to shun the appearance of outward strength and pride. S/he conveys the message, "I am a weak, inferior person."

The maladaptive form is called the masochistic personality. Such a person feels inferior and unworthy and is obsessed with matters of right and wrong. S/he presents a facade of guilty submissiveness and may appear glum, weak, and withdrawn.

There are obvious connections between this and the lower neutral position, though Leary demonstrates a conspicuous inability to conceive of a truly positive version of it.

The PG Position (Corresponds in Place to Lower Distant)

Called adjustment through rebellion. The typical FG person maintains a realistic, accurate skepticism toward the accepted way of doing things. S/he derives a retaliatory pleasure in rejecting the conventional and challenging taboos, commitments, and expectations. S/he handles anxiety by establishing distance between her/himself and others.

The maladaptive form is called the distrustful personality. Such a person is overly bitter, cynical, passively resistant, and resentful. S/he has a grievance against the world and is pessimistic and disappointed.

This has the distance but not the lowerness of the lower distant position; it is as close as Leary got to describing neutral distance. It should have been shunted up a place.

The DE Position (Corresponds in Place to Neutral Distant)

Called adjustment through aggression. The typical DE person delights in combat and feels comfortable only when engaged in a threatening attack. S/he threatens others by verbal, moral, or physical means. S/he imposes discipline and provokes guilt. S/he conveys the message "I am a dangerous, fearsome person."

The maladaptive form is called the sadistic personality. Such a person is overly hostile and punitive and indulges in hurtful, mocking, destroying, and threatening actions. S/he experiences no qualms about hurting others.

This again should have been shunted up a place. What Leary is describing here comes closest to upper distant behavior, though again he demonstrates an inability to conceive of a truly positive version of it.

The BC Position (Corresponds in Place to Upper Distant)

Called adjustment through competition. The typical BC person is independent and confident. S/he invests considerable energy in protecting and increasing her/his prestige. S/he feels most secure when s/he is independent of other people and feels s/he is triumphing over them. S/he conveys the message that s/he feels superior.

The maladaptive form is called the narcissistic personality. Such a person is smug, cold, boastful, rejecting, selfish, competitive, and exploitative. S/he indulges in exhibitionism and proud self-display.

This is another variant of upper distance, but now it is in the corresponding place. The independence, coldness, narcissism, exploitation, rejection, and selfishness are right, but the competition and prestige belong more to the upper neutral position. Again, it is deficient in positive characteristics.

The PA Position (Corresponds in Place to Upper Neutral)

Called adjustment through power. The typical PA person expresses strength, force, energy, and leadership and wins from others respect, approbation, and deference. S/he feels secure when exerting control over people and things, and s/he wins awe, admiration, and obedience from others. S/he conveys the message, "I know something you don't know."

The maladaptive form is called the autocratic personality. Such a person is

FIGURE 7
Early Modifications of the Leary Circle

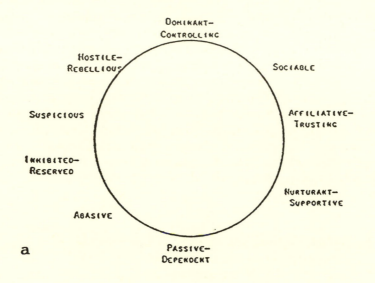

a

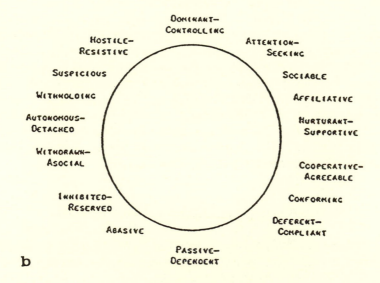

b

a and b are from Lorr and McNair, "An Interpersonal Behavior Circle." Journal of Abnormal and Social Psychology, 67, pages 70 and 73. Copyright (1963) by the American Psychological Association. Reprinted by permission.

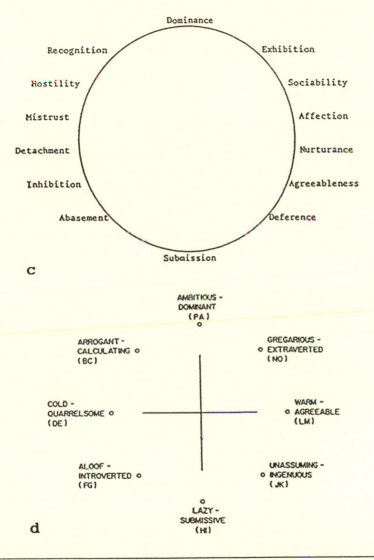

Dominance

Recognition
Exhibition

Hostility
Sociability

Mistrust
Affection

Detachment
Nurturance

Inhibition
Agreeableness

Abasement
Deference

Submission

c

AMBITIOUS -
DOMINANT
(PA)
o

ARROGANT -
CALCULATING o
(BC)

GREGARIOUS -
o EXTRAVERTED
(NO)

COLD -
QUARRELSOME o
(DE)

WARM -
o AGREEABLE
(LM)

ALOOF -
INTROVERTED o
(FG)

UNASSUMING -
o INGENUOUS
(JK)

o
LAZY -
SUBMISSIVE
(HI)

d

c is from Lorr and McNair, "Expansion of the Interpersonal Behavior Circle." Journal of Personality and Social Psychology, 2:6, page 828. Copyright (1965) by the American Psychological Association. d is from Wiggins, "A Psychological Taxonomy of Trait-Descriptive Terms: The Interpersonal Domain" Journal of Personality and Social Psychology, 37:3, page 399. Copyright (1979) by the American Psychological Association. Both reprinted by permission.

domineering, power-ridden, and overambitious. S/he exhibits a compulsive need to appear competent, organized and authoritative.

This corresponds reasonably well with the upper neutral position, though the concern with power and control fit better into upper distance. Leary also has called this the managerial position, which would be appropriate for upper neutrality. The range of negative forms is limited.

The NO Position (Corresponds in Place to Upper Close)

Called adjustment through responsibility. The typical NO person strives to be close to others, to help, protect, counsel, support, and sympathise. S/he appears sound, sympathetic, and considerate. S/he is most secure when involved in a close, friendly, protective relationship with a dependent other.

The maladaptive form is called the hypernormal personality. Such a person is driven by relentless ideals of service and contribution to others. S/he is compulsively popularity-seeking and overprotective.

The correspondence between this and the upper close position is good, though it is questionable whether the upper close person seeks popularity.

LATER MODIFICATIONS OF THE INTERPERSONAL CIRCLE

From an early stage, following the introduction of the interpersonal circle there were many attempts to improve upon it. Early on the scene were Lorr and McNair (1963), who replaced LaForge and Suczek's (1955) Interpersonal Check List with their own Interpersonal Behavior Inventory (IBI), by which therapists were asked to rate the behavior of their patients. The statistical analyses of their data generated Circle *a* of Figure 7. In this, *nurturant* had shifted from the upper right to the lower right position and been replaced by *sociable*. A new construct, *inhibited-reserved,* now appeared in the lower left position. On the basis of data from the ICL, the IBI, and two unpublished scales (Stern's Need Scales and Campbell's Interpersonal Need Scales) they proposed the hypothetical sixteen-segment Circle *b* of Figure 7, which brought *nurturant-supportive* up to the due east position but had *attention-seeking* and *sociable* in the upper right position. A new construct, *autonomous-detached,* now appeared in the due west position, which corresponded exactly with neutral distance of the interpersonal octagon. Using a revised version of the IBI, Lorr and McNair (1965) generated Circle *c* of Figure 7, which apart from retaining *detachment* in the due west position, corresponded less well than did the original interpersonal circle with the interpersonal octagon.

Wiggins (1979) placed the highest priority upon the construction of a circle that conformed precisely with the requirements of Guttman's (1954) circumplex (see Chapter 3). He observed, as had Lorr and McNair (1965) and Stern (1970), that when the variables generated from the ICL are factored by the method of principal components, and loaded on the first two factors, a plotting of these loadings does not produce a perfect circumplex. The close apposition of LM and NO leaves a hole in the upper right position, which Lorr and McNair (1963) and later Wiggins (1979) himself filled with a gregarious factor. It also concerned him that a number of the pairs of vectors that appeared on opposite sides of the Leary circle did not constitute bipolar opposites. He therefore developed a new measure, based upon single adjectives, called the Interpersonal Adjective Scales (IAS). According to Paddock & Nowicki (1986), when the factor loadings are plotted, data from these scales generate four sets of bipolar variables (comprising eight octants), which are almost evenly spaced around the circle and show no significant gaps in any quadrant. These are shown in Circle *e* of Figure 7.

Wiggins & Broughton (1985) pooled the data from six different questionnaires (including those of Stern and Campbell, cited previously, and the IAS) and selected the most representative items. Because they relied upon brief questionnaire items, their classification suffers from a paucity of detail. Much more serious than this, it fails to distinguish between positive and negative features. As a result, some factors are predominantly positive and others are predominantly negative. What follows is a listing of the eight factors with comments about the appropriateness of their placing.

LM (Corresponds in Place to NC) *Warm-Agreeable*

This factor includes the attributes kind, soft-hearted, cooperative, sympathetic, appreciative, sympathetic, and forgiving. These reflect a disposition to be warm, nurturant, and caring. This is an entirely positive factor, which comes nearest to upper closeness.

JK (Corresponds in Place to LC) *Unassuming-Ingenuous*

This factor includes the attributes mild, gentle, conventional, timid, and obliging, which reflect a disposition to be obedient, deferent, and easily intimidated. This is a strange mixture, which is generally negatively lower but does not represent lower closeness.

HI (Corresponds in Place to LN) *Lazy-Submissive*

This factor includes the attributes inactive and avoidant of power or achievement, timid, meek, self-doubting, worried, fearful, and anxious. The factor is generally negatively lower and therefore reasonably correctly placed.

FG (Corresponds in Place to LD) *Aloof-Introverted*

This factor includes the attributes distant, introverted, inward, silent, reserved, inhibited, shy, bashful, bitter, and aloof. This comes nearest to negative neutral distance. It appears to have been pushed into the LD position in order to be opposite the gregarious-extravert factor in the UC position. The (upper) aloof component appears to be completely out of place.

DE (Corresponds in Place to ND) *Cold-Quarrelsome*

This factor includes the attributes cruel, coldhearted, hardhearted, and ruthless, which reflect a disposition to avoid people. Although this is generally negatively distant, the cruel and ruthless features push it more toward upper distance.

BC (Corresponds in Place to UD) *Arrogant-Calculating*

This factor includes the attributes boastful, flaunty, bigheaded, swellheaded, conceited, tricky, cunning, crafty, wily, sly, and exploitative. These reflect a disposition to maximize gains in relation to others and to express irritability and anger. This seems to be a mixture of negative upper neutral and upper distant qualities.

PA (Corresponds in Place to UN) *Ambitious-Dominant*

This factor includes the attributes forceful, assertive, dominant, self-assured, self-confident, industrious, domineering, persistent, firm and persevering, which reflect a disposition to take charge and assume responsibility. This is an almost entirely positive factor and is correctly place. It appears to be a positive version of BC.

NO (Corresponds in Place to UC) *Gregarious-Extraverted*

This factor includes the attributes extroverted, cheerful, pleasant, good-natured, outgoing, sociable, perky, enthusiastic, and vivacious, which reflect a disposition to enjoy social events and gatherings. This is another entirely positive factor, which was introduced by Lorr and McNair and retained by Wiggins. It has nothing to do with the nurturant caring qualities of upper closeness, though it is related to neutral closeness.

In this classification, the original circle has been seriously distorted by the insertion of the old Jungian/Eysenckian distinction of introversion-extroversion across the upper-right, lower-left diameter. As a result, the neutral close and lower close positions have been completely lost and the upper close position has been moved down to where the neutral close one should be. This may have produced a more perfect circumplex, but it is no longer an accurate reflection of reality.

The "1982" Interpersonal Circle

Kiesler's (1983) "1982" circle (see Figure 8a) is a theoretical system, intended to be an update of the original Freedman/Leary circle, in the light of the modifications made by Lorr and McNair and by Wiggins. It reverts to the sixteen-segment format, and re-introduces the moderate-extreme distinction, but incorporates Wiggins's bipolar principle. Kiesler, like Freedman and Leary, has no clear conception of positive and negative relating, so some of the segments are positive (e.g., *warm-pardoning*) and others are negative (e.g., *cold-punitive*) and the moderate-extreme distinction is simply a matter of intensity. For each one of the sixteen segments there is a set of (three to five) moderate terms and (three to five) extreme terms, and for each term there is a set of (three to nine) short descriptive statements. There are, in all, 700 statements. The statements are intended to allow researchers to classify observed behavior. Determining the psychometric qualities of the instrument would indeed be a formidable task.

The distribution of the segments retains all the disadvantages of the IAS. The horizontal dimension ranges from cooperative-helpful at the right extreme to antagonistic-harmful at the left, and the vertical dimension ranges from controlling at the top to docile at the bottom. The upper right quadrant continues to be dominated by the extroversion theme, its three segments being *confident, spontaneous,* and *outgoing.* Because of this the upper close, neutral close, and lower close functions have had to be squeezed into the lower right quadrant. Strong et al. (1988, page 808) observed that "Kiesler changed the relative positions of several behavior categories from those proposed by Leary, and our results do not support his changes."

The Strong and Hills Interpersonal Circle

Strong et al. (1988) reported upon yet another variant of the interpersonal circle (see Figure 8b) which was developed by Strong and Hills (1986). In line with the Freedman/Leary model, it has a friendly-hostile horizontal axis and a dominant-submissive vertical axis. Superimposed upon these, however, is the Wiggins extravert-introvert axis extending from the upper right to the lower left quadrant, and quite ingeniously, a separated-connected axis (equivalent in many respects to a distance-closeness axis) extending from the upper left to the lower right quadrant. This creates, *in the spaces between these four axes*, eight octants,

FIGURE 8
Later Modifications of the Leary Circle

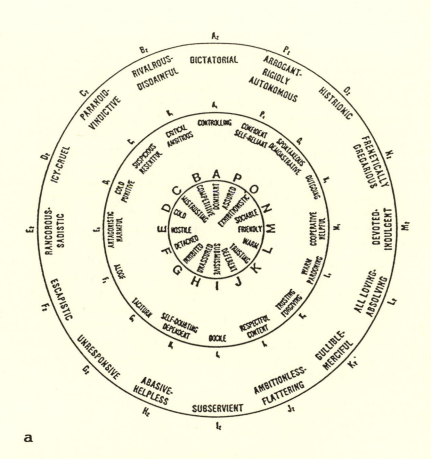

a

a is from Kiesler, "The 1982 Interpersonal Circle: A Taxonomy for Complementarity in Human Transactions" Psychological Review, 90, page 189. Copyright (1983) by the American Psychological Association. Reprinted by permission.

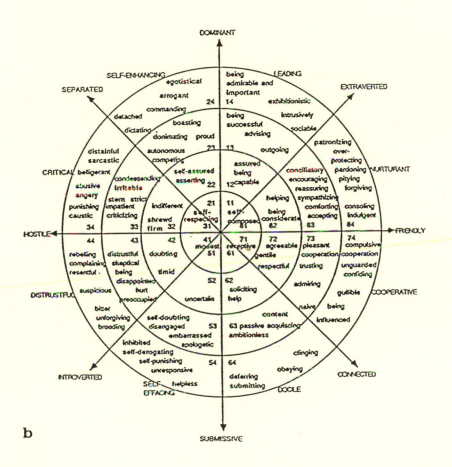

DOMINANT

SELF-ENHANCING

SEPARATED

LEADING

EXTRAVERTED

being admirable and important

egotistical

arrogant

commanding

24   14

exhibitionistic

detached

being successful advising

boasting

intrusively sociable

dictating

dominating   proud

patronizing

distainful

autonomous

23   13

outgoing

over-protecting

sarcastic

competing

assured

conciliatory

pardoning   NURTURANT

CRITICAL   belligerent

self-assured   being

encouraging   pitying

condescending

asserting   22

12 capable

reassuring   forgiving

abusive

irritable

angery

stern   strict

helping   sympathizing

punishing   impatient

indifferent

21   11

comforting   consoling

caustic   criticizing

self-

self-

being   accepting   indulgent

shrewd   respecting   composed   considerate

34   33   firm 32   31   81   82   83   84

HOSTILE

44   43   42   41   71   72   73   74

FRIENDLY

modest   receptive   agreeable   pleasant   compulsive

51   61

rebeling   distrustful   doubting   gentle   cooperation   cooperation

complaining   skeptical   respectful   trusting   unguarded

resentful   being   timid   confiding

disappointed   52   62   admiring

DISTRUSTFUL   suspicious   hurt   gullible   COOPERATIVE

preoccupied   soliciting   naive   being

bitter   help   influenced

unforgiving   self-doubting   content

brooding   disengaged   53   63 passive acquiescing

embarrassed   ambitionless

Inhibited   apologetic   clinging

self-derogating   self-punishing   54   64   obeying

unresponsive   deferring   CONNECTED

INTROVERTED   SELF   helpless   submitting

EFFACING   DOCILE

b

SUBMISSIVE

---

b is from Strong et al., "The Dynamic Relations among Interpersonal Behaviors: A Test of Complementarity and Anticomplementarity." Journal of Personality and Social Psychology, 54, page 799. Copyright (1988) by the American Psychological Association. Reprinted by permission.

FIGURE 9
Interpersonal Circles for Parents and Children

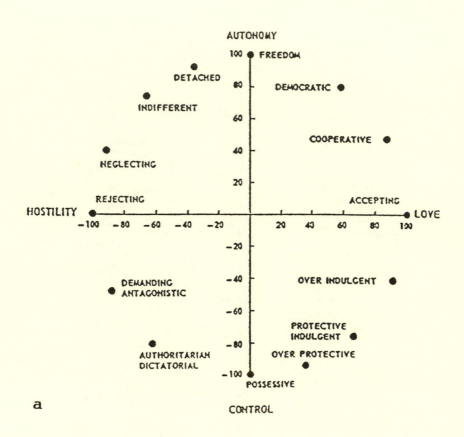

a is Schaefer's (1959) system for classifying the behavior of a mother toward her child. It is from Schaefer, "A Circumflex Model for Maternal Behavior." Journal of Abnormal and Social Psychology, 59, page 232.

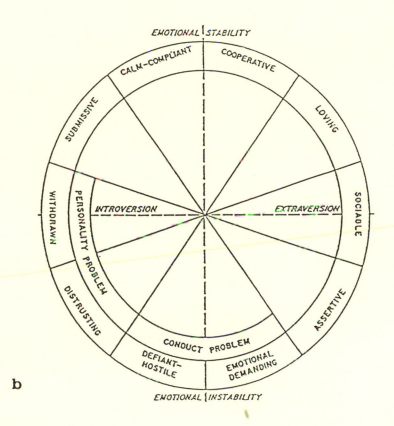

b is Becker and Krug's system for classifying the behavior of a child toward its mother. It is from Becker and Krug, "A Circumflex Model for Social Behavior in Children." <u>Child Development</u>, 35, page 373. Copyright The Society for Research in Child Development, 1964. Reproduced by permission.

the proposed characteristics of which were described in a series of paragraphs. On the basis of these, a carefully worked out coding system was developed, by which trained raters could classify units of interpersonal behavior. One advantage of this circle (over the circles of Lorr and McNair, Wiggins and Kiesler) is that *nurturant* has been returned to the upper right quadrant. Its disadvantages are as follows: (1) it does not allow for pure forms of relating, (e.g., pure separatedness or pure connectedness), since all octants have to be intermediate octants, (2) it is not based upon a sound theoretical system and simply draws upon existing systems, (3) some of its octants are positive (e.g., *leading*), and some are negative (e.g., *distrustful*), and (4) although the function of its four concentric circles is not explained, it appears to incorporate a measure of intensity (see criticism 10 of the interpersonal circle).

Schaefer's Classification of Maternal Behavior

Schaefer's (1959) system is not strictly a modification of the interpersonal circle. As far as is known, when he developed it he was not aware of the work of the Berkley group, and his system was designed specifically for the classification of a mother's relating to her child. However, he was aware of Guttman's (1954) writing, organized his system in the form of a hypothetical circumplex (see Figure 9a), constructed correlation matrices, and fitted behavior ratings into a two-dimensional circumplex. His horizontal axis concerned accepting versus rejecting, and his vertical axis concerned being controlling versus encouraging autonomy. He later (1965) added the variant firm control versus lax control.

Becker and Krug's Classification of Children's Behavior

Becker and Krug (1964) also apparently were unaware of the work of the Berkley group but, like Schaefer, were aware of Guttman's writing. They developed a system for the classification of the relating of children toward their parents and teachers that complemented Schaefer's system. They too proposed a hypothetical circumplex (see Figure 9b), constructed correlation matrices of ratings, and plotted these against the two main factors. Their horizontal axis concerned being loving and sociable versus being mistrusting and withdrawn, and their vertical axis concerned being defiant and demanding versus being compliant and cooperative.

Benjamin's Three Surfaces

Benjamin (1974) acknowledged her indebtedness to Leary and Schaefer but, strangely, not to Becker and Krug. Although she was concerned with the relating of adults, she recognized the importance of distinguishing between what she called *parentlike* and *childlike* behaviors. The former she called *active;* it concerned doing things to or for another person. The latter she called *reactive;* it concerned having things done to or for oneself. (This should not be confused with a different use of these terms in Chapter 1 of this book.) This idea came to her through trying to reconcile the circles of Leary and Schaefer. The only solution, she realized, was to construct two circles or, as she put it, *"surfaces"* or *"planes,"* one concerned with relating (the *other* plane), the other with being related to (the *self* plane). She was the only interpersonal psychologist to reach this conclusion. Both surfaces have the same two axes: the horizontal axis she called *affiliation,* which concerned Leary's love versus hate; the vertical axis she called *interdependence,* which concerned Shaefer's control versus encourage autonomy - only the terms she used were *"dominate"* versus *"emancipate."*

The important point about Benjamin's (1979a) system (see Figure 10) is that each surface is concerned only with opposites; in this respect it differs even from the interpersonal octagon, for in the interpersonal octagon, as was stated in Chapter 3, lowerness is the complement and not the opposite of upperness. In Benjamin's system, surface one would be concerned mainly with upper characteristics and surface two with lower ones. There is also a third surface, which is concerned with how the person relates to her/himself. Each surface takes the form of a diamond, not a circle. The four corners of the diamond represent the four poles, which Benjamin calls *primitive basics* (i.e., love, hate, dominate, and emancipate). Along each side there are eight steps, called *tracks:* approach-avoidance, need-fulfilment, attachment, logic communications, attention to self-development, balance in relationships, intimacy-distance, and identity. The meaning of these terms is not normally explained. Each item in the system is identified not by Leary's letters of the alphabet but by a set of three digits (e.g., 135). The first digit refers to the surface (1, 2, or 3), the second to the side of the diamond (1, 2, 3 or 4); and the third to the track number, that is the point along the side of the diamond (1 to 8). The opposite of any given track is the point on the opposite side of the diamond with the same third digit. Its complement is the point on the other surface with the same third digit. A complete listing of the items is provided in Benjamin, 1979a. Benjamin was a firm adherent to Guttman's statistical approach. She demonstrated that opposite items were highly negatively correlated and that each surface conformed to a true circumplex. One point she did not attend to was the distinction between positive and negative relating.

Benjamin called her system the *structural analysis of social behavior.* She has used it (1) to generate questionnaires, which measure either a person's general style of relating to others or her/his style of relating to a specified other, or a named other's relating to her/him (Benjamin, 1974, 1979a) and (2) as the basis for a method of coding interpersonal behavior from videotapes of individuals or families. For this purpose, she has compiled coding manuals and developed a number of computer programs for scoring and analyzing data (Benjamin et al., 1986).

Combining the systems of Leary and Shaefer has created difficulties for Benjamin. Her horizontal axis ranges from "tender sexuality" to "annihilating attack." It creates a markedly positive-negative division. Sexuality is not a good anchor point for closeness. Attack has upper qualities as well as distant ones. It also is an activity that involves moving toward people. Her vertical axis ranges from "Manage, control" to "Endorse freedom." Although this might be a useful axis for rating parental activities, it is not very appropriate for rating adult-to-adult behavior. Endorsing freedom is a form of giving distance. Moving around the four sides of the *other* plane, the items amount to (1) giving positive neutral closeness, (2) negatively neutral to upper distant, (3) negatively upper to negatively upper distant, and (4) positively upper distant. Moving round the four sides of the *self* plane, they amount to (1) positively neutral close, (2) positively to negatively neutral distant, (3) negatively lower distant, and (4) positively lower to neutral close.

THE INTERPERSONAL CIRCLE AND PSYCHIATRIC NOSOLOGY

Leary's (1957) objective to replace the existing medical classifications of psychiatric conditions with one based upon the interpersonal circle has never been far from the minds of the interpersonal psychologists. Adams (1964) expressed the view that the major differences between mental illness and mental health were to be found in the characteristic frequency, intensity, and nature of interpersonal acts. McLemore and Benjamin (1979) argued that an interpersonal classification would avoid the continued endorsement of a disease conceptualization of abnormality. Kiesler (1986) considered that mounting evidence indicates that the interpersonal circle offers considerable advantages to psychiatric classification. Wiggins (1982) thought it unlikely that there would be a one-to-one correspondence between psychiatric categories and the octants of an interpersonal system, though he felt there could be characteristic profiles of interpersonal variables associated with each category. Benjamin (1986) reported that the results of her research strongly support the idea that her system could provide a scientific description of dynamic and social variables involved in DSM III, Axis I and II syndromes. It will be recalled that in Chapters 5 through 8, most of the major psychiatric conditions were accommodated within the four

FIGURE 10
Benjamin's Three Surfaces

INTERPERSONAL

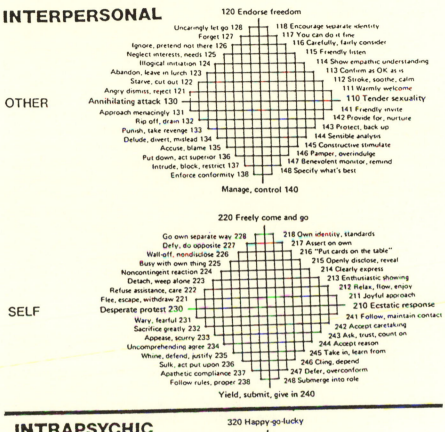

120 Endorse freedom
118 Encourage separate identity
117 You can do it fine
116 Carefully, fairly consider
115 Friendly listen
114 Show empathic understanding
113 Confirm as OK as is
112 Stroke, soothe, calm
111 Warmly welcome
110 Tender sexuality
141 Friendly invite
142 Provide for, nurture
143 Protect, back up
144 Sensible analysis
145 Constructive stimulate
146 Pamper, overindulge
147 Benevolent monitor, remind
148 Specify what's best
Manage, control 140

Uncaringly let go 128
Forget 127
Ignore, pretend not there 126
Neglect interests, needs 125
Illogical initiation 124
Abandon, leave in lurch 123
Starve, cut out 122
Angry dismiss, reject 121
Annihilating attack 130
Approach menacingly 131
Rip off, drain 132
Punish, take revenge 133
Delude, divert, mislead 134
Accuse, blame 135
Put down, act superior 136
Intrude, block, restrict 137
Enforce conformity 138

OTHER

220 Freely come and go
218 Own identity, standards
217 Assert on own
216 "Put cards on the table"
215 Openly disclose, reveal
214 Clearly express
213 Enthusiastic showing
212 Relax, flow, enjoy
211 Joyful approach
210 Ecstatic response
241 Follow, maintain contact
242 Accept caretaking
243 Ask, trust, count on
244 Accept reason
245 Take in, learn from
246 Cling, depend
247 Defer, overconform
248 Submerge into role
Yield, submit, give in 240

Go own separate way 228
Defy, do opposite 227
Wall-off, nondisclose 226
Busy with own thing 225
Noncontingent reaction 224
Detach, weep alone 223
Refuse assistance, care 222
Flee, escape, withdraw 221
Desperate protest 230
Wary, fearful 231
Sacrifice greatly 232
Appease, scurry 233
Uncomprehending agree 234
Whine, defend, justify 235
Sulk, act put upon 236
Apathetic compliance 237
Follow rules, proper 238

SELF

INTRAPSYCHIC

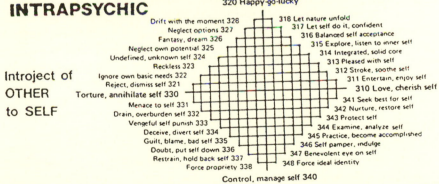

320 Happy-go-lucky
318 Let nature unfold
317 Let self do it, confident
316 Balanced self acceptance
315 Explore, listen to inner self
314 Integrated, solid core
313 Pleased with self
312 Stroke, soothe self
311 Entertain, enjoy self
310 Love, cherish self
341 Seek best for self
342 Nurture, restore self
343 Protect self
344 Examine, analyze self
345 Practice, become accomplished
346 Self pamper, indulge
347 Benevolent eye on self
348 Force ideal identity
Control, manage self 340

Drift with the moment 328
Neglect options 327
Fantasy, dream 326
Neglect own potential 325
Undefined, unknown self 324
Reckless 323
Ignore own basic needs 322
Reject, dismiss self 321
Torture, annihilate self 330
Menace to self 331
Drain, overburden self 332
Vengeful self punish 333
Deceive, divert self 334
Guilt, blame, bad self 335
Doubt, put self down 336
Restrain, hold back self 337
Force propriety 338

Introject of
OTHER
to SELF

From Lorna S. Benjamin, "Structural Analysis of Differentiation Failure." Psychiatry, 42, page 6. Copyright Guilford Publications, Inc. 1979. Reproduced by permission.

main spatial positions; this appears to be a more constructive arrangement.

THE INTERPERSONAL CIRCLE AND PSYCHOTHERAPY

In a final, brief chapter to his book, Leary indicated a possible application of his theory to psychotherapy. Others have carried this lead further. Kiesler (1979, 1982, 1983, 1986) has developed an entirely new method of psychotherapy based largely on Carson's (1969) proposed rules of complementarity and anticomplementarity. Carson maintained that when a person adopts a particular form of behavior, s/he is inviting a complementary response on both the horizontal and the vertical dimensions. "Complementary" means from the same pole of the horizontal dimension (love pulls love) and from the opposite pole of the vertical dimension (dominance pulls submission). If the other's response is complementary on only one dimension, it is called non-complementary; if it is complementary on neither, it is called anticomple-mentary. It was Kiesler's (1983) intention, when he constructed the 1982 circle, to produce "eight pairs of exact segment opposites" (page 200) to which he could apply Carson's rules in his particular form of psychotherapy. The object of therapy is to reduce both the rigidity and the extremeness of the patient's relating by responding in an anticomplementary way to it. The therapy will be effective only if Kiesler's axes are truly bipolar and Carson's rules apply. A question mark hangs over both these possibilities.

Benjamin's principal objective always has been the development of a system that would enable clinicians to describe and code patients' interpersonal feelings and behavior; but also she always has been keen to apply this to psychotherapy (Benjamin, 1979a and 1979b, 1982, 1987; Benjamin et al., 1986). She considered the system to be applicable to any psychotherapeutic school, but some of the methods she advocated are strikingly similar to those of Kiesler. What she called the *SASB Shaurette principle* closely resembles Kiesler's method of responding to rigid and extreme behavior in an anticomplementary way. A more complex maneuver she called prescribing an *antithetical* or *antidotal* response. The antithesis is the opposite of the complement. The object of this is to try to elicit a behavior in someone that is the opposite of that which is being shown.

SUMMARY

The Freedman/Leary interpersonal circle comprised sixteen segments, representing generic interpersonal themes, labeled alphabetically in a counterclockwise direction, constructed around a horizontal love-hate axis and a vertical dominate-submit axis. People express their interpersonal styles reflexively, and such reflexes initiate or invite complementary responses. The circle and its variants, and the associated measuring instruments, have come to form the basis of an area of study known as interpersonal psychology. This has had the effect of fixing it in a form that cannot easily be changed; yet at a fundamental level it has a number of serious defects. Two objectives of the interpersonal school are (1) replacement of conventional psychiatric nosology and (2) the development of a new form of psychotherapy based upon complementarity.

Ironically, it is the original version of the circle that resembles the interpersonal octagon most closely. The poorest correspondences in this arrangement are in the neutral distant and lower distant positions, and there is a general lack of positive characteristics. Lorr and McNair and, later, Wiggins distorted the circle by imposing an extravert/introvert dimension across the NO/FG axis and pushing upper close into the neutral close position. This arrangement lacked a positive/negative distinction. Kiesler's sixteen-segment "1982" circle perpetuated this distortion and added others. Its emphasis on bipolarity was to facilitate Kiesler's complementarity-based psychotherapy. The Strong and Hills circle returns to an octant format and reinstates nurturance in the NO position, but it lacks a positive/negative distinction. Benjamin replaces the classical circle with three diamonds concerned, respectively, with active relating, reactive relating, and relating to the self. Her vertical axis, concerned with control versus emancipate, is taken from Schaefer's system for classifying parental behavior.

11

Conclusion

The theory presented here represents a departure from conventional thinking, and though the ideas expressed are clear enough, they are not always easily understood or accepted. In these last few pages, some of the more problematic areas will be considered in a little more detail.

EXPLAINING ADAPTIVE AND MALADAPTIVE RELATING

The Question of Intensity

Leary (1957) was preoccupied with Sullivan's (1953) concept of continuity; that is, that behavior ranges from *adaptive adjustment,* which Leary placed at the center of the interpersonal circle, to the *psychiatric extremes*, which Leary placed at the periphery of the circle. The movement outward along any radius of the circle represents progressively more extreme forms of behavior, and such progression was called by Leary *intensity*. This concept does not stand up to scrutiny. Extreme forms of behavior are not necessarily pathological. On the horizontal dimension, a person may love or hate with great intensity; on the vertical dimension, a person may be extremely powerful or extremely weak without being pathological. It has been argued, particularly in Chapter 1, that the difference between adaptive and maladaptive behavior is qualitative, not quantitative; and various criteria for distinguishing between them have been proposed (e.g., secure versus insecure, respectful versus disrespectful). Providing one remains within an adaptive or maladaptive mode, it may be meaningful, and even useful, to describe a form of relating in terms of its intensity.

People talk glibly of intensity without giving much thought to what it really means. Intensity sometimes is applied to love. An insecurely close person might ask, "How much do you love me?" expecting some kind of quantitative reply. It is reasonable to ask questions such as how cold, how bossy, or how dependent somebody is. One normally answers with an example, saying s/he is so cold that s/he would do such and such. Conventionally, intensity is measured by counting the number of different forms of a particular quality the person shows evidence of. With the PROQ and CREOQ measures, described in Chapter 9 and illustrated in Figures 4 and 5, scores were generated by summating the ratings of items within any negative category. It is reasonable to assume that the more intense a form of relating may be, the more aspects of it become recruited.

Continuous versus Categorical Measures

Psychometricians distinguish between continuous and categorical measures. A continuous measure is one that has a range, such as height or weight; a categorical measure is one that concerns separate categories, such as gender or race. However, the distinction is not as clear-cut as it may seem. One can have categories of height, such as tall and short, and gender may be continuous, in that one can talk of degrees of masculinity or femininity. Bipolarity appears to be a mixture of the continuous and the categorical, in that although one pole may be construed as the opposite of the other, low scores of one measure start turning into high scores of another. The horizontal axis is more continuous; for, around its mid-point, the distinction between closeness and distance has got to be arbitrary. The vertical dimension is more categorical; for, provided the area of activity is defined, it should always be possible to say who is being upper and who is being lower.

The circumplex embraces a different kind of continuity, namely a continuity around the circumference of the circle. The present system is less in accord with what Wiggins (1979) has referred to as slicing the circumplex pie into progressively thinner segments; it is more concerned with defining the characteristics of the main positions. This is one reason for representing it as an octagon rather than a circle.

Is Positive versus Negative Relating an Additional Dimension?

Some have argued that the positive negative distinction ought to amount to an additional dimension of the system. Gilbert (1992, page 97), in a graphic representation of the system, added what he called the control dimension: whether the individual has any control over her/his attaining a particular state of relatedness. His contention was that having control generates positive affect and not having control generates negative affect. Control is not necessarily the factor that determines the individual's affective state. It is more a matter of whether the arrangement meets with her/his approval. A baby has no control over its lowerness, but being lower does not make it depressed. What Gilbert was referring to was the distinction between imposed relating and relating that occurs through negotiation or mutual agreement. Imposed relating is but one form of negative relating. If that warrants an additional dimension, then so do all the others. A dimension is not only a form of continuousness, it is a bipolar form of continuousness. It is preferable to consider the various forms of negative relating as categories, rather than dimensions, though it is possible that some (e.g., insecurity) could be converted into continuous measures.

The Attainment of States of Relatedness

The key to the distinction between positive and negative forms of relating lies in the individual's success or failure in attaining a particular state of relatedness. A person who (1) is confident of her/his ability to attain a particular state of relatedness, (2) has good experiences of attaining it in the past, (3) has accumulated adequate stores of it, (4) can draw upon a number of different sources of it and (5) is aware of no immediate danger to the loss of any of her/his stores or sources of it will be a positive relater. Such a person, at least within that particular sector of relating, will be calm, secure, considerate, respectful of and generous toward others. A person who is not will be a negative relater, that is, s/he will be frightened and desperate in her/his attempts to defend what stores and sources s/he has and ruthless and unscrupulous in her/his efforts to gain new sources. In this regard, it helps to view states of relatedness as commodities. When a commodity is in ample supply, people are relaxed and reasonable toward each other. When there is a shortage, it brings out the worst in people and gives rise to a dog-eat-dog situation.

The shortage or danger hypothesis does not explain all forms of negative relating. There is a form that arises from a lack of concern for others. A person may have adequate stores of a particular state of relatedness yet continue to relate negatively. Someone in a position of power, for example, may be unnecessarily arrogant and callous toward others either because s/he is not aware of the effect s/he is having upon them or because s/he does not care what they think of her/him. The capacity to perceive and care about the effect one has upon others must be a form of closeness, yet some people are disrespectfully close in just this kind of way.

THE INTERPLAY BETWEEN THE AXES

In the opening paragraph of the book the point was made that though relating, like gravity, has always existed, we have tended not to pay attention to it. Later in Chapter 1 it was observed that relating is something we never stop doing, even when we are asleep; from the moment we are born to the moment we die, we go on doing it; and mostly it occurs automatically without our awareness. It is for reasons such as this that we do not pay attention to it, and in order to study it, we have had to focus upon it consciously. Because it is a continuous process, its components are in a state of continuous interaction. These have been separated out artificially, and we have examined frame by frame what normally is a moving picture.

The drives for hunger and thirst appear to operate independently of each other, so that satisfying one does not satisfy the other, and at any one time one could be seeking to satisfy both. The same appears to apply to the four main positions. The four intermediate positions are evidence that we can function on two different axes at the same time, and the four paradoxical positions are evidence that we can function at both poles of an axis at the same time - but probably, for much of the time, while our attention is directed toward satisfying the needs of one position, our interest in the other three positions is temporarily held in abeyance.

There appear to be *background processes* and *foreground processes*. All the time we seem to be monitoring the extent to which our relating needs are being met in all four positions, and most of this monitoring is in the form of background processes. Concurrent with this we may be involved in some more immediate activity directed toward one particular position. Whilst we are engaged in a game of chess, our primary concern is most likely to be (though not necessarily) winning the game (upperness). At the same time we are concerned about keeping to the rules of the game (lowerness), remaining on good terms with the person we are playing against (closeness), and maintaining an adequate degree of personal space (distance). Also going on somewhere inside us may be thoughts about how well our investments are doing (upperness), whether our boss is satisfied with the standard of our work (lowerness), when we can next have some friends over for dinner (closeness), and when we are going to complain to the neighbors about the noise their stereo makes (distance). Further back in our minds are all kinds of considerations of the sources of our upperness, lowerness, closeness and distance.

AN IMPORTANT DISTINCTION BETWEEN THE TWO AXES

Whereas closeness and distance are opposites, upperness and lowerness are complementary to each other. Consequently, whereas loss of closeness almost invariably gives rise to distance and loss of distance to closeness, loss of upperness does not necessarily give rise to lowerness, or loss of lowerness to upperness. When a person's child grows up and becomes able to fend for itself, s/he loses her/his upper function but s/he does not become lower to the child. When a person's leader and mentor goes away, the person loses that source of lowerness but does not become upper, either to the leader and mentor or to anyone else. Ranking theorists (see Gilbert, 1992) find these points difficult to follow, for in ranking theory, which is based upon confrontation and competition, you either win or you lose. If you win you go up and if you lose you go down. In ranking theory there is no place for being helpfully upper or gratefully lower.

Ranking theory draws direct parallels between the relating of animals and the relating of humans. On the vertical dimension in particular, the relating of animals is predominantly negative (dog-eat-dog), and upperness is mainly malevolent (see Chapter 7). The malevolently (insecure) upper person is intent on keeping or putting the other one down. In this kind of situation up is good and down is bad. Ranking theory and spatial theory are both evolutionary theories, but ranking theory does not take adequate account of the behavioral innovations that humans have acquired.

INTO WHICH DISCIPLINE DOES SPATIAL THEORY FIT?

The object of this book has been to develop a theory of relating. Since no adequate theory of relating exists, there is no obvious category of knowledge into which it can be slotted. Its focus shifts from animals to humans, from momentary interactions to enduring personality characteristics, from subjective experiences to objective observations, and from the behavior of individuals to the organization of societies. It is not a question of which of these areas the book is concerned with: Since relating is a fundamental characteristic, it has relevance to all of them. Animals, humans, groups, institutions, societies, and nations all relate. Sometimes animals relate to humans, humans relate to groups, groups relate to nations, and so on. Sometime the relating is momentary and sometimes it is maintained over long periods. Confusion often arises between relating and a relationship. Relating is a characteristic of an individual; when a group, society, or nation relates, it is behaving as though it were an individual. A relationship is that which happens or exists between two animals, individuals, groups or nations; but a knowledge of the relating characteristics of the respective relaters contributes to an understanding of the relationship.

INTERRELATING

The issue of interrelating was dealt with briefly at the end of Chapter 1. At that stage, the axes and their characteristics had not been introduced. The application of the rules of interrelating to the functions of the four main positions is too complex to be encompassed within the confines of this book. As was mentioned in Chapter 10, Leary (1957) always envisaged his theory as one that should be concerned with the interactions between people. However, the rules of complementarity as laid down by himself, Carson (1969), Kiesler (1983), and others fall far short of what would be required. Essentially they say: If A does X to B, what does it make B do in return? Interrelating is much more complicated than this. A and B are two individuals, each with a set of relating needs. When they come together it is not so much a matter of one doing something to the other and seeing what the other does back as both putting their cards on the table and seeing what kind of deal they can do together. Either one can offer, invite, or impose a particular course of action; and how the other responds depends upon what the other's relating needs happen to be at that particular moment. It is not simply a matter of A offering upperness and B responding with lowerness. It depends entirely on what form the upperness takes and whether it is offered in a positive or a negative manner. Clearly there are rules of interrelating, but they need to be worked out much more carefully than the interpersonal psychologists have done so far.

ARE THERE REALLY ONLY TWO AXES?

Many have complained that restricting relating processes to two axes is a gross oversimplification. However complex a system may be, it can still be reduced to a simple, central framework. An important first step in understanding the system is to identify that simple, central framework. Once the framework is in place, the rest will follow. It is essential, however, to get it right; for if it is wrong, everything that is derived from it will also be wrong.

Wiggins (1982) observed that from the mid 1950s onward, there was a proliferation of two-dimensional models of interpersonal behavior, most of them having been developed independently of each other. This important observation strongly suggests that there is a two-dimensional basis to human relating; the question is, what are the two dimensions? As the Preface points out, the present system was developed independently of all others. That so many two-dimensional systems already existed, and that the dimensions of such systems bore a striking resemblance to each other, indicates that everyone was approximately on the right track - but which system was the correct one? Lorr (personal communication, 1987) was of the opinion that the two dimensions represent *higher order factors* and that subsumed under these are probably twenty or so lower dimensions. This is in keeping with the view of Eysenck (1983) that there might be a hierarchy of personality factors such that higher order ones contain within them lower order ones.

UPON WHICH PROCESS IS RELATING BASED?

The advantages of the present system over Leary's system were enumerated in Chapter 9. They are, incidentally, advantages over most of the other systems referred to by Wiggins. A point to be stressed, however, is that Leary's system, together with most of the other proposed systems, grew out of considerations of psychopathology and can be traced, through Horney and Sullivan, back to Freudian psychoanalysis. Because of this, it is founded on the principle that interpersonal strategies essentially are means of allaying anxiety. Views as to the origin of such anxiety have gradually shifted from Freud's preoccupation with the ego's attempts to exert control over the instinct-driven id, to Horney's concern with feelings of insecurity and isolation. Although Leary wrote a great deal about defenses against anxiety, he never made it clear where he considered such anxiety came from. A theory that interpersonal behavior should be construed as a flight from anxiety, particularly when there is little agreement about the source of such anxiety, carries serious limitations. One is that it could not apply to all animal forms. Although many animals experience anxiety, it is far from certain that they all do; and it would be hard to imagine a source of anxiety that could be common to all of them.

A central feature of spatial theory is that relating is not based upon a negative flight from something, but on a positive move towards something. The concept of states of relatedness and the similarity of these to physiological needs such as hunger and thirst, represents a significant advance upon existing theories. The importance of this concept is that it establishes relating as a normal activity rather than a pathological one; and it is significant that so much of the book has been concerned with normal behavior.

THE ESSENTIAL LINK WITH EVOLUTION

No other two-dimensional system has a firm basis in evolutionary theory. The link with evolution is essential. The relating of humans did not just happen: It must have evolved from the relating of earlier animal forms. The dimensions, if they are correct, must be as applicable to the relating of other animals as they are to humans. They must therefore be extremely simple, yet capable of development. It was argued in Chapter 1 that relating did not become a possibility until organisms became mobile, and the simplest and most fundamental form of mobility is approach and avoidance. This inevitably defined the horizontal dimension. If approaching and avoiding is horizontal movement, moving up and moving down, with all that it implies, must be vertical movement. There is a simple elegance to the fact that these two dimensions are readily transferable to lines on a sheet of graph paper.

WHERE NOW?

If all human relating can be reduced to two lines, once the lines are in place their outward ramifications must be enormous. Within the confines of a single book, it has been possible to present only the barest outline of what the characteristics of the four main positions might be. If the system proves to be useful, further elaborations will follow and the representations of interpersonal behavior will become more complex.

Despite the contrasts which have been drawn between the present theory and Leary's theory, it remains reasonable to consider spatial theory to be a variant of interpersonal theory. If this is so it seems likely that a number of modifications to existing theory will have to be made. Since there exists a large body of literature and research in the field of interpersonal theory, this is no small consideration. An important feature of the four central chapters, 5, 6, 7, and 8, was an indication of the contribution which spatial theory can make to the classification of (1) personality disorders and (2) psychiatric conditions. Throughout the book, references have been made to psychotherapy. Already there exists a form of therapy called interpersonal psychotherapy (Anchin and Kiesler (1987) and spatial theory can make contributions to this. Beyond this, it can provide a basis for understanding and monitoring the processes involved in a range of psychotherapies. The PROQ can be administered before and after individual psychotherapy and the CREOQ can be administered before and after marital therapy. All these are useful developments, but most of all, it is hoped that the book will form the basis of what will become a science of relating.

References

Abraham, K. (1924) A short study of the development of the libido. In *Selected Papers in Psychoanalysis*. Hogarth Press: London, 1949.

Abramson, Y.L., Metalsky, G.I., and Alloy, L.B. (1989) Hopelessness: A theory-based subtype of depression. *Psychological Review*, 96, 358-372.

Adair, J. (1987) *Not Bosses But Leaders*. Kogan Page: London.

Adams, H.B. (1964) "Mental illness" or interpersonal behaviour. *American Psychologist*, 19, 191-197.

Adler, A. (1931) *What Life Should Mean to You*. Allen & Unwin: London.

Adorno, T.W., Frenkel-Brunswick, E., Levinson, D.J., and Sanford, R.N. (1950) *The Authoritarian Personality*. Harper: New York.

Ainsworth, M.D. (1963) The development of infant-mother interaction among the Ganda. In Foss, B.M. (Ed.) *Determinants of Infant Behavior, vol. 2.* Wiley: New York.

--------. (1989) Attachments beyond infancy. *American Psychologist*, 44, 709-716.

Ainsworth, M.D., Blehar, M.C., Waters, E., and Wall, S. (1978) *Patterns of Attachment: A Psychological Study of the Strange Situation*. Erlbaum: Hillsdale, N.J.

Akiskal, H.S., Hirschfeld, R.M.A., and Yerevanian, B.I. (1983) The relationship of personality to affective disorders. *Archives of General Psychiatry*, 40, 801-810.

Alexander, R.D. (1974) The evolution of social behavior. *Annual Review of Ecology and Systematics*, 5, 325-383.

Allee, W.C. (1926) Studies in animal aggregations: Causes and effects of bunching in land isopods. *Journal of Experimental Zoology*, 45, 255-277.

Alloy, B., Abramson, L.Y., Metalsky, G.I., and Hartledge, S. (1988) The hopelessness theory of depression: Attributional aspects. *British Journal of Clinical Psychology*, 27, 5-12.

Altman, I. (1975) *The Environment and Social Behavior: Privacy, Personal Space, Territory and Crowding*. Brooks/Cole: Monterey, Calif.

---------. (1979) Privacy as an interpersonal boundary process. In von Cranach, M., Foppa, K., Lepenies, W., and Ploog, D. (Eds.) *Human Ethology: Claims and Limits of a New Discipline*. Cambridge University Press: Cambridge.

American Psychiatric Association. (1980) *Diagnostic and Statistical Manual of Mental Disorders*, 3d. Edition. American Psychiatric Association: Washington, D.C.

---------. (1987) *Diagnostic and Statistical Manual of Mental Disorders*, 3d. Edition, Revised. American Psychiatric Association: Washington, D.C.Anchin, J.C. and Kiesler, D.J. (1987) *Handbook of Interpersonal Psychotherapy*. Pergamon: New York.

Anderson, N. (1923) *The Hobo: The Sociology of the Homeless Man*. University of Chicago Press: Chicago, Ill.

Ansbacher, H.L., and Ansbacher, R.R. (1958) *The Individual Psychology of Alfred Adler*. George Allen & Unwin: London.

Anzieu, D. (1989) *The Skin Ego*. Yale University Press: New Haven, Conn.

Argyle, M. (1972) *The Psychology of Interpersonal Behaviour*. Penguin: Harmondsworth, Middlesex.

Asch, S.E. (1951) Effects of group pressure upon the modification and distortion of judgement. In Guetzkow, H. (Ed.) *Groups, Leadership and Men*. Carnegie: Pittsburgh, Pa.

Badcock, C.R. (1986) *The Problem of Altruism*. Blackwell: Oxford.

Bahr, S.J. (1982) Exchange and control in married life. In Nye, F.I. (Ed.) *Family Relationships: Rewards and Costs*. Sage: Beverly Hills, Calif.

Bailey, K.G. (1988) Psychological kinship: Implications for the helping professions. *Psychotherapy*, 25, 132-141.

Balint, M. (1952) *Primary Love and Psychoanalytic Technique*. Hogarth Press: London.

Bandura, A., Underwood, B., and Fromson, M.E. (1975) Disinhibition of aggression through diffusion of responsibility and dehumanisation of victims. *Journal of Research in Personality*, 9, 253-269.

Bannister, D. (1987) The psychotic disguise. In W. Dryden (Ed.) *Therapists' Dilemmas*. Harper & Row: London.

Barber, T.X. (1984) Changing "unchangeable" bodily processes by (hypnotic) suggestions: A new look at hypnosis, cognitions, imagining and the mind-body problem. In Sheikh, A.A. (Ed.) *Imagination and Healing* Baywood: Farmingdale, N.Y.

Barker, J.C. (1962) The hospital addiction syndrome (Munchausen syndrome). *Journal of Mental Science*, 108, 167-182.

Barkow, J.H. (1975) Prestige and culture: A biosocial interpretation. *Current Anthropology*, 16, 533-572.

———. (1980) Prestige and self-esteem: A biosocial interpretation. In Omark, D.R., Strayer, D.R. & Freedman, J. (Eds.) *Dominance Relations: An Ethological View of Social Conflict and Social Interaction*. Garland STPM Press: New York.

Baron, R.A., and Byrne, D. (1991) *Social Psychology*. Allyn & Bacon: London.

Barsky, A.J., and Klerman, G.L. (1983) Overview: Hypochondriasis, bodily complaints and somatic styles. *American Journal of Psyciatry*, 140, 273-283.

Bartholomew, K. (1990) Avoidance of intimacy: An attachment perspective. *Journal of Social and Personal Relationships*, 7, 147-178.

Barton, R. (1959) *Institutional Neurosis*. John Wright & Sons: Bristol.

Barton, R., and Whitehead, T.A. (1969) The gaslight phenomenon. *The Lancet*, 1, 1258-1260.

Beck, A.T. (1983) Cognitive therapy of depression: New perspecives. In Clayton, P.J., and Barrett, J.E. (Eds.) *Treatment of Depression Old Controversies and New Approaches*. Raven Press: New York.

Beck, A.T., Epstein, N., Harrison, R.P., and Emery, G. (1983) *Development of the Sociotropy-Autonomy Scale: A Measure of Personality Factors in Psychopathology*. Center for Cognitive Therapy, University of Pennsylvania: Philadelphia, Pa.

Beck, A.T., Steer, R.A., Kovacs, M., and Garrison, B. (1985) Hopelessness and eventual suicide: A 10-year prospective study of patients hospitalised with suicidal ideation. *American Journal of Psychiatry*, 142, 559-563.

Becker, W.C. and Krug, R.S. (1964) A circumplex model for social behavior in children. *Child Development*, 35, 371-396.

Bemporad, J. (1980) Psychotherapy of mild depression. In Arieti, S., and Bemporad, J. *Severe and Mild Depression: The Psycothotherapeutic Approach*. Tavistock: London.

Benedek, T. (1956) Toward the biology of the depressive constellation. *Journal of the American Psychoanalytic Association*, 4, 389-427.

Benjamin, L.S. (1974) Structural analysis of social behavior. *Psychological Review*, 81, 394-425.

———. (1979a) Structural analysis of differentiation failure. *Psychiatry*, 42, 1-23.

———. (1979b) Use of structural analysis of social behavior (SASB) and Markov chains to study dyadic interactions. *Journal of Abnormal Psychology*, 88, 303-319.

———. (1982) Use of structural analysis of social behavior (SASB) to guide intervention in psychotherapy. In Anchin, J.C., and Kiesler, D.J. (Eds.) *Handbook of Interpersonal Psychotherapy*. Pergamon: New York.

---------. (1986) Adding social and intrapsychic descriptors to Axis I of DSM III. In Millon, T., and Klerman, G.L. (Eds.) *Contemporary Directions in Psychopathology*. Guilford: New York.

---------. (1987) Use of the SASB dimensional model to develop treatment plans for personality disorders. I: Narcissism. *Journal of Personality Disorders*, 1, 43-70.

Benjamin, L.S., Foster, S.W., Roberto, L.G., and Estroff, S.E. (1986). Breaking the family code: Analysis of videotapes of family interactions by structural analysis of social behavior (SASB). In Greenberg, L.S. and Pinsoff, W.M. (Eds.) *The Psychotherapeutic Process: A Research Handbook*. Guilford Press: New York.

Bergman, J.A., O'Mally, H., and Segars, H. (1980) Legal research and services for the elderly. In *Select Committee on Aging, Elder Abuse: The Hidden Problems*. U.S. Government Printing Office: Washington, D.C.

Bergson, H. (1912) *An Introduction to Metaphysics*. Pitman: London.

Berke, J.E. (1987) Shame and envy. In Nathanson, D.L. (Ed.) *The Many Faces of Shame*. Guilford Press: New York.

Berkowitz, L. (1989) Frustration-aggression hypothesis: Examination and reformulation. *Psychological Bulletin*, 106, 59-73.

Berne, E. (1975) *What Do You Say after You Say Hello?* Corgi: London.

Bibring, E. (1953) The mechanism of depression. In Greenacre, P. (Ed.) *Affective Disorders: Psychoanalytic Contributions to Their Study*. International Universities Press: New York.

Birney, R.C., Burdick, H., and Teevan, R.C. (1969) *Fear of Failure*. Van Nostrand-Reinhold: New York.

Birtchnell, J. (1983) Psychotherapeutic considerations in the management of the suicidal patient. *American Journal of Psychotherapy*, 37, 24-36.

---------. (1984) Dependence and its relationship to depression. *British Journal of Medical Psychology*, 57, 215-225.

---------. (1986) The imperfect attainment of intimacy: A key concept in marital therapy. *Journal of Family Therapy*, 8, 153-172.

---------. (1987) Attachment-detachment, directiveness-receptiveness: A system for classifying interpersonal attitudes and behaviour. *British Journal of Medical Psychology*, 60, 17-27.

---------. (1988) Defining dependence. *British Journal of Medical Psychology*, 61, 111-123.

---------. (1990) Interpersonal theory: Criticism, modification and elaboration .*Human Relations*, 43, 1183-1201.

---------. (1991a) Redefining dependence: A reply to Cadbury's critique. *British Journal of Medical Psychology*, 64, 253-261.

---------. (1991b) The measurement of dependence by questionnaire. *Journal of Personality Disorders*, 5, 281- 295.

--------. (1993a) The interpersonal octagon: An alternative to the interpersonal circle. *Human Relations* (in press)

--------. (1993b) A new approach to the conceptualisation and assessment of the relating of marital partners. Unpublished ms.

Birtchnell, J., Falkowski, J., and Steffert, B. (1992) The negative relating of depressed patients: A new approach. *Journal of Affective Disorders*, 24, 165-176.

Birtchnell, S.A. (1988) Dysmorphophobia: A centenary discussion. *British Journal of Psychiatry*, 153, 41-43.

Blackburn, I.M. (1974) The pattern of hostility in affective illness. *British Journal of Psychiatry*, 125, 141-145.

Blatt, S.J. (1974) Levels of object representation in anaclitic and introjective depression. *The Psychoanalytic Study of the Child*, 29, 107-157.

Blatt, S.J., and Behrends, R.S. (1987) Internalisation, separation-individuation, and the nature of therapeutic action. *International Journal of Psycho-Analysis*, 68, 279-297.

Blatt, S.J., and Shichman, S. (1983) Two primary configurations of psychopathology. *Psychoanalysis and Contemporary Thought*, 6, 187-249.

Blatt, S.J., and Wild, C.M. (1976) *Schizophrenia: A Developmental Analysis*. Academic Press: New York.

Blos, P. (1967) The second individuation process of adolescence. *Psychoanalytic Study of the Child*, 22, 162-186.

Bonner, R.I., and Rich, A.R. (1988) Negative life stress, social problem solving, self-appraisal and hopelessness: Implications for suicde research. *Cognitive Therapy and Research*, 12, 849-856.

Bowen, M. (1978) *Family Therapy in Clinical Practice*. Aronson: London.

Bowlby, J. (1960) Separation anxiety. *International Journal of Psycho-Analysis*, 41, 89-113.

--------. (1961) Processes of mourning. *International Journal of Psycho-Analysis*, 42, 317-339.

--------. (1969) *Attachment and Loss. Vol. 1: Attachment*. Hogarth Press/Institute of Psycho-Analysis: London.

--------. (1973a) *Attachment and Loss. Vol. 2: Separation, Anxiety and Anger*. Hogarth Press/ Institute of Psycho-Analysis: London.

--------. (1973b) Self-reliance and some conditions that promote it. In Gosling, R. (Ed.) *Support, Innovation and Autonomy*. Tavistock: London.

--------. (1977) The making and breaking of affectional bonds, 1. Aetiology and psychopathology in the light of attachment theory. *British Journal of Psychiatry*, 130, 201-210.

--------. (1980) *Attachment and Loss. Vol. 3: Loss, Sadness and Depression*. Hogarth Press/Institute of Psycho-Analysis: London.

Boyd-Franklin, N. (1984) Issues in family therapy with black families. *Clinical Psychologist*, 37, 54-58.

Branden, N. (1980) *The Psychology of Romantic Love*. Bantam: Toronto.

Brenner, C. (1957) *An Elementary Textbook of Psychoanalysis*. Doubleday Anchor: New York.

Bretherton, I., Biringen, Z., Ridgeway, D., Maslin, C., and Sherman, M. (1989) Attachment: The parental perspective. *Infant Mental Health Journal*, 10, 203-221.

Bruch, H. (1957) *The Importance of Overweight*. Norton: New York.

Buber, M. (1937) *I and Thou*. Clark: Edinburgh.

Burney, C. (1952) *Solitary Confinement*. Clark & Cockeran: New York.

Burns, J.M. (1978) *Leadership*. Harper & Row: New York.

Buss, A.H. (1988) *Personality: Evolutionary Heritage and Human Distinctiveness*. Erlbaum: Hillsdale, N.J.

Buss, D.M., and Craik, K.H. (1986) Acts, dispositions and clinical assessment: The psychopathology of everyday conduct. *Clinical Psychology Review*, 6, 387-406.

Buunk, A., and Bringle, R.G. (1987) Jealousy in love relationships. In D. Perlman & S. Duck (Eds.) *Intimate Relationships*. Sage: Newbury Park, Calif.

Byrne, D. (1971) *The Attraction Paradigm*. Academic Press: New York.

Byrne, D., McDonald, R.D., and Mikawa, J. (1963) Approach and avoidance affiliation motives. *Journal of Personality*, 31, 21-37.

Carpenter, C.C. (1978) Ritualistic social behaviors in lizards. In Greenberg, N., and MacLean, P. (Eds.) *Behavior and Neurology of Lizards*. National Institute of Mental Health: Rockville, Md.

Carson, R.C. (1969) *Interaction Concepts of Personality*. Aldine: Chicago, Ill.

Chagnon, N.A., and Irons, W. (Eds.) (1979) *Evolutionary Biology and Human Social Behavior: An Anthropological Perspective*. Duxbury: North Scituate, Mass.

Chance, M.R.A. (1984) Biological systems synthesis of mentality and the nature of the two modes of mental operation: Hedonic and agonic. *Man-Environment Systems*, 14, 143-157.

---------. (1988) Introduction. In Chance, M.R.A. (Ed.) *Social Fabrics of the Mind*. Erlbaum: Hillsdale: N.J.

Chapman, R., and Rutherford, J. (1988) *Male Order: Unwrapping Masculinity*. Lawrence & Wishart: London.

Chodoff, P. (1972) The depressive personality. *Archives of General Psychiatry*, 27, 666-673.

Christian, J.J. (1959) The roles of endocrine and behavioral factors in the growth of mammalian populations. In Gorbman, A. (Ed.) *Comparative Endocrinology*. Wiley: New York.

Clark, L.A., Mills, J.R., and Corcoran, D.M. (1989) Keeping track of needs and inputs of friends and strangers. *Personality and Social Psychology Bulletin*, 15, 533-542.

Cobb, J. (1979) Morbid jealousy. *British Journal of Hospital Medicine*, 21, 511-518.

Cochrane, N., and Neilson, M. (1971) Depressive illness: The role of aggressiveness further considered. *Psychological Medicine*, 7, 282-288.

Collins, N.L., and Read, S.J. (1990) Adult attachment, working models and relationship quality in dating couples. *Journal of Personality and Social Psychology*, 58, 644-663.

Conger, J.A., and Kanungo, R.N. (1988) *Charismatic Leadership: The Elusive Factor in Organizational Effectiveness*. Jossey-Bass: San Francisco, Calif.

Coopersmith, S. (1967) *The Antecedendts of Self-Esteem*. Freman: San Francisco, Calif.

Cornell-Pedrick, C.P., and Gelles, R.J. (1982) Adolescent to parent violence. *Urban and Social Change Review*, 15, 8-14.

Cosmides, L. (1989) The logic of social exchange: Has natural selection shaped how humans reason? Studies with the Wason selection task. *Cognition*, 31, 187-276.

Crisp, A.H. (1980) *Anorexia Nervosa: Let Me Be*. Academic Press: London.

Crook, J.H. (1970) Social organisation and the environment: Aspects of contemporary social ethology. *Animal Behavior*, 18, 197-209.

---------. (1980) *The Evolution of Human Consciousness*. Oxford University Press: Oxford.

---------. (1986) The evolution of leadership: A preliminary skirmish. In Graumann, C.F., and Moscovici, S. (Eds.) *Changing Conceptions of Leadership*. Springer Verlag: New York.

Cumming, J. (1961) The family and mental disorders: An incomplete essay. In *Causes of Mental Disorder: A Review of Epidemiological Knowledge*. Millbank Memorial Fund: New York.

Curtis, L. (1974) *Criminal Violence: National Patterns and Behavior*. D.C. Heath: Lexington, Mass.

Dawidowicz, L. (1975) *The War against the Jews*. Penguin: Harmondsworth, Middlesex.

Dawkins, R. (1976) *The Selfish Gene*. Oxford University Press: London.

DeCasper, A.J., and Fifer, W.P. (1980) Of human bonding: Newborns prefer their mother's voices. *Science*, 208, 1174-1176.

de Rivera, J. (1977) A structural theory of the emotions. *Psychological Issues*, 10, No. 40.

Derlega, V.J., and Berg, J.H. (Eds.) (1987) *Self-Disclosure: Theory, Research and Therapy*. Plenum: New York.

Deutsch, H. (1933) The psychology of manic-depressive states. In *Neuroses and Character Types*. International Universities Press: New York.

---------. (1942) Some forms of emotional disturbance and their relationship to schizophrenia. *Psychoanalytic Quarterly*, 11, 301-321.

De Vore, I. (1965) *Primate Behavior: Field Studies of Monkeys and Apes*. Holt: Toronto.

Downing, G. (1973) *The Massage Book*. Wildwood House: London.

Dowrick, S. (1992) *Intimacy and Solitude*. The Womens' Press: London.

Draper, E. (1976) A developmental theory of suicide. *Comprehensive Psychiatry*, 17, 67-79.

Dublin, J.E. (1985) The terrorized patient as brutalized person. In Stern, E.M. (Ed.) *Psychotherapy and the Terrorized Patient*. The Hawthorn Press: New York.

Dubois, C. (1944) *The People of Alor: A Socio-Psychological Study of an East Indian Island*. Harper & Bros.: New York.

Duck, S. (Ed.) (1990) *Personal Relationships and Social Support*. Sage: London.

---------. (1992) *Human Relationships*. Sage: London.

Duke, M.P., and Nowicki, S. (1987) A social learning theory analysis of interactional theory concepts and a multidimensional model of human interaction constellations. In Anchin, J.C., and Kiesler, D.J. (Eds.) *Handbook of Interpersonal Psychotherapy*. Pergamon: New York.

Durant, J.R. (1981) The beast in man: An historical perspective on the biology of human aggression. In Brain, P.F., and Benton, D. (Eds.) *The Biology of Aggression*. Sijthoff & Noordhoff: Rockville, Md.

Durkheim, E. (1897) *Suicide*. Free Press: New York, 1951.

Dyer, J.A., and Kreitman, N. (1984) Hopelessness, depression and suicidal intent in parasuicide. *British Journal of Psychiatry*, 144, 127-133.

Edwards, A.L. (1959) *The Edwards Personal Preference Schedule*. University of Washington: Washington, D.C.

Egeland, B., and Farber, E.A. (1984) Infant-mother attachment: Factors related to its development and changes over time. *Child Development*, 55, 753-771.

Eibl-Eibesfeldt, I. (1970) *Ethology: The Biology of Behavior*. Holt, Rinehart and Winston: New York.

---------. (1989) *Human Ethology*. Aldine de Gruyter: New York.

Eisenberg, N. (1986) *Altruism, Emotion, Cognition and Behavior*. Erlbaum: Hillsdale, N.J.

Ellis, E.M. (1985) Primitive agonies. In Stern, E.M. (Ed.) *Psychotherapy and the Terrorised Patient*. The Hawthorn Press: New York.

Ellis, H. (1898) Auto-erotism: A psychological study. *Alienation and Neurology*, 19, 260-299.

Erikson, E. (1965) *Childhood and Society*. Penguin: London.

Everett, C.A. (Ed.) (1991) *Marital Instability and Divorce Outcomes: Issues for Therapists and Educators.* The Haworth Press: New York.

Eysenck, H.J. (1947) *Dimensions of Personality.* Routledge and Kegan Paul: London.

---------. (1970) *The Structure of Human Personality*, Revised Edition. Methuen: London.

---------. (1983) A biometrical-genetical analysis of impulsive and sensation-seeking behavior. In Zuckerman, M. (Ed.) *Bilogical Bases of Sensation Seeking, Impulsivity and Anxiety.* Erlbaum: Hillsdale, N.J.

---------. (1989) Personality, primary and secondary suggestibility and hypnosis. In Gheorghiu, V.A., Netter, P., Eysenck, H.J., and Rosenthal, R. (Eds.) *Suggestion and Suggestibility: Theory and Research.* Springer-Verlag: New York.

Fagan, J., and Shepherd, I.L. (Eds.) (1970) *Gestalt Therapy Now.* Science and Behavior Books: Palo Alto, Calif.

Fairbairn, W.R.D. (1940) Schizoid factors in the personality. In *Psychoanalytic Studies of the Personality.* Routledge and Kegan Paul: London, 1952.

---------. (1941) A revised psychopathology of the psychoses and psychoneuroses. In *Psychoanalytic Studies of the Personality.* Tavistock: London, 1952.

Fast, I. (1967) Some relationships of infantile self-boundary development to depression. *International Journal of Psycho-Analysis*, 48, 259-266.

Feinman, S. (1980) Infant response to race, size, proximity and movement of strangers. *Infant Behavior and Development*, 3, 187-204.

Feldman, L.B. (1976) Depression and family interaction. *Family Process*, 15, 389-395.

---------. (1979) Marital conflict and marital intimacy: An integrative psychodynamic-behavioral-systemic model. *Family Process*, 18, 69-78.

Fenichel, O. (1945) *The Psychoanalytic Theory of Neurosis.* Norton: New York.

---------. (1968) Depression and Mania. In Gaylin, W. (Ed.) *The Meaning of Despair.* Science House: New York.

Ferenczi, S. (1916) Stages in the development of the sense of reality. In *Contributions to Psychoanalysis.* Richard C. Bager: Boston, Mass.

Ferreira, A.J. (1964) The intimacy need in psychotherapy. *American Journal of Psychoanalysis*, 24, 190-194.

Fisher, S. (1973) *Body Consciousness.* Prentice Hall: Englewood Cliffs, N.J.

Foa, U.G. (1961) Convergencies in the analysis of the structure of interpersonal behaviour. *Psychological Review*, 68, 341-353.

Foulds, G., Caine, T.M., and Creasy, M.A. (1960) Aspects of extra- and intro-punitive expression in mental illness. *Journal of Mental Science*, 106, 599-610.

Fraiberg, S. (1969) Libidinal object constancy and mental representation. *Psychoanalytic Study of the Child*, 24, 9-47.

---------. (1975) The development of human attachments in infants blind from
    birth. *Merrill-Palmer Quarterly*, 21, 315-334.
Frankl, V.E. (1967) *Psychotherapy and Existentialism: Selected Papers on
    Logotherapy*. Souvenir: London.
Freedman, M.B. (1950) *The Interpersonal Dimension of Personality: Concepts
    and Measurement Methods*. Doctoral Dissertation, University of
    California: Berkley, Calif.
Freedman, M.B., Leary, T., Ossorio, A.G., and Coffey, H.S. (1951) The
    interpersonal dimension of personality. *Journal of Personality*, 20,
    143-161.
Freeman, T. (1971) Psychoanalysis and the schizophrenias. In Ramsey, I.T., and
    Porter, R. (Eds.) *Personality and Science*. Churchill Livingstone:
    London.
French, N. (1984) *Successful Hypnotherapy*. Thorsons: Wellingborough,
    Northants.
Freud, A. (1949) *The Ego and the Mechanisms of Defence*. International
    Universities Press: New York.
Freud, A., and Burlingham, D. (1944) *Infants without Families*. International
    Universities Press: New York.
Freud, S. (1895) Project for a scientific psychology. *Standard Edition*, Vol. 1,
    Hogarth Press: London, 1950.
---------. (1905) Three essays on sexuality (translated by J. Strachey). *Standard
    Edition*, Vol. 7. Hogarth Press: London, 1953.
---------. (1911a) Formulations regarding the two principles in mental functioning
    (translated by M.N. Searl). *Collected Papers*, Vol. 4. Hogarth Press:
    London, 1925.
---------. (1911b) Psychoanalytic notes on an autobiographical account of a case
    of paranoia (dementia paranoides) (Translated by J. Strachey). *Standard
    Edition*, Vol. 12. Hogarth Press: London, 1958.
---------. (1914) On narcissism: An introduction (translated by J. Strachey).
    Standard Edition, Vol. 14. Hogarth Press: London, 1957.
---------. (1915a) Observations on transference-love (translated by J. Strachey).
    Standard Edition, Vol. 12. Hogarth Press: London, 1958.
---------. (1915b) The unconscious (translated by J. Strachey). *Standard Edition*,
    Vol. 14. Hogarth Press: London, 1957.
---------. (1917) Mourning and melancholia (translated by J. Riviere). *Collected
    Papers*, Volume 4. Hogarth Press: London, 1935.
---------. (1921) Group psychology and the analysis of the ego (translated by J.
    Strachey). *Standard Edition*, Vol. 18. Hogarth Press: London, 1948.
---------. (1923) *The Ego and the Id* (translated by J. Riviere). Hogarth Press:
    London, 1927.
---------. (1926a) *The Problem of Anxiety* (translated by H.A. Bunker). Norton:

New York, 1936.

---------. (1926b) Inhibitions, symptoms and anxiety (translated by J. Strachey). *Standard Edition*, Vol. 20. Hogarth Press: London, 1959.

---------. (1927) The future of an illusion (translated by J. Strachey). *Standard Edition*, Vol. 21. Hogarth Press: London, 1961.

---------. (1933) *New Introductory Lectures on Psychoanalysis* (translated by W.J.H. Sprott). Norton: New York.

---------. (1937) Analysis terminable and interminable (translated by J. Strachey). *Standard Edition*, Vol. 23. Hogarth Press: London, 1964.

---------. (1939) *Civilisation and Its Discontents* (translated by J. Riviere). Hogarth Press: London.

---------. (1950) "Why War?" (translated by J. Strachey). *Collected Papers*, Vol. 5. Hogarth Press: London.

Friday, N. (1986) *Jealousy*. Collins: London.

Fromm, E. (1947a) *Escape from Freedom*. Rinehart: New York.

---------. (1947b) *Man for Himself*. Rinehart: New York.

Fromm-Reichmann, F. (1959) Loneliness. *Psychiatry*, 22, 1-25.

Frude, N. (1991) *Understanding Family Problems: A Psychological Approach*. Wiley: Chichester.

Galdston, R. (1965) Observations on children who have been physically abused by their parents. *American Journal of Psychiatry*, 122, 440-443.

Gardner, R. (1982) Mechanisms in manic-depressive disorder: An evolutionary model. *Archives of General Psychiatry*, 39, 1436-1441.

---------. (1988) Psychiatric syndromes as infrastructure for intra-specific communication. In Chance, M.R.A. (Ed.) *Social Fabrics of the Mind*. Erlbaum, Hillsdale, N.J.

---------. (1992) X-Y plotting used in the spatial model. *Across-Species Comparisons and Psychiatry Newsletter*, 4, No. 12, 3-10.

Gelles, R. (1974) *The Violent Home: A Study of Physical Aggression between Husbands and Wives*. Sage: Newbury Park, Calif.

---------. (1976) Abused wives: Why do they stay? *Journal of Marriage and the Family*, 38, 659-668.

George, C., and Main, M. (1979) Social interactions of young, abused children: Approach, avoidance and aggression. *Child Development*, 50, 306-318.

Gibb, J.R. (1961) Defensive communication. *Journal of Communication*, 11, 141-148.

Gibbens, T.C.N. (1970) Hooliganisn and vandalism. *Medico-Legal Journal*, 38, 122-134.

Gibran, K. (1968) *The Prophet*. Alfred A. Knopf: New York.

Gilbert, P. (1988) Shame and guilt. *Changes*, 6, 50-53.

---------. (1989) *Human Nature and Suffering*. Erlbaum: Hillsdale, N.J.

---------. (1992) *Depression: The Evolution of Powerlessness*. Erlbaum: Hillsdale,

N.J.

Gilligan, C. (1982) *In a Different Voice: Psychological Theory and Women's Development*. Harvard University Press: Cambridge, Mass.

Giovacchini, P.L. (1990) Regression, reconstruction and resolution: Containment and holding. In Giovacchini, P.L. (Ed.) *Tactics and Techniques in Psychoanalytic Therapy. Vol. 3: The Implications of Winnicott's Contributions*. Jason Aronson: Northvale, N.J.

Godelier, M. (1979) Territory and property in primitive society. In von Cranach, M., Foppa, K., Lepenies, W., and Ploog, D. (Eds.) *Human Ethology: Claims and Limits of a New Discipline*. Cambridge University Press: Cambridge.

Goffman, E. (1963) *Behavior in Public Places: Notes on the Social Organisation of Gatherings*. Free Press (Macmillan): New York.

---------. (1968) *Stigma: Notes on the Management of a Spoiled Identity*. Penguin: Harmondsworth, Middlesex.

Gollwitzer, P.M., Wicklund, R.A., and Hilton, J.L. (1982) Admission of failure and symbolic self-completion: Extending Lewinian theory. *Journal of Personality and Social Psychology*, 43, 358-371.

Gournay, K. (Ed.) (1989) *Agoraphobia: Current Perspectives on Theory and Treatment*. Routledge: London.

Grassian, S. (1983) Psychopathological effects of solitary confinement. *American Journal of Psychiatry*, 140, 1450-1454.

Green, M. (1984) *Marriage*. Fontana: London.

Green, R., and Money, J. (Eds.) (1969) *Transsexualism and Sex Reassignment*. Johns Hopkins University Press: Baltimore, Md.

Greenson, R.R. (1968) Dis-identifying from mother: Its special importance for the boy. *International Journal of Psycho-Analysis*, 49, 370-374.

Groddeck, G.W. (1923) *The Book of the It*. Mentor Books: New York, 1961.

Grossmann, K.E., Grossmann, K., and Schwan, A. (1986) Capturing the wider view of attachment: A reanalysis of Ainsworth's Strange Situation. In Izard, C.E., and Read, P.B. (Eds.) *Measuring Emotions in Infants and Children*, Vol. 2. Cambridge University Press, Cambridge.

Groth, A.N., Burgess, A.W., and Holmstrom, L.L. (1977) Rape: Power, anger and sexuality. *American Journal of Psychiatry*, 134, 1239-1243.

Guntrip, H. (1969a) *Schizoid Phenomena, Object Relations and the Self*. Hogarth Press: London.

---------. (1969b) Religion in relation to personal integration. *British Journal of Medical Psychology*, 42, 323-333.

Guttman, L.A. (1954) A new approach to factor analysis: The radex. In Lazarsfeld, P.R. (Ed.) *Mathematical Thinking in the Social Sciences*. Free Press: Glencoe, Ill.

Hall, E.T. (1966) *The Hidden Dimension*. Doubleday: New York.

Hamilton, W.D. (1963) The evolution of altruistic behavior. *American Naturalist*, 97, 354-356.

---------. (1964) The genetical evolution of social behaviour, I and II. *Journal of Theoretical Biology*, 7, 1-16 and 17-62.

Haney, C., Banks, C., and Zimbardo, P. (1973) Interpersonal dyamics in a simulated prison. *International Journal of Criminology and Penology*, 1, 69-97.

Hansen, G.L. (1991) Jealousy and its conceptualisation, measurement and integration with family stress theory. In P. Salove (Ed.) *The Psychology of Jealousy and Envy*. Guilford: New York.

Haritos-Fatouros, M. (1988) The official torturer: A learning model for obedience to authority of violence. *Journal of Applied Social Psychology*, 18, 1107-1120.

Harlow, H., and Zimmermann, R.R. (1959) Affectional responses in the infant monkey. *Science*, 130, 421-432.

Harris, A. (1959) Sensory deprivation and schizophrenia. *Journal of Mental Science*, 105, 235-237.

Hartup, W.W. (1989) Social relationships and their developmental significance. *American Psychologist*, 44, 120-126.

Hayward, M.L., and Taylor, J.E. (1956) A schizophrenic patient describes the action of intensive psychotherapy. *Psychiatric Quarterly*, 30, 211-248.

Hazan, C., and Shaver, P. (1987) Romantic love conceptualised as an attachment process. *Journal of Personality and Social Psychology*, 52, 511-524.

---------. (1990) Love and Work: An attachment-theoretical perspective. *Journal of Personality and Social Psychology*, 59, 270-280.

Heard, D.H., and Lake, B. (1986) The attachment dynamic in adult life. *British Journal of Psychiatry*, 149, 430-438.

Heidegger, M. (1927) *Being and Time* (translated by A. Macquarrie and E. Robinson). Harper: New York, 1962.

Henderson, A.S. (1974) Care-eliciting behavior in man. *Journal of Nervous and Mental Disorders*, 159, 172-181.

Hilgard, E.R., Atkinson, R.L., and Atkinson, R.C. (1979) Chapter 14, Conflict and Stress. In *Introduction to Psychology*, 7th Edition. Harcourt Brace Jovanovich, Inc.: New York.

Hirschfeld, R.M.A., Klerman, G.L., Gough, H.G., Barrett, J., Korchin, S.J., and Chodoff, P. (1977) A measure of interpersonal dependency. *Journal of Personality Assessment*, 41, 610-619.

Hollender, M., Luborsky, L., and Harvey, R.B. (1970) Correlates of the desire to be held in women. *Journal of Psychosomatic Research*, 14, 387-390.

Hollender, M., Luborsky, L., and Scaramella, T.J. (1969) Body contact and sexual excitement. *Archives of General Psychiatry*, 20, 188-191.

Horney, K. (1937) *The Neurotic Personality of Our Time*. Norton: New York.

----------. (1942) *Self Analysis*. Norton: New York.

----------. (1945) *Our Inner Conflicts*. Norton: New York.

Hudson, L., and Jacot, B. (1991) *The Way Men Think*. Yale University Press: London.

Jacobson, E. (1964) *The Self and the Object World*. International Universities Press: New York.

Jevrons, F.B. (1927) *An Introduction to the History of Religion*. Methuen: London.

Jones, E.E., and Archer, R.L. (1976) Are there special effects of personalistic self-disclosure? *Journal of Experimental Social Psychology*, 12, 180-193.

Jones, W.H., Cavert, C.W., Snider, R.L., and Bruce, T. (1985) Relational stress: An analysis of situations and events sociated with loneliness. In Duck, S.W., and D. Perlman (Eds.) *Understanding Personal Relationships*. Sage: London.

Jung, C.J. (1921) *Psychological Types. The Collected Works*, Vol. 6. (Edited by Read, H., Fordham, M., and Adler, G.). Routledge & Kegan Paul: London, 1971.

----------. (1964) *Two Essays on Analytical Psychology*. Meridian: New York.

Kalma, A. (1991) Hierarchisation and dominance assessment at first glance. *European Journal of Social Psychology*, 21, 165-181.

Kaltenbach, K., Weinraub, M., and Fullard, W. (1980) Infants' wariness towards strangers reconsidered: Infants' and mothers' reactions to unfamiliar persons. *Child Development*, 51, 1197-1202.

Kasper, S., and Rosenthal, N.E. (1989) Anxiety and depression in seasonal affective disorder. In Kendall, P.C., and Watson, D. (Eds.) *Anxiety and Depression: Distinctive and Overlapping Features*. Academic Press: New York.

Kernberg, O. (1979) Regression in organisational leadership. *Psychiatry*, 42, 29-39.

Kets de Vries, M.F.R., and Miller, D. (1985) Narcissism and leadership: An object relations perspective. *Human Relations*, 38, 583-601.

Kierkegaard, S. (1944) *The Concept of Dread* (translated by W. Lowrie). Princeton University Press: Princeton, N.J.

Kiesler, D.J. (1979) An interpersonal communication analysis of relationship in psychotherapy. *Psychiatry*, 42, 299-311.

----------. (1982) Confronting the client-therapist relationship in psychotherapy. In Anchin, J.C., and Kiesler, D.J. (Eds.) *Handbook of Intepersonal Psychotherapy*. Pergamon: New York.

----------. (1983) The 1982 interpersonal circle: A taxonomy for complementarity in human transactions. *Psychological Review*, 90, 185-214.

----------. (1986) Interpersonal methods of diagnosis and treatment. In Cavenar, J.O. (Ed.) *Psychiatry*, Vol. 1, 1-23. Lippincott: Philadelphia.

---------. (1987) Complementarity: Between whom and under what conditions? *Clinician's Research Digest: Supplemental Bulletin*, 5, No. 20 (October).

---------. (1990) Interpersonal methods of assessment and diagnosis. In Snyder, C.R., and Forsyth, D.R. (Eds.) *Handbook of Social and Clinical Psychology: The Health Perspective.* Pergamon: Elmsford, N.Y.

---------. (1992) Interpersonal circle inventories: Pantheoretical applications to psychotherapy research and practice. *Journal of Psychotherapy Integration*, 2, 77-99.

Klaus, M.H., and Kennell, J. H. (1976) *Maternal-Infant Bonding.* Mosby: St. Louis, Mo.

Klein, M. (1934) A contribution to the psychogenesis of manic-depressive states. In *Contributions to Psychoanalysis 1921-1945.* Hogarth: London, 1950.

---------. (1950) *Contributions to Psychoanalysis 1921-1945.* Hogarth: London.

---------. (1957) *Envy and Gratitude: A Study of Unconscious Sources.* Tavistock: London.

Kohut, H. (1971) *The Analysis of the Self: A Systematic Approach to the Psychoanalytic Treatment of Narcissistic Personality Disorders.* International Universities Press: New York.

---------. (1977) *The Restoration of the Self.* International Universities Press: New York.

---------. (1978) Creativeness, charisma, group psychology. In Ornstein, P.H. (Ed.) *The Search for the Self,* Vol. 2. International Universities Press: New York.

---------. (1984) *How Does Analysis Cure?* University of Chicago Press: Chicago.

Kohut, H., and Wolf, E.S. (1978) The disorders of the self and their treatment: An outline. *International Journal of Psycho-Analysis*, 59, 413-426.

Konner, M.J. (1972) Aspects of the developmental ethology of a foraging people. In Blurton-Jones, N. (Ed.) *Ethological Studies of Child Behavior.* Cambridge University Press: London.

Krell, R., and Miles, J.E. (1976) Marital therapy in couples in which the husband is a physician. *American Journal of Psychotherapy*, 30, 267-275.

Krohn, A. (1978) Hysteria: The elusive neurosis. *Psychological Issues*, Monograph 45/46. International Universities Press: New York.

Kummer, H. (1967) Tripartite relationships in hamadryas baboons. In Altmann, S. (Ed.) *Primate Communication.* Chicago University Press: Chicago.

LaForge, R., Freedman, M.B., and Wiggins, J. (1985) Interpersonal circumplex models: 1948-1983 (Symposium) *Journal of Personality Assessment*, 49, 613-631.

LaForge, R., and Suczek, R. (1955) The interpersonal dimension of personality, III: An interpersonal check list. *Journal of Personality*, 24, 94-112.

Laing, R.D. (1965) *The Divided Self.* Penguin: Harmondsworth, Middlesex.

Laing, R.D., and Esterson, A. (1964) *Sanity, Madness and the Family*. Penguin: Harmondsworth, Middlesex.

Laing, R.D., Phillipson, H., and Lee, A.R. (1966) *Interpersona Perception*. Tavistock Publications: London.

Lambert, M.J., Shapiro, D.A., and Bergin, A.E. (1986) The effetiveness of psychotherapy. In Garfield, S.L., and Bergin, A.E. (Eds.) *The Handbook of Psychotherapy and Behavior Change*. Wiley: New York.

Lancaster, J.B. (1975) *Primate Behavior and the Emergence of Human Culture*. Holt, Rinehart & Winston: New York.

Lange, A., and van der Hart, O. (1983) *Directive Family Therapy*. Brunner/Mazel: New York.

Larson, J.H., and Bell, N.J. (1988) Need for privacy and its effect upon interpersonal attraction and interaction. *Journal of Social and Clinical Psychology*, 6, 1-10.

Lasch, C. (1984) *The Minimal Self*. Picador: London.

Lawick-Goodall, J. van. (1965) New discoveries among Africa's chimpanzees. *National Geographic*, 128, 802-831.

---------. (1968) The behavior of free living chimpanzees in the Gombe Stream Reserve. *Animal Behaviour   Monographs*, 1, 161-311.

Leary, T. (1957) *Interpersonal Diagnosis of Personality*. Ronald Press: New York.

Lederer, W.J., and Jackson, D.D. (1968) *The Mirages of Marriage*. Norton: New York.

Levin, J.D. (1987) *Treatment of Alcoholism and Other Addictions*. Jason Aronson: Northvale, N.J.

Lewis, H.B. (1986) The role of shame in depression. In Rutter, M., Izard, C.E., and Read, P.B. (Eds.) *Depression in Young People*. Guilford: New York.

Lifton, R.J. (1986) *The Nazi Doctors: Medical Killing and the Psychology of Genocide*. Basic Books: New York.

Lilly, J.C. (1956) Mental effects of reduction of ordinary levels of physical stimuli on intact, healthy persons. *Pychiatric Research Reports*, No. 5, 1-9. American Psychiatric Association: Washington, D.C.

Liss, J. (1974) *Free to Feel: Finding Your Way through the New Therapies*. Wildwood House: London.

Livesley, W.J., Schroeder, M.L., and Jackson, D.N. (1990) Dependent personality disorder and attachment problems. *Journal of Personality Disorders*, 4, 131-140.

Lord, R.G., De Vader, C.L., and Alliger, G.M. (1986) A meta-analysis of the relationship between personality traits and leadership perceptions: An application of validity generalisation procedures. *Journal of Alied Psychology*, 71, 401-410.

Lorenz, K.Z. (1957) Fellow members of the species as releasers of social behavior. In Schiller, C. H. (Ed. and Trans.) *Instincte Behavior*. International Universities Press: New York.

---------. (1966) *On Aggression*. Methuen: London.

---------. (1974) *Civilized Man's Eight Deadly Sins*. Harcourt Brace Jovanovich: New York.

---------. (1981) *The Foundations of Ethology*. Springer Verlag: New York.

Lorr, M., and McNair, D.M. (1963) An interpersonal behavior circle. *Journal of Abnormal and Social Psychology*, 67, 68-75.

---------. (1965) Expansion of the interpersonal behaviour circle. *Journal of Personality and Social Psychlogy*, 2, 823-830.

Lovejoy, C.O. (1981) The origin of man. *Science*, 211, 341-350.

Lowen, A. (1967) *The Betrayal of the Body*. Collier Macmillan: London.

---------. (1975) *Bioenergetics*. Coventure: London.

Luborsky, L., Crits-Christoph, P., Mintz, J., and Auerbach, A. (1988) *Who Will Benefit from Psychotherapy? Predicting Therapeutic Outcomes*. Basic Books: New York.

Lynn, D.B. (1969) *Parental and Sex Role Identification*. McCutchan: Berkeley, Calif.

Lyons, J., Hirschberg, N., and Wilkinson, L. (1980) The radex structure of the Leary interpersonal behavior circle. *Multivariate Behavioral Research*, 15, 249-257.

Macdiarmid, D. (1989) Self-cathexis and other-cathexis: Vicissitudes in the history of an observation. *British Journal of Psychiatry*, 154, 844-852.

MacFarlane, J. (1975) Olfaction in the development of social preferences in the human neonate. In M. Hoffer (Ed.) *Parent-Infant Interaction*. Elsevier: New York.

Mackie, R.E. (1969) Intimate and non-intimate relations in therapy. *British Journal of Medical Psychology*, 42, 371-382.

MacLean, P.D. (1973) *A Triune Concept of Brain and Behavior*. University of Toronto Press: Toronto.

---------. (1975) Sensory and perceptive factors in emotional functins of the triune brain. In L. Levi (Ed.) *Emotions: Their parameters and Measurement*. Raven: New York.

---------. (1985) Brain evolution relating to family, play and the separation call. *Archives of General Psychiatry*, 42, 405-417.

Mahler, M. (1961) On sadness and grief in infancy and childhood. *Psychoanalytic Study of the Child*, 16, 332-351.

---------. (1963) Thoughts about development and individuation. *Psychoanalytic Study of the Child*, 18, 307-324.

Main, M., Kaplan, N., and Cassidy, J. (1986) Security in infancy, childhood and adulthood: A move to the level of representation. In Bretherton, I., and Waters, E. (Eds.) *Growing Points in Attachment Theory and Research*.

Monograph of the Society for Research in Child Development, 50, Nos. 1-2.

Martin, T.C., and Bumpass, L. (1989) Recent trends in marial disruption. *Demography*, 26, 37-51.

Masterson, J.F. (1972) *Treatment of the Borderline Adolescent*. Wiley: New York.

May, R. (1953) *Man's Search for Himself*. Norton: New York.

Maynard Smith, J. (1964) Group selection and kin selection. *Nature*, 20, 1145-1147.

Mazur, A. (1977) Interpersonal spacing on public benches in "contact" vs. "noncontact" cultures. *Journal of Social Psychology*, 101, 53-58.

McBride, G., King, M.G., and James, J.W. (1965) Social proximity: Effects on galvanic skin response in humans. *Journal of Psychology*, 61, 153-157.

McLemore, C.W., and Benjamin, L.S. (1979) Whatever happened to interpersonal diagnosis? A psychosocial alternative to DSM-III. *American Psychologist*, 34, 17-34.

Mechanic, D. (1966) Response factors in illness: The study of illness behaviour. *Social Psychiatry*, 1, 11-20.

Mikulincer, M. and Erev, I. (1991) Attachment style and the structure of romantic love. *British Journal of Social Psychology*, 30, 273-291.

Milgram, S. (1974) *Obedience to Authority*. Harper and Row: New York.

Miller, A. (1987) *For Your Own Good*. Virago: London.

Millon, T. (1969) *Modern Psychopathology: A Biosocial Approach to Maladaptive Learning and Functioning*. Saunders: Philadelphia, Pa.

---------. (1981) *Disorders of Personality, DSM III, Axis II*. Wiley, New York.

Minuchin, S. (1974) *Families and Family Therapy*. Harvard University Press: Cambridge, Mass.

Mitchell, K.M., Bozarth, J.D. & Krauft, C.C. (1977) A reappraisal of the therapeutic effectiveness of accurate empathy, non-possessive warmth and genuineness. In Gurman, A.S. & Radzin, A.M. (Eds.) *Effective Psychotherapy: A Handbook of Research*. Pergamon: New York.

Montagu, A. (1986) *Touching: The Human Significance of the Skin*. Harper & Row: New York.

Morris, L.W. (1979) *Extraversion and Introversion: An Interactional Perspective*. Wiley: New York.

Mowrer, O.H. (1964) *The New Group Therapy*. Van Nostrand: New York.

Mullen, P.E. and White, G.L. (1989) *Jealousy, Theory, Research and Clinical Strategies*. Guilford, New York

Murdock, G.P. (1968) The current status of the world's hunting and gathering peoples. In Lee, R.B., and DeVore, I. (Eds.) *Man the Hunter*. Aldine: New York.

Murray, H. (1938) *Explorations in Personality*. Oxford University Press: New

York.

Myers, B.J. (1984) Mother-infant bonding: the status of this critical period hypothesis. *Developmental Review*, 4, 240-274.

Nemiah, J.C. (1975) Depressive neurosis. In Freedman, A.M., Kaplan, H.I., and Sadock, B.J. (Eds.) *Comprehensive Textbook of Psychiatry II*, Vol.1. Williams & Wilkins: Baltimore, Md.

Nesse, R.M. (1990) Evolutionary explanations of emotions. *Human Nature*, 1, 261-289.

Nunberg, H. (1948) Problems of therapy. In *Practice and Theory of Psychoanalysis*, Vol. 1. International Universities Press: New York.

---------. (1961) *Curiosity*. International Universities Press: New York.

Oates, W. (1971) *Confessions of a Workaholic. The Facts about Work Addiction.* World Publishing Company: New York.

Olds, J., and Milner, P. (1954) Positive reinforcement produced electrical stimulation of septal area and other regions of the rat brain. *Journal of Comparative and Physiological Psychology*, 47, 419-427.

Oppong, C. (1979) Changing family structure and conjugal love: The case of the Akan of Ghana. In Cook, M, and Wilson, G. (Eds.) *Love and Attraction*. Pergamon: Oxford.

Orford, J. (1986) The rules of interpersonal complementarity: Does hostility beget hostility and dominance, submission? *Psychological Review*, 93, 365-377.

Orlinsky, D.E. (1979) Structural features of the romantic love relationship. In Cook, M., and Wilson, G. (Eds.) *Love and Attraction*. Pergamon Press: Oxford.

Orlofsky, J.L., Marcia, J.E., and Lesser, I.M. (1973) Ego identity status and the intimacy versus isolation crisis of young adulthood. *Journal of Personality and Social Psychology*, 27, 211-219.

Orne, M.T. (1962) On the social psychology of the psychological experiment: With particular reference to demand characteristics and their implications. *American Psychologist*, 17, 776-783.

Ornitz, E.M. (1983) The functional neuroanatomy of infantile autism. *International Journal of Neuroscience*, 19, 85-124.

Packer, M., and Richardson, E. (1991) Analytic hermeneutics and the study of morality in action. In Kurtines, W.M., and Gewirtz, J.L. (Eds.) *Handbook of Moral Behavior and Development, Vol. 1: Theory*. Erlbaum: Hillsdale, N.J.

Paddock, J.R., and Nowicki, S. (1986) An examination of the Leary circumplex through the Interpersonal Check List. *Journal of Research in Personality*, 20, 107-144.

Parens, H., and Saul, L.J. (1971) *Dependence in Man*. International Universities Press: New York.

Parker, G.A. (1974) Assessment strategy and the evolution of fighting behaviour. *Journal of Theoretical Biology*, 47, 223-243.

---------. (1984) Evolutionarily stable strategies. In Krebs, J.R. & Davies, N.B. (Eds.) *Behavioral Ecology: An Evolutionary Approach.* Blackwell: Oxford.

Parkes, C.M. (1965) Bereavement and mental illness. Part 2, A classification of bereavement reactions. *British Journal of Medical Psychology*, 38, 13-26.

---------. (1973) Factors determining the persistence of phantom in in the amputee. *Journal of Psychosomatic Research*, 17, 97-108.

Parsons, T. (1951) *The Social System.* Free Press: New York.

Parsons, T., and Bales, R. F. (1955) *Family, Socialisation and Interaction Process.* The Free Press: New York.

Pedersen, J., Schelde, J.T.M., Hannibal, E., Benke, K., Neilsen, B.M., and Hertz, M. (1988) An ethological description of depression. *Acta Psychiatrica Scandinavica*, 78, 320-330.

Pilkonis, P.A. (1988) Personality prototypes among depressives: Themes of dependency and autonomy. *Journal of Personality Disorders*, 2, 144-152.

Pilkonis, P.A., and Frank, E. (1988) Personality pathology in recurrent depression: Nature, prevalence and relationship to treatment response. *American Journal of Psychiatry*, 145, 435-441.

Pilowsky, I. (1969) Abnormal illness behaviour. *British Journal of Medical Psychology*, 42, 347-351.

Poppen, R. (1988) *Behavioral Relaxation Training and Assessment.* Pergamon: New York.

Power, M. (1988) The cohesive foragers: Human and chimpanzee. In Chance, M.R.A. (Ed.) *Social Fabrics of the Mind.* Erlbaum: Hillsdale, N.J.

Price, J.S. (1967) Hypothesis: The dominance hierarchy and the evolution of mental illness. *The Lancet*, 2, 243-246.

---------. (1968) Neurotic and endogenous depression: A phylogenetic view. *British Journal of Psychiatry*, 114, 119-120.

---------. (1972) Genetic and phylogenetic aspects of mood variation. *International Journal of Mental Health*, 1, 124-144.

---------. (1988) Alternative channels for negotiating asymmetry in social relationships. In Chance, M.R.A. (Ed.) *Social Fabrics of the Mind.* Erlbaum: Hillsdale, N.J.

---------. (1991) Change or homeostasis? A systems theory approach to depression. *British Journal of Medical Psychology*, 64, 331-344.

Price, J.S., and Sloman, L. (1987) Depression as yielding behavior: An animal model based on Schelderup-Ebbe's pecking order. *Ethology and Sociobiology*, 8, 85S-98S.

Rado, S. (1951) Psychodynamics of depression from the etiological point of view. *Psychosomatic Medicine*, 13, 51-55.

Rank, O. (1923) *The Trauma of Birth*. Harper and Row: London.

Raskin, P.M. (1985) The application of identity status and intimacy status research to counselling with couples. *Psychotherapy*, 22, 201-212.

Ray, J.J. (1976) Do authoritarians hold authoritarian attitudes? *Human Relations*, 29, 307-325.

---------. (1981) Authoritarianism, dominance and assertiveness. *Journal of Personality Assessment*, 45, 390-397.

Reich, W. (1933) *Character Analysis*. Simon & Schuster: New York, 1972.

Reynolds, V. (1966) Open groups in hominid evolution. *Man*, 1, 441-452.

Reynolds, V., and Kellett, J. (Eds.) (1990) *Mating and Marriage*. Oxford University Press: London.

Rheingold, H.L., and Eckerman, C.O. (1970) The infant separates himself from his mother. *Science*, 168, 78-83.

Richards, G. (1987) *Human Evolution: An Introduction for the Behavioral Sciences*. Routledge & Kegan Paul: London.

Riley, W.T., Treiber, F.A., and Woods, M.G. (1989) Anger and Hostility in Depression. *Journal of Nervous and Mental Disease*, 177, 668-674.

Rioux, B. (1963) A review of folie à deux, the psychosis of association. *Psychiatric Quarterly*, 37, 405-428.

Rochlin, G. (1961) The dread of abandonment: A contribution to the etiology of the loss complex and to depression. *Psychoanalytic Study of the Child*, 16, 451-470.

Rogers, C.R. (1957) The necessary and sufficient conditions of therapeutic personality change. *Journal of Consulting Psychology*, 21, 95-103.

Roth, S., and Cohen, L.J. (1986) Approach, avoidance, and coping with stress. *American Psychologist*, 41, 813-819.

Rowe, C.E., and MacIsaac, D.S. (1989) *Empathic Attunement: The Technique of Psychoanalytic Self Psychology*. Aronson: Northvale, N.J.

Rubin, L.B. (1985) *Intimate Strangers*. Fontana/Collins: London.

Rushton, J.P. (1988) Epigenetic rules in moral development: Distal-proximal approaches to altruism and aggression. *Aggressive Behavior*, 14, 35-50.

Ryan, R.M., and Lynch, J.H. (1989) Emotional autonomy versus detachment: Revisiting the vicissitudes of adolescence and young adulthood. *Child Development*, 60, 340-356.

Rycroft, C. (1972) *A Critical Dictionary of Psychoanalysis*. Penguin: Harmondsworth, Middlesex.

Sainsbury, P. (1955) *Suicide in London: An Ecological Study*. Maudsley Monographs, No.1. Chapman & Hall: London.

Sargant, W. (1957) *Battle for the Mind: A Physiology of Conversion and Brain Washing*. Heinemann: London.

Schachter, S. (1959) *The Psychology of Affiliation.* Stanford University Press: Stanford, Calif.

Schaefer, E.S. (1959) A circumplex model for maternal behaviour. *Journal of Abnormal and Social Psychology*, 59, 226-235.

----------. (1965) A configurational analysis of children's reports of parental behavior. *Journal of Consulting Psychology*, 29, 552-557.

Schafer, R. (1984) The pursuit of failure and the idealization of unhappiness. *American Psychologist*, 39, 398-405.

Scheff, T.J. (1988) Shame and conformity. The defense emotion system. *American Sociological Review*, 53, 395-406.

Schjelderup-Ebbe, T. (1935) Social behavior of birds. In Murchison, C. (Ed.) *Handbook of Social Psychology.* Clark University Press: Worcester, Mass.

----------. (1975) Contributions to the social psychology of the domestic chicken. In Schein, M.W. (Ed.) *Social Hierarchy and Dominance.* Benchmark Papers in Animal Behavior, Series 3. Academic: Orlando, Fa.

Schneider, K. (1950) *Psychopathic Personalities,* 9th Edition, (English translation). Cassell: London.

Schotte, D.E., and Clum, G.A. (1982) Suicidal ideation in a college population: A test of a model. *Journal of Consulting and Clinical Psychology*, 50, 690-696.

Schumaker, J.F. (Ed.) *Human Suggestibility.* Routledge: New York.

Schwartz, D.A., Flinn, D.E., and Slawson, P.F. (1974) Treatment of the suicidal character. *American Journal of Psychotherapy*, 28, 194-207.

Seeman, M.V. (1978) Delusional loving. *Archives of General Psychiatry*, 35, 1265-1267.

Segal, H. (1964) *Introduction to the Work of Melanie Klein.* Heineman: London.

Seligman, M.E.P. (1975) *Helplessness: On Depression, Development and Death.* Freeman: San Francisco, Calif.

Seyfarth, R., and Cheney, D. (1992) Inside the mind of a monkey. *New Scientist*, 133, No. 1802, 25-29.

Shepherd, M. (1961) Morbid jealousy: Some clinical and social aspects of a psychiatric symptom. *Journal of Mental Science*, 107, 687-753.

Shibutani, T. (1961) *Society and Personality: An Interactionist Approach to Social Psychology.* Prentice Hall: Englewood Cliffs, N.J.

Siebenaler, J.B., and Caldwell, D.K. (1956) Co-operation among adult dolphins. *Journal of Mammalogy*, 37, 126-128.

Simons, R.C. (1987) Applicability of DSM-III to psychiatric education. In Tischler, G.L. (Ed.) *Diagnosis and Classification in Psychiatry: A Critical Appraisal of DSM- III.* Cambridge University Press: Cambridge.

Simpson, J.A. (1990) Influence of attachment styles on romantic relationships. *Journal of Personality and Social Psychology*, 59, 971-980.

Slocum, J. (1948) *Sailing Alone around the World*. Rupert Hart-Davis: London.

Sloman, L., and Price, J.S. (1987) Losing behavior (yielding subroutine) and human depression: Proximate and selective mechanisms. *Ethology and Sociobiology*, 8, 99(S)-109(S)

Smith, C.G., and Sinanan, K. (1972) The gaslight phenomenon returns. *British Journal of Psychiatry*, 120, 685-686.

Smith, L., and Martinsen, H. (1977) The behavior of young children in a strange situation. *Scandinavian Journal of Psychology*, 18, 43-52.

Spitzberg, B.H., and Canary, D. (1985) Loneliness and relationally competent communication. *Journal of Social and Personal Relationships*, 2, 387-402.

Spurgeon, C. (1970) *Mysticism in English Literature*. Kenikat Press: Port Washington, N.Y.

Stagner, R. (1937) *Psychology of Personality*. McGraw: New York.

Stengel, E. (1941) On the aetiology of fugue states. *Journal of Mental Science*, 87, 572-599.

---------. (1943) Further studies on pathological wandering. *Journal of Mental Science*, 89, 224-241.

Stern, G.G. (1970) *People in Context: Measuring Person-Environment Congruence in Education and Industry*. Wiley: New York.

Stoller, R.J. (1979) *Sexual Excitement: Dynamics of Erotic Life*. Marefield Library: London.

Stone, L. (1984) *Transference and Its Context*. Aronson: New York.

Storr, A. (1983) A psychotherapist looks at depression. *British Journal of Psychiatry*, 143, 431-435.

---------. (1988) *Solitude*. Collins: London.

Straus, M. (1974) Leveling, civility and violence in the family. *Journal of Marriage and the Family*, 36, 13-29.

Straus, M., Gelles, R., and Steinmetz, S. (1980) *Behind Closed Doors: Violence in the American Family*. Doubleday/Anchor: New York.

Strong, S.R., and Hills, H.I. (1986) *Interpersonal Communication Rating Scale*. Virginia Commonwealth University: Richmond, Va.

Strong, S.R., Hills, H.I., Kilmartin, C.T., DeVries, H., Lanier, K., Nelson, B.N., Strickland, D., and Meyer, C.W., III, (1988). The dynamic relations among interpersonal behaviors: A test of complementarity and anticomplementarity. *Journal of Personality and Social Psychology*, 54, 798-810.

Suedfeld, P. (1980) *Restricted Environmental Stimulation: Research and Clinical Applications*. Wiley: New York.

---------. (1991) Groups in isolation and confinement: Environments and experiences. In Harrison, A.H, Clearwater, Y.A., and McKay, C.P. (Eds.) *From Antarctica to Outer Space: Life in Isolation and*

Confinement. Springer-Verlag: New York.

Suedfeld, P., and Kristeller, J.L. (1982) Stimulus reduction as a technique in health psychology. *Health Psychology*, 1, 337-357.

Suedfeld, P., and Roy, C. (1975) Using social isolation to control the behavior of disruptive inmates. *International Journal of Offender Therapy and Comparative Criminology*, 19, 90-99.

---------. (1947) *Conceptions of Modern Psychiatry*. Norton: New York.

---------. (1949) Multidisciplined coordination of interpersonal data. In Sargent, S.S., and Smith, M.W. (Eds.) *Culture and Personality*. Viking Fund: New York.

Sullivan, H. S. (1953) *The Interpersonal Theory of Psychiatry*. Norton: New York.

Suls, J., and Wills, T.A. (1991) *Social Comparison: Contemporary Theory and Research*. Lawrence Erlbaum: Hillsdale, NJ.

Suttie, I.D. (1935) *The Origins of Love and Hate*. Kegan Paul: London.

Szasz, T. (1956) Malingering: "Diagnosis" or social condemnation? *Archives of Neurology and Psychiatry*, 76, 432-443.

---------. (1972) *The Myth of Mental Illness*. Paladin: London.

Tabachnick, N. (1961) Interpersonal relations in suicidal attempts. *Archives of General Psychiatry*, 4, 16-21.

Tattum, D.B. (1989) Violence and aggression in schools. In Tattum, D.B. (Ed.) *Bullying in Schools*. Trentham Books: Stoke-on-Trent, Staffs.

Taylor, G.J. (1975) Separation-individuation in the psychotherapy of symbiotic states. *Canadian Psychiatric Association Journal*, 20, 521-526.

Tedeschi, J.T., Lindskold, S., and Rosenfeld, P. (1985) *Introduction to Social Psychology*. West Publishing: St. Paul, Minn.

Thibaut, J.W., and Kelley, H.H. (1959) *The Social Psychology of Groups*. Wiley: New York.

Titus, H.E., and Hollander, E.P. (1957) The California F Scale in psychological research: 1950-1955. *Psychological Bulletin*, 54, 47-64.

Trivers, R. (1971) The evolution of reciprocal altruism. *Quarterly Review of Biology*, 46, 35-57.

---------. (1985) *Social Evolution*. Benjamin/Cummings: Redwood City, Calif.

Tsuang, M.T. (1982) *Schizophrenia: The Facts*. Oxford University Press: London.

Vernon, J. (1963) *Inside the Black Room*. Potter: London.

Vincent, J-D. (1990) *The Biology of Emotions*. Blackwell: Oxford.

Vinge, L. (1967) *The Narcissus Theme in Western Literature*. University of Lund Publications: Lund, Sweden.

Von Witzleben, H.D. (1958) On loneliness. *Psychiatry*, 21, 37-51.

Wagstaff, G.F. (1986) Hypnosis as compliance and belief: A socio-cognitive view. In Naish, P.L.N. (Ed.) *What Is Hypnosis?* Open University Press:

Milton Keynes.

----------. (1991) Suggestibility: A social psychological approach. In Schumaker, J.F. (Ed.) *Human Suggestibility: Advances in Theory, Research and Application*. Routledge: New York.

Waldroop, J.A., and Hurst, J.C. (1982) The psychotherapist and one-way intimacy. *Psychotherapy: Research and Practice*, 19, 48-53.

Waters, W., Matas, L., and Sroufe, L.A. (1975) Infants' reactions to an approaching stranger: Description, validation and functional significance of wariness. *Child Development*, 46, 348-356.

Weber, M. (1947) *The Theory of Social and Economic Organisations*. Oxford University Press: New York.

Weigert, E. (1960) Loneliness and trust: Basic factors of human existence. *Psychiatry*, 23, 121-131.

Weiss, R.S. (1969) The fund of sociability. *Trans-Action*, 6, 36-43.

Wenegrat, B. (1984) *Sociobiology and Mental Disorder: A New View.* Addison-Wesley: Redwood City, Calif.

West, M.A. (1987) Traditional and psychological perspectives on meditation. In West, M.A. (Ed.) *The Psychology of Meditation*. Clarendon Press: Oxford.

Wiggins, J.S. (1979) A psychological taxonomy of trait-descriptive terms: The interpersonal domain. *Journal of Personality and Social Psychology*, 37, 395-412.

----------. (1982) Circumplex models of interpersonal behavior in clinical psychology. Chapter 6, Kendall, P.C., and Butcher, J.N. (Eds.) *Handbook of Research Methods in Clinical Psychology*. Wiley: New York.

Wiggins, J.S., and Broughton, R. (1985) The interpersonal circle: A structural model for the integration of personality research. In Hogan,. (Ed.) *Perspectives in Personality*. JAI Press, Inc.: Greenwich, Conn.

Wimmer, H., and Perner, J. (1983) Beliefs about beliefs: Representation and constraining function of wrong beliefs in young children's understanding of deception. *Cognition*, 13, 103-128.

Wing, J.K., Cooper, J.E., and Sartorius, N. (1974) *The Measurement and Classification of Psychiatric Symptoms*. Cambridge University Press: London.

Winnicott, D.W. (1948) Paediatrics and psychology. *British Journal of Medical Psychology*, 21, 229-240. Reprinted in *Collected Papers by D.W. Winnicott*. Tavistock: London.

----------. (1952) Anxiety associated with insecurity. In Winnicott, *Collected Papers*. Tavistock: London.

----------. (1953) Transitional objects and transitional phenomena. *International Journal of Psycho-Analysis*, 34, 89-97.

----------. (1956) On transference. *International Journal of Psycho-Analysis*, 37, 382-395.

----------. (1958) The capacity to be alone. *International Journa of Psycho-Analysis*, 9, 420-438.

Wood, J.V. (1989) Theory and research concerning social comparison of personal attributes. *Psychological Bulletin*, 106, 231-248.

World Health Organization (1989) *International Classification of Diseases*, 10th Edition (ICD-10). World Health Organization, Division of Mental Health: Geneva.

Yardley, K., and Honess, T. (1987) *Self and Identity: Psychosocial Perspectives*. Wiley: New York.

Yukl, G. (1981) *Leadership in Organisations*. Prentice Hall: Englewood Cliffs, N.J.

Zaleznik, A. (1977) Managers and leaders: Are they different? *Harvard Business Review*, 55, 67-78.

Zilboorg, G. (1938) Loneliness. *The Atlantic Monthly* CL 11 (January).

Zuckerman, M., and Eisen, B. (1962) Relationship of acquiescence response set to authoritarianism and dependency. *Psychological Reports*, 10, 95-102.

Author Index

Subject Index

About the Author

John Birtchnell is a Senior Lecturer at the Institute of Psychiatry and a Consultant Psychiatrist at the Maudsley Hospital in London. He was trained in medicine at the University of Edinburgh. He is a Fellow of the Royal College of Psychiatrists and has a postgraduate qualification in psychotherapy from the University of Aberdeen. For over twenty years he was employed as a Scientific Officer by the Medical Research Council and has published extensively in the psychiatric literature. He is Editor of the *British Journal of Medical Psychology*.